STUDY GUIDE

FINANCIAL ACCOUNTING

STUDY GUIDE
Thomas G. Evans
University of Central Florida

FINANCIAL ACCOUNTING
Principles and Issues
Fourth Edition

Michael H. Granof
University of Texas

Philip W. Bell
Boston University

Englewood Cliffs, New Jersey 07632

Editorial/Production Supervision: **Christine McLaughlin**
Supplements Acquisitions Editor: **Jenny Sheehan**
Acquisitions Editor: **Joe Heider**
Pre-press Buyer: **Trudy Pisciotti**
Manufacturing Buyer: **Bob Anderson**

 © 1991 by Prentice-Hall, Inc.
A Simon & Schuster Company
Englewood Cliffs, New Jersey 07632

All rights reserved. No part of this book may be
reproduced, in any form or by any means,
without permission in writing from the publisher.

Printed in the United States of America

10 9 8 7 6 5 4 3 2 1

ISBN 0-13-321886-4

Prentice-Hall International (UK) Limited, *London*
Prentice-Hall of Australia Pty. Limited, *Sydney*
Prentice-Hall Canada Inc., *Toronto*
Prentice-Hall Hispanoamericana, S.A., *Mexico*
Prentice-Hall of India Private Limited, *New Delhi*
Prentice-Hall of Japan, Inc., *Tokyo*
Simon & Schuster Asia Pte. Ltd., *Singapore*
Editora Prentice-Hall do Brasil, Ltda., *Rio de Janeiro*

CONTENTS

Accounting: A Dynamic Discipline	1
The Accounting Equation and the Three Fundamental Financial Statements	7
The Accounting Cycle	17
Accruing Revenues and Expenses	33
Measuring and Reporting Revenues	57
Valuation of Assets: Cash and Marketable Securities	73
Receivables and Payables	87
Inventories and Cost of Goods Sold	105
Long-Lived Assets and the Allocation of Their Costs	121
Liabilities and Related Expenses	135
Transactions Between a Firm and Its Owners	157
Special Problems of Measuring and Reporting Dividends and Earnings	179
Intercorporate Investments and Earnings	197
Statement of Cash Flows	217
Accounting for Changes in Prices	225
Financial Reporting and Analysis in Perspective	249
Glossary	267
Appendix	285

PREFACE

This study guide is designed to facilitate your use of <u>Financial Accounting: Principles and Issues</u>, Fourth Edition, in a number of ways. It is a supplement to this text and contains features for each chapter to help you.

1. **Key Points**. The key points of each text chapter are presented in outline form. By reviewing this outline after having studied the corresponding chapter in the text, you will reinforce your understanding of the key points. You can also determine whether or not you are familiar with the major concepts presented in the text chapter. This outline will also be useful to you for reviewing before examinations and tests.

2. **Key issues focused upon in this chapter**. This section indicates some of the more important issues presented in the text chapter. A central theme of this text is that there are few "correct" answers in accounting (contrary to popular opinion) and there are many important accounting issues that are unresolved. This section directs your attention to some of the key issues raised in the chapter in the text.

3. **Key words and phrases**. A list of key words and phrases from the text chapter is presented. Accounting, like any specialized profession employs a number of technical terms that are critical to your understanding of the principles. You should review the terms listed to see whether or not you can recall their meaning. Definitions are provided for all terms listed in a glossary at the end of this guide.

4. **Illustrations for review**. Additional problem illustrations are presented for your solution and study. There are few better ways to test your understanding of the text material than by working problems and examples. The problems presented in this section are solved for you. However, sufficient space is provided beneath each problem so that you can work it before looking at the solution. Many of the illustrations are of a "self-teaching" type; that is, a fairly difficult and complex problem is broken down into relatively simple steps which you are asked to solve. By the time you have completed all the steps, you have solved the complex problem.

5. **Exercises**. This section presents additional numerical exercises and problems for you to solve. Many of these involve fundamental accounting procedures and practices that must be understood with the more conceptual issues raised in the text. It is essential that you take the time to work these problems in conjunction with your study of the text. Solutions to these exercises and problems are provided at the end of the study guide chapter.

Accounting is a difficult subject. There are relatively few to whom the study of the principles of accounting is not a challenge. But if you have a firm grasp of the material presented in Financial Accounting: Principles and Issues, Fourth Edition, you can take pride in the fact that you have obtained an unusually sophisticated overview of financial accounting in a short time. We sincerely hope that this study guide will make your learning process a little easier. Special thanks to Scott Wilson, UCF, for able research assistance in preparing this study guide.

        M.H.G.   T.G.E.
        Austin, Texas   Orlando, Florida

{ Chapter 1 }

ACCOUNTING:

A DYNAMIC DISCIPLINE

Chapter 1 is intended to provide an introduction to the study of accounting, to set forth the central themes of the text and to dispel some common misconceptions of accounting. The chapter is designed to inform you that the study of accounting is not just a matter of learning a set of established rules and procedures. Accounting is indeed a dynamic discipline and there are few "correct" answers to many of the questions which accountants are called upon to address.

KEY POINTS

I. **Description of Accounting**

   A. Accounting is a discipline involved with the collection, summarization and reporting of financial information.

   B. Accounting is concerned with describing economic events, measuring resources and determining periodic changes in those resources.

II. **Purposes of Accounting**

   A. One purpose of accounting is to facilitate the allocation of the scarce resources of our society.

   B. Another purpose is to provide a basis on which to manage and direct the resources of an organization. Managers of both profit and non-profit organizations rely on accounting information to assist them in directing and controlling their enterprises.

   C. A third purpose is to provide a basis on which managers or public officials can report to stockholders or citizens on how well they are carrying out the duties end responsibilities with which they have been entrusted.

III. **Standards that Accounting Information Should Satisfy.**

A. Accounting information must be relevant. It must bear upon or be associated with the decisions it is designed to facilitate. In other words, it must be useful for a particular purpose.

B. Accounting information should be reliable; it must be objective and verifiable. It should not be based upon the subjective judgments of the individuals who have prepared it.

C. Financial reports should be neutral. They should present economic information as objectively as possible.

D. Accounting information should be comparable. Similar firms should base their financial statements on the same accounting policies.

E. This accounting information should be consistent; financial statements should be based on accounting practices that do not change from year to year.

IV. **Common Misconceptions about Accounting Information and Financial Statements.**

A. Financial statements are not "accurate" or "precise." They are necessarily based on estimates and judgments.

B. Financial Information is not certain. It is based on predictions.

V. **The Accounting Profession.**

A. The professional accountant is most closely associated with the practice of public accounting. The public accountant who has satisfied various state requirements, foremost of which is passing a nationally administered examination, is recognized as a Certified Public Accountant (CPA).

B. The public accounting profession is characterized by three main functions.

   1. **Auditing**. The CPA attests to (vouches for) the fairness of the financial statements issued by companies or other organizations. Based upon an independent examination of the financial records of the firm, the CPA issues a report in which he expresses an opinion as to whether the financial statements express fairly the financial position and results of operations of the firm in accordance with generally accepted accounting principles applied on a consistent basis.

      a. Generally accepted accounting principles are, to a large extent, those that are adhered to by a large number of companies. These principles are used to prepare external financial reports.

        b.   Specific principles and standards, however, are established by professional and governmental bodies. Predominant of these bodies is the <u>Financial Accounting Standard Board</u> (FASB), a seven-member, standard-setting body composed of members drawn from the public accounting profession, industry, and government. The board periodically issues pronouncements on matters of accounting practice. <u>The Securities and Exchange Commission</u> (SEC), a federal agency, has the legal authority to regulate financial reporting practice of publicly held corporations, and in recent years, it has issued regulations intended, in large measure, to increase the amount of information that corporations disclose about their financial affairs.

    2.   **Tax services**. CPAs provide tax advice and assistance to their clients.

    3.   **Management advisory services**. Many CPAs provide advice and consulting services to their clients on a broad range of business matters.

C.   Not all accountants are public accountants. Many are employed directly by industrial firms, non-profit firms, non-profit organizations, and governmental agencies.

KEY ISSUES FOCUSED UPON IN THIS CHAPTER

1. Why should I study Financial Accounting if I'm not planning a career as an accountant?

   Financial accounting provides financial information for decisions by all aspects of society--investors, managers, the financial community, and the public. A knowledge of financial accounting concepts, financial accounting principles and limitations will benefit almost everyone in one way or another.

2. Why isn't accounting more precise and scientific like everyone thinks it should be?

   Accounting processes and communicates financial information about business activity. Business is an art, not a science and involves judgement and estimation and human activity. Thus, accounting parallels those aspects of business phenomena and must necessarily use judgment and estimation.

KEY WORDS AND PHRASES

Definitions for the following words and phrases can be found in the Glossary at the end of this study guide.

Assets	Fixed Costs
Audit	Historical Cost
Balance Sheet	Income
Common Stock	Income Statement
Depreciation	Liability
Financial Accounting	Managerial Accounting
Fixed Assets	Market Value

EXERCISES

1. The J & R Manufacturing Company produces drilling machines for resale. The company produces 100 machines per month at an average cost of $50.00 per machine.

   If the company were able to sell an entire month's production for $7,500, what would be the net income from the month's sales? $_____

   What would be the selling price per machine? $ __75.00__

2. The Farm Equipment Sales Company buys three tractors for the following prices:

   Tractor 1 - $350.00
   Tractor 2 - $400.00
   Tractor 3 - $450.00

   What would be the profit from the sale of two tractors for $1,000.00 per tractor under each of the following assumptions as to the tractors sold:

   a. Tractors one and two are sold.

   b. Tractors two and three are sold.

4

c. The company determines the cost of tractors sold based upon the average cost of all tractors purchased for resale.

3. The Domicile Heating Company was organized on January 1, 1991 and sold stock investors for $5,000,000 cash which was then used to acquire facilities and equipment. These should last five years and then be worthless.

During 1991 the firm purchased two million gallons of heating oil at a total cost of $8,000,000 and sold all of it for $14,000,000. The firm had 1991 cash operating cost which totalled $2,000,000. At the end of 1991, an independent appraisal of the facilities and equipment gave them a market value of $5,500,000, the inflation rate for 1991 was 10 percent. The market value of their common stock on the American Exchange was $5,250,000 at year end.

Using generally accepted accounting principles (GAAP) determine the 1991 income for Domicile Heating Company.

SOLUTIONS TO CHAPTER ONE EXERCISES

1. | | |
    |---|---|
    | Sales Revenue | $ 7,500.00 |
    | Less: Cost of Machines Sold* | 5,000.00 |
    | Net income from Sales | $ 2,500.00 |

*Cost of machines sold is calculated by multiplying the number of machines sold (produced) by the average cost of producing a machine.

100 X $50.00 = $5,000.00

$7,500.00/100 machines = $75.00 selling price per machine

2. a. Revenue = 2 x $1,000 = $2,000
        Cost of tractors sold: #1   350
                                      #2   400
        Profit $1,250

    b. Revenue $2,000
        Cost of tractors: #2   400
                                  #3   450
        Profit $1,150

    c. Revenue $2,000
        Cost of tractors:
        $\frac{\$350 + \$400 + \$450}{3} \times 2$ 800
                             $1,200

3.
	Revenues	$14,000,000
	Cost of Oil Sold	8,000,000
	Cash operating expenses	2,000,000
	Depreciation ($5,000,000/5)	1,000,000
	Net Loss	$ 3,000,000

{ Chapter 2 }

THE ACCOUNTING EQUATION AND THE THREE FUNDAMENTAL FINANCIAL STATEMENTS

Chapter 2 considers the accounting equation and provides an introduction to the three primary financial statements - the balance sheet, the income statement, and the statement of cash flows. The chapter presents an overview of several fundamental accounting relationships.

KEY POINTS

Financial accounting is basically a means for processing data. The final results, the output, are In the form of accounting reports, called financial statements.

I. **The Balance Sheet** (also called the Statement of Financial Position)

    A. The balance sheet reports the status of an enterprise as of a specific point in time (e.g., the close of business, December 31, 1991).

    B. It indicates the financial resources (assets) available to the firm to carry out its activities as well as the claims (equities) against those resources. There are two types of equities. The claims against the business owners (those to whom the company is indebted) are known as <u>liabilities</u>. The claims against the business by its owners are known as <u>owners' equity</u>.

    C. The balance sheet is based upon the fundamental accounting equation:

$$\text{Assets} = \text{Equities}$$

That is, the assets of an enterprise equal the claims (both those of owners and creditors) against those assets. In an expand form:

$$\text{Assets} = \text{Liabilities} + \text{Owners' Equity}$$

This equation also serves as the foundation for the double entry record keeping process.

D. Owners' equity of a firm increases as a consequence of the two events: 1) the owners of the enterprise make direct contributors to the firm (for example, they contribute cash or other assets in exchange for shares of common stock or some other form of ownership interest); 2) the firm earns income (assuming no change in liabilities, then the assets of the firm increase; so too, therefore, must the claims of the owners against the assets). Owners' equity decreases as the result of two opposite types of events.

II. **The Income Statement**

A. The income statement indicates changes in owners' equity that result from operations of the business.

B. The income statement reports both the revenues and the expenses of the period.

1. Revenues are the inflows of cash of other assets attributable to the goods or services provided by the enterprise.

2. Expenses are the outflows of cash and other assets attributable to the profit-directed activities of the firm.

C. Whereas the balance sheet is <u>as of</u> a particular point in time, an income statement is for a <u>period ending</u> as of a particular point in time. The balance sheet indicates the level of net assets (assets less liabilities) possessed by a firm at a given time. The income statement indicates the rate (expressed as dollars per period of time) that net assets are flowing into or out of the firm.

III. **The Balance Sheet - A Closer Look**

A. The balance sheet is divided into two main sections - one indicating assets and the other indicating equities (liabilities and owners' equity).

B. The asset section is further divided into sections for current and for non-current assets.

1. Current assets include cash and other assets that will either be transformed into cash or will be sold or consumed within one year (or one normal operating cycle of the business if it is greater than one year).

2. Non-current assets are those assets that are not expected to be sold or consumed within one year (or one normal operating cycle of the business if it is greater than one year). They are considered to be "long-lived" assets.

C. Assets, in general, represent future services to be received in money or which are convertible into money. They can be viewed as "bundles of services" available for use or sale by a particular entity. Assets are recorded initially on the balance sheet at the price paid to acquire them. As their service potential declines over time, their reported value is reduced proportionately. The process by which the recorded value is reduced is known as either depreciation or amortization.

D. The liability section is divided into sections for current and for non-current liabilities.

1. Current liabilities are those expected to be satisfied out of current assets (or through the creation of other current liabilities) or to be satisfied within a relatively short period of time.

2. Non-current liabilities represent all other amounts owed. They include long-term notes and bonds payable.

3. Included among liabilities (both current and non-current) are obligations to provide goods or services to customers. Such obligations result from customer advance payments. These obligations are generally labeled advances from customers, revenues received but not yet earned, or deferred credits.

E. The owners' equity section of the balance sheet indicates the interest of the owners in the enterprise. The owners' equity section of a corporate balance sheet is divided into two sections.

1. The first section reveals the capital contributed by the shareholders-either at the time the corporation was first formed or when additional shares were issued throughout the corporation's existence. The amounts contributed by owners (stockholders) are included in the accounts, common stock, preferred stock, and additional paid-in capital or capital in excess of par.

2. The second section indicates the accumulated earnings of the business. Such earnings are usually referred to as retained earnings.

3. If a firm is either a sole proprietorship (owned by a single individual or a partnership (owned by two or more parties) then the equity of the equity of the owners is generally reported in a single account for each owner; no distinction is made between owners' contributions and accumulated earnings.

IV. **The Income Statement - A Closer Look**

A. Income statements take a variety of forms but each indicate the major categories of revenue and expenses, commonly in summary form.

B. Extraordinary items - those which are exceptional in nature and infrequent in occurrence - are indicated separately in the income statement, usually beneath the income from the ordinary operations of the firm.

V. **Statement of Cash Flows**

    A.   This is the third primary financial statement. It reports on the firm's cash position and changes in that position during a period of time. This is vitally important information because investors and creditors are interested in the firm's cash flows. Cash flows may differ from accounting net income for a variety of reasons.

    B.   The Statement of Cash Flows is basically a summary of where a firm acquired its cash from and what it did with it. The cash transactions of a firm are classified into three groups:

        1.   Operating activities
        2.   Investing activities
        3.   Financing activities

VI. **The Statement of Changes in Retained Earnings**

    A.   The Statement of Changes in Retained Earnings serves as the link between the income statement and the balance sheet.

    B.   It Is based on the following fundamental relationship: retained earnings, beginning of year + income for year-dividends declared during the year = retained earnings, end of year.

    C.   Retained earnings represent the claims of owners, against the assets of the firms earnings over one or more accounting periods that have been left in the business. But retained earnings do not represent claims against specific assets. Retained earnings, for example, are not the equivalent of cash of any other asset.

    D.   Dividends represent distributions of assets to the owners of an enterprise. When dividends are paid to stockholders, both the assets (generally cash) and the claims of the owners against those assets, are reduced. As a consequence, a declaration of a dividend results in a reduction of retained earnings. Dividends are sometimes said to be "charged against" or "paid out of" retained earnings. in fact, of course, those are assets that are distributed to stockholders.

KEY ISSUES FOCUSED UPON IN THIS CHAPTER

1.   How are the two financial statements, the Balance Sheet the Income Statement, related?

The Balance Sheet presents, as of a point in time, the assets, liabilities, and the their difference, the owners' equity, in the firm. The Income Statement, by concentrating on revenues and expenses, indicates the rate at which the owners equity in the firm is increasing or decreasing.

2. What determines whether or not an asset is current or non-current?

The critical test is whether or not management reasonably expects to transform the asset into cash or to use it up within one year or the operating cycle of the firm. For example, a farm tractor is a current asset to a farm equipment dealer who expects to sell it within the normal course of his business, the same tractor would be a non-current assets to the farmer who expects to use it within his operations over the long life of the tractor.

KEY WORDS AND PHRASES

Accounts Receivable	Fiscal Year
Amortization	Inventory
Capital in Excess of Par	Loss
Consolidated Financial Statements	Non-Current Assets
Cost of Goods Sold	Non-Current Liabilities
Current Assets	Operating Cycle
Current Liabilities	Owners' Equity
Deferred Charges	Partnership
Deferred Credits	Par Value
Dividends	Preferred Stock
Double-Entry Bookkeeping	Prepaid Expenses
Equities	Retained Earnings
Executory Contracts	Revenues
Expenses	Sole Proprietorship
Extraordinary Item	Working Capital

ILLUSTRATIONS FOR REVIEW

1. Indicate the impact of each of the following financial events on the basic accounting equation.

                                                Assets = Liabilities + Owners' Equity

Event	Assets	Liabilities	Owners' Equity
A company issues 1,000 shares of common stock at $5 per share.	+ $5,000		+ $5,000
It acquires equipment for $1,500 paying cash of $500 and giving a note for the balance	+ $1,500 − 500		+ $1,000
It purchases merchandise for $600 cash.	+ $ 600 − 600		
It sells for $500 merchandise that had cost $300	+ $ 500 − 300		+ 200 − $ 200

2. You have been provided with the following summary information for a business which began operations on January 1, 1991.

Balance Sheet as of December 31

	1991	1992	1993
Assets			
Cash	$ 100	$ 200	$ 400
Inventory	(1)	400	400
Machinery	400	350	300
Delivery truck	300	550	500
Liabilities and Owners' Equity			
Accounts Payable	$ 300	$ 400	$ 300
Wages Payable	100	(5)	200
Common Stock	400	400	400
Retained Earnings	300	(4)	(8)

Income Statement for the Year Ending December 31

	1991	1992	1993
Sales	$ (3)	$4,000	$6,000
Less: Cost of Goods Sold and Other Operating Expenses	$1,000	(6)	5,700
Net Income	(2)	600	(7)
Dividends Paid During Year	$ 300	$ 400	$ (9)

Required: Determine the missing balance.

The missing balance may be determined in the following manner:

(1) Total assets = total liabilities + owners' equity. Therefore total assets must equal $1,100 (the sum of the balances in the liability and owners' equity accounts). Hence Inventory = $1,100 - ($100+400=$300) = $300.

(2) Retained earnings, 12/31/91 = $300, and since $300 was paid in dividends, net income must equal $600. Net income=retained earnings, 12/31/91 + dividends paid-retained earnings, 1/1/91. Net income = $300+$300-$0 = $600.

(3) Sales-expenses ($1,000) = net income ($600), therefore sales must equal $1,600.

(4) Retained earnings, 12/31/91 ($300)+net income ($600)-dividends paid ($400) = retained earnings, 12/31/91; or $300+$600-$400 = $500.

(5) Total liability and owner' equity must equal $1,500 (sum of the asset accounts) hence wages payable = $1,500-($400+$400+$500) = $200.

(6) Sales ($4,000)-expenses = net income ($600). Therefore, expenses-$4,000-$600 = $3,400.

(7) Sales ($6,000)-expenses ($5,700) = net income, $6,000-$5,700 = $300.

(8) Total liabilities and owners' equity must equal $1,600 (sum of the asset accounts). Hence retained earnings, 12/31/93 = $1,600 - ($300+$200+$400) = $700.

(9) Retained earnings, 12/31/92 ($500)+net income ($300)-dividends paid = retained earnings, 12/31/93 ($700), therefore dividends paid must equal $500 = $300-$700 = $100.

The answers provided by the above calculations are included in the financial statements that follow:

Balance Sheet as of December 31

	1991	1992	1993
Assets			
Cash	$ 100	$ 200	$ 400
Inventory	300(1)	400	400
Machinery	400	350	300
Delivery truck	300	550	500
Total Assets	$1,100	$1,500	$1,600
Liabilities and Owners' Equity			
Accounts Payable	$ 300	$ 400	$ 300
Wages Payable	100	200(5)	200
Common Stock	400	400	400
Retained Earnings	300	500(4)	700(8)
Total liabilities and Owners' Equity	$1,100	$1,500	$1,600

Income Statement for the Year Ending December 31

Sales	$1,600(3)	$4,000	$6,000
Less: Cost of Goods Sold and Other Operating Expenses	1,000	(6)	5,700
Net Income	600(2)	600	300(7)
Dividends Paid During Year	$ 300	$ 400	$ 100(9)

EXERCISES

The Presto Appliance Company
Balance Sheet
As of December 31, 1991

Assets

Current Assets:
Cash		$ 70,000
Marketable Securities		80,000
Accounts Receivable		100,000
Inventories		125,000
Total Current Assets		$375,000

Non-Current Assets:
Operating Vehicles and Machinery	$125,000		
Less: Accumulated Depreciation	25,000	$100,000	
Buildings	$250,000		
Less: Accumulated Depreciation	50,000	200,000	
Land		75,000	
Total Non-Current Assets			$375,000
Total Assets			$750,000

Liabilities and Owners' Equity

Current Liabilities:
Accounts Payable	$ 85,000	
Notes Payable	75,000	
Accrued Salaries Payable	15,000	
Taxes Payable	75,000	$250,000

Non-Current Liabilities:
Notes Payable	$ 25,000		
Bonds Payable	300,000	325,000	
Total Liabilities			$575,000

Stockholders' Equity:
Common Stack, $10 Par Value		$100,000	
Retained Earnings		74,500	
Total Stockholders' Equity			$174,500
Total Liabilities and Stockholders' Equity			$750,000

The Presto Appliance Company
Income Statement
For the Year Ended December 31, 1991

Revenues:

From Sales Operations	$1,000,000	
From Service Operations	400,000	$1,400,000

Less: Expenses

Cost of Appliances Sold	$ 700,000	
Operating Supplies	200,000	
Selling and Administrative	179,400	
Interest	50,500	
Property and State Taxes	60,100	1,190,000
Income Before Taxes		$ 210,000
Taxes on income from Operations		105,000
Net income from Operations		$ 105,000

Respond to questions 1-5 using the information contained in the financial statements of the Presto Appliance Company (presented above):

1. What was the amount of dividends declared in 1991 if the balance in the Retained Earnings account on December 31, 1990 was $64,000?

2. How many shares of common stock are outstanding:

3. What were the earnings per share of the company in 1991:

4. What was the percentage return earned by owners in 1991 on their investment?

5. What was the balance in working capital as of December 31, 1991?

SOLUTIONS TO CHAPTER TWO EXERCISES

1. Retained Earnings as of December 31, 1990 $ 64,000
    +Net Income for 1991 (per income Statement)   105,000
    -Dividends Declared   ?
    Retained earnings as of December 31, 1991 $ 74,500

    Dividends declared = Retained earnings, 12/31/84
      +Net income, 1991-Retained earnings,12/31/85
    Dividends declared = 64,000+105,000-74,500+ $ 94,500

2. Balance in common stock = $100,000
    $$\frac{\text{Balance in common stock} = \$100{,}000}{\text{Par Value per share (\$10)} \quad \$10} = 10{,}000 \text{ shares of common stock outstanding}$$

3. Earnings per share = Net income/Shares of common stock outstanding

    $$\text{Earnings Per share} = \frac{\$105{,}000}{10{,}000} = \$10.50$$

4. Return on owners' investment = Net income/Owners' equity

    $$\text{Return on owners' investment} = \frac{\$105{,}000}{\$174{,}000} = 60.2\%$$

5. Current assets - Current liabilities = Working capital
        $375,000   - $250,000   = $125,000

{ Chapter 3 }

THE ACCOUNTING CYCLE

Chapter 3 is directed to an explanation of the details in the accounting cycle--the manner in which transactions are recorded, accounting records maintained, and financial reports prepared.

Accounting is best viewed as a system for processing information. The raw material in that system is the transaction. In this chapter are presented the processing activities typically found in accounting systems.

KEY POINTS

I. **Recording Transactions**

    A. The basic accounting equation, Assets = Liabilities + Capital Contributed by Owners + Retained Earnings, serves as the basis for all accounting transactions.

    B. Every transaction affects one or more elements of the equation but preserves the equality between the left hand side and the right hand side of the equation.

    C. A separate page in a ledger is maintained for each of the firm's accounts. The sum of the balances of the asset accounts must, at all times, equal the sum of the balances in the liability accounts plus the owners' equity accounts.

        1. An increase in an asset account is recorded on the left side of the page (a debit); a decrease is recorded on the right (a credit).

        2. An increase in a liability or an owners' equity account is recorded on the right side of the page (a credit), a decrease is recorded on the left (a debit).

        3. At any given point in time, asset accounts would ordinarily have debit balances, liability and owners' equity accounts, credit balances.

    D. In order to maintain a complete record of all financial events affecting a firm, transactions are recorded initially by means of journal entries.

        1. A Journal entry indicates the one or more accounts to be debited, along with the amounts, and the one or more accounts to be credited, along

with the amounts. The sum of the debits must equal the sum of the credits. A journal entry takes the following form:

Equipment	$100,000	
Cash		$ 20,000
Notes payable		80,000

To record purchase of equipment.
(Firm paid $20,000 cash and gave a note for the balance.

2. The amounts indicated in the journal entries are <u>posted</u> to (entered in) the appropriate accounts in the ledger.

E. A trial balance can be prepared at any time simply by determining the balances in each of the ledger accounts and listing them. The sum of the debit balances (the asset accounts) must equal the sum of the credit balances (the liability and owners' equity accounts); If they do not, then the accounts are in error.

II. **Accounting for Revenues and Expenses**

A. Some transactions affect <u>only</u> asset and liability accounts. The 'level' of net assets (assets less liabilities) remains unchanged, the interests of the owners, likewise remain unchanged. Other transactions increase or decrease the interests of the owners in the enterprise. They result in revenues or expenses and enter into the determination of periodic income.

B. Since the reason for change is usually of utmost importance to the users of financial information, it is necessary to divide the retained earnings account into sub-accounts-each of which is used to record specific types of inflows (revenues) or outflows (expenses) of net assets.

C. Revenue and expense accounts are maintained for each of the major categories of inflows and outflows.

1. <u>Revenues</u>: The inflows of assets into the firm as the result of production or delivery of goods and/or the rendering of services.

2. <u>Expenses</u>: The outflow of assets in the course of the profit directed activities of the firm.

3. <u>Income</u>: The excess of revenues over expenses.

D. Revenue and expense accounts are temporary accounts. At the end of each accounting period, the balances in the accounts are transferred to the ""parent" account, retained earnings. As a consequence of the journal entry which the transfer is made, retained earnings are increased by the difference between the revenues and the expenses (i.e. income). The revenue and expense accounts are "zeroed out" ready to be used to record revenues and expenses in the next accounting period.

E. The entries by which the balances in the revenue and expense accounts are transferred to the retained earnings are known as <u>closing entries</u>. Closing entries generally take the following form:

Revenue accounts
(each individual account)   xxxx
    Retained earnings   xxxx

To close revenue account.

Retained earnings   xxxx
  Expense accounts
(each individual account)   xxxx

To close expense accounts.

III. The Complete Accounting Cycle

A. The accounting cycle consists of the following steps:

1. Journalizing the transactions and other financial events. Transactions and other economic events are first recorded in the form of journal entries.

2. Updating the accounts by recognizing other economic events. This is necessary at month end, prior to preparing the financial statements.

3. Posting to ledger accounts and computing account balances. At the end of an accounting period, the entries to each of the ledger accounts are summarized. The ending balance is equal to the beginning balance plus the difference between the sum of the debit and credit entries to the account.

4. Taking a trial balance. All the balances of the individual accounts are listed on a worksheet. Debit balances are indicated in one column, credit balances in another. The sum of the debit balances must equal the sum of the credit balances.

5. Preparing the income statement. The revenue and expense accounts are taken from the trial balance and re-arranged in the form of an income statement. Net income is the difference between the total revenues and expenses.

6. Closing revenues, expenses, and dividends. Journal entries are made to close the revenue and expense accounts. The entries serve to

transfer the balances in those accounts to Retained Earnings and to "zero-out" the balances. This is accomplished through an Income Summary account.

7. Taking a post-closing trial balance. This trial balance should only contain balance sheet accounts.

8. Preparing a balance sheet.

9. Preparing a statement of cash flows.

KEY ISSUES FOCUSED UPON IN THIS CHAPTER

Why are revenues and expenses accounted for in accounts separate from retained earnings? What Is the relationship between revenue and expense accounts. retained earnings, and closing entries?

Revenue and expenses are temporary sub-accounts of the retained earnings account to keep detailed record of the major operating components of the firm without "cluttering up" retained earnings with many entries. At the end of the accounting period, their balances are closed out and the net differences, profit or loss, is transferred to the retained earnings account.

KEY WORDS AND PHRASES

Accounting Cycle	Net Assets
Closing Entries	Organizational Costs
Credit	Posting
Debit	T-Account
General Ledger	Trial Balance
Journal	Turnover

ILLUSTRATING FOR REVIEW

This example is intended to Illustrate the effects of various types of business transactions on the basic accounting equation, Assets = Liabilities + Owners' Equity, or the expanded form of the equation, Assets = Liabilities + Contributed Capital + Beginning Retained Earnings + Revenues − Expenses − Dividends. The effects of the following business transactions of the Ajax Company are indicated in the journal entries. They are summarized in the table that follows.

1. January 1, 1991. The company sells 100 shares of stock for $100 per share.

        Cash (asset+) $ 10,000
            Common stock (contributed capital+) $ 10,000

        To record the sale of 100 shares of common stock.

2. January 2, 1991. The company purchases $4,000 of inventories from the Johnson Supply Company.

        Merchandise inventory (asset +) $ 4,000
            Accounts payable (liability+) $ 4,000

        To record the purchase, on account, of merchandise inventory.

3. January 5, 1991. Salaries of $600 earned by employees, but not yet paid, are given accounting recognition.

        Salary expense (expense+) $ 600
            Accrued salaries payable (Liability+) $ 600

        To record the accrual of salary expenses for the first week of January.

4. January 9, 1991. The company pays Its employees salaries earned in the first week of the month.

        Accrued Salaries payable (liability-) $ 600
            Cash (asset-) $ 600

        To record the payment of accrued salaries to employees.

5. January 10, 1991. The company sells for $5,000 (on account) merchandise which costs $3,000.

        Accounts receivable (asset+) $ 5,000
            Sales revenue (revenue+) $ 5,000

        To record the sale of merchandise.

        Cost of goods sold (expense+) $ 3,000
            Merchandise inventory (asset-) $ 3,000

        To record the cost of merchandise sold.

6. January 10, 1991. The company borrows $10,000 from the First National Bank and signs a 3-year note requiring payment of interest at an annual rate of 8 percent.

        Cash (asset+) $ 10,000

            Notes payable (liability+) $ 10,000

        To record the receipt of a $10,000 loan. (No recognition of interest need be given at this time.)

7. January 11, 1991. The company's Board of Directors declares a $1 per share cash dividend to common stockholders of record as of January 18. It is payable on January 21st.

        Dividend (owners' equity-) $ 100
            Dividends payable (Liability+) $ 100

To record the declaration of a $1 per share cash dividend payable, to stockholders of record as of January 18th, on January 21st.

8. January 14, 1991. The company receives a $500 payment on an open account from one of its customers.

        Cash (asset+) $ 500
            Accounts receivable (asset-) $ 500

To record payment received from customer.

9. January 15, 1991. The company pays in advance $1,200 for one year's rental on a duplicating machine.

        Prepaid rent (asset+) $ 1,200
            Cash (asset-) $ 1,200

To record the payment, in advance, of rent on a duplicating machine.

10. January 16, 1991. The company pays $500 of the amount included in account payable.

        Accounts payable (liability-) $ 500
            Cash (asset) $ 500

Record payment on account to the Johnson Supply Company

11. January 21,1991. The company pays the cash dividend declared on January 11th.

        Dividends payable (liability-) $ 100
            Cash (asset-) $ 100

To record the payment of a cash dividend declared on January 11th.

12. January 10, 1991. The company pays $400 to the First National Bank. The payment includes $44 for interest on the note and $356 as prepayment of the amount borrowed.

        Interest expense (expense+) $ 44
        Notes payable (liability-)   356
            Cash (asset-) $ 400

To record the payment of interest and principal to the First National Bank.

13. January 13, 1991. The company records the expiration of one-half month's prepaid rent on a duplicating machine.

    Machine rental expense (expense+) $ 50
        Prepaid rent (asset-) $ 50

    To record the expiration of one-half month's prepaid rent on a duplicating machine.

14. January 31, 1991. The company "closes" its revenue, expense, and dividend accounts.

    Sales revenue (revenue-) $ 5,000
        Income Summary (owners' equity+) $5,000

    To close the revenue account at month's end.

    Income Summary (owners' equity-) $ 3,694
        Salary expense (expense-) $ 600
        Cost of goods sold (expense-)   3,000
        Interest expense (expense-)   44
        Machine rental expense (expense-)   50

    To close the expense accounts at month's end.

    Income Summary $ 1,036
        Retained earnings $1,036

    To close the Income Summary account.

    Retained earnings (owners' equity-) $ 100
        Dividends (owners' equity+) $ 100

    To close dividend accounts at month's end.

EFFECTS OF TRANSACTIONS OF ACCOUNTING EQUATION

	ASSETS	=	LIABILITIES	+	CONTRIBUTED CAPITAL	+	RETAINED EARNINGS 12-31-90	+	REVENUES	-	EXPENSES	-	DIVIDENDS
1.	Cash (+10,000)				Common Stock (+10,000)								
2.	Merchandise inventory		Accounts payable (+4,000)										
3.			Accrued salaries payable (+600)								Salary expense (+600)		
4.	Cash		Accrued salaries payable (-600)										
5.	Accounts receivable (+5,000)								Sales (+5,000)				
	Merchandise inventory (-3,000)										Cost of goods sold (+3,000)		
6.	Cash (+10,000)		Notes payable (+10,000)										
7.			Dividends payable (+100)										Dividends (+100)
8.	Cash (+500) Accounts receivable (-500)												

24

EFFECTS OF TRANSACTIONS OF ACCOUNTING EQUATION (cont.)

ASSETS	=	LIABILITIES	+	CONTRIBUTED CAPITAL	+	RETAINED EARNINGS 12-31-90	+	REVENUES	-	EXPENSES	-	DIVIDENDS
9. Prepaid rent (+1,200) Cash (-1,200)												
10. Cash (-500)		Accounts payable (-500)										
11. Cash (-100)		Dividends Payable (-100)										
12. Cash (-400)		Notes payable (-356)								Interest (+44)		
13. Prepaid rent (-50)										Machine rental (+50)		
14.						Retained earnings (+5,000)		Sales (-5,000)				
						Retained earnings (-3,694)				Salary expense (-600)		
										Cost of goods sold (-3000)		
										Interest (-44)		
										Machine rental (-50)		
						Retained earnings (-100)						Dividends (-100)
Totals $ 24,350		$ 13,144		$10,000		$1,206		$ 0		$ 0		$0

25

EXERCISES

1. You are provided with the following revenue and expense account balances of the E. F. Burroughs Company as of December 31, 1991 (000 omitted).

Advertising Expense	$ 20
Bad Debt Expense	7
Cost of Goods Sold	52
Deprecation Expense	15
Income Tax Expense	20
Rental Expense	18
Sales Revenue	215
Wage Expense	30

   How much income did the E. F. Burroughs Company earn in 1991?

2. Prepare the journal entries required to close the E. F. Burroughs Company's revenue and expense accounts indicated above.

3. Prepare journal entries, as required, to give accounting recognition to each of the following financial events that take place during 1991.

   a) March 20. The company purchases and pays for 20 acres of land at $300 per acre.

   b) April 15th. The company pays $1,000 to the Internal Revenue Service to satisfy its estimated income tax liability for the first quarter of the year.

   c) May 11th. A customer sends the company a $200 payment on his account.

   d) July 3rd. The company sells for $100 cash merchandise which cost $50. (Assume the cost of goods sold is recorded at the time of sale.)

   e) September 15th. The company pays $1,500 in salaries (not previously recorded) to its employees.

   f) December 15th. The company signs a contract with the Acme Electrical Supply Company to buy electrical supplies at a 15% discount for a two year period starting January 1, 1992. You are provided with the Trial balance Of the Antique Furniture Corporation as of December 31, 1991.

4. You are provided with the trial balance for the Antique Furniture Corporation as of December 31, 1991.

Antique Furniture Corporation
Trial Balance
As of December 31, 1991

	Debit	Credit
Cash in Bank	$ 8,500	
Accounts Receivable	85,000	
Allowance Of Uncollectible Accounts		$ 9,500
Prepaid insurance	2,400	
Merchandise inventory	68,300	
Machinery and Equipment	50,000	
Accumulated Depreciation-Machinery and Equipment		20,000
Building	70,000	
Accumulated Depreciation-Building		25,000
Land	10,000	
Accounts Payable		6,250
Interest Payable		375
Notes Payable		15,000
Preferred Stock		50,000
Common Stock		100,000
Retained Earnings		25,375
Sales Revenue		150,000
Rent Revenue		15,000
Cost of Goods Sold	75,000	
Depreciation Expense	10,000	
Wages Expense	27,975	
Insurance Expense	1,200	
Miscellaneous Expenses	8,125	
Total	$ 416,500	$416,500

Required:

a) Prepare an income statement for the year ended December 31, 1991.

SOLUTIONS TO CHAPTER THREE EXERCISES

1. Revenues - Expenses = Net Income
   215 - (20+7+52+15+20+18+30) = $ 53

2. a) Sales revenue $ 215
       Income Summary $ 215

   To close revenue account.

   b) Income Summary $ 162
       Advertising expense $ 20
       Bad debt expense   7
       Cost of goods sold   52
       Deprecation expense   15
       Income expense   20
       Rent expense   18
       Wage expense   30

   To close expense accounts.

   c) Income Summary $ 53
       Retained earnings $ 53

   To transfer income to retained earnings.

3. a) March 20

   Land $ 6,000
       Cash $ 6,000
   To record the Cash purchase of 20 acres of land at $300 per acre.

   b) April 15

   Income tax expense $ 1,000
       Cash $ 1,000
   To record the payment of the first quarter's estimated income.

   c) May 11

   Cash $ 200
       Accounts receivable $ 200
   To record the receipt of $200 from a customer.

   d) July 3

   Cash $ 100
       Sales Revenue $ 100
   To record the sale of merchandise.

   Cost of goods sold $ 50
       Merchandise inventories $ 50
   To record the cost of merchandise sold.

e) September 15

    Salary expense $ 1,500
        Cash $ 1,500
    To record the payment of salaries to employees.

f) December 15

    No journal entry is required.

4. a)

Antique Furniture Corporation
Income Statement
For the Year Ended December 31, 1991

Revenues:		
From Sales	$150,000	
From Rent	15,000	$165,000
Less Expenses:		
Cost of Goods Sold	$ 75,000	
Depreciation	10,000	
Wages	27,975	
Insurance	1,200	
Miscellaneous	8,125	122,300
Net Income from Operations		$ 42,700

Antique Furniture Corporation
Balance Sheet
As of December 31, 1991

Assets

Current Assets:			
Cash		$ 8,500	
Accounts Receivable	$ 85,000		
Less: Allowance for			
Uncollectible Accounts	9,500	75,500	
Prepaid Insurance		2,400	
Merchandise Inventory		68,300	$154,700
Non-Current Assets:			
Machinery and Equipment	$ 50,000		
Less: Accumulated Depreciation	20,000	$ 30,000	
Buildings	$ 70,000		
Less: Accumulated Depreciation	25,000	45,000	
Land		10,000	85,000
Total Assets			$239,700

Liabilities and Owners' Equity

Current Liabilities:
    Accounts payable $ 6,250
    Interests payable   375 $ 6,625

Non-Current Liabilities:
    Notes payable   15,000

Stockholders' Equity:
    Preferred Stock $ 50,000
    Common Stock   100,000
    Retained Earnings   68,075   218,075
        Total Liabilities and Owners' Equity $239,700

c) Closing entries:

    (1)   Revenue from sales $150,000
                 Revenue from rent   15,000
                     Income summary $165,000
         To close the revenue accounts.

    (2)   Income summary $122,300
                     Cost of goods sold $ 75,000
                     Deprecation expense   10,000
                     Wages expense   27,975
                     Insurance expense   1,200
                     Miscellaneous expenses   8,125

         To close the expense accounts.

    (3)   Income Summary $ 42,700
                     Retained earnings $42,700
         To transfer income to retained earnings.

d)   The difference amounts to $42,700, the same as the Net income for the year.

         Retained Earnings per Balance Sheet $ 68,075
         Less: Retained Earnings per Trial Balance   25,375
               Difference (Net Income) $ 42,700

The difference arises because the balance in retained earnings per the trial balance, is that before taking into account the income for the period. The balance per the trial balance is a <u>pre-closing</u> balance; that on the balance sheet is a <u>post-closing</u> balance.

{Chapter 4}

ACCRUING REVENUES AND EXPENSES

Chapter 4 explains some important features of the basic accounting cycle. It focuses upon the accrual concept-the idea that revenues and expenses should be reported in the accounting period in which they have their primary ECONOMIC impact, not necessarily when the related cash is received or disbursed.

KEY POINTS

I. **The Accrual Concept**

The accrual concept is the notion that the effects of transactions and other financial events on the assets and liabilities of an enterprise should be accorded accounting recognition at the time that they have their primary economic impact, not necessarily when the related cash is received or disbursed.

    A.   Revenues should be assigned to that period in which they are earned; revenues are said to be <u>realized</u> at this point when they are earned. This period may be one either before or after the related cash is received.

    B.   Costs are charged as expenses in the period in which they provide their expected services, when revenues are recognized.

        1.   When costs intended to provide future services are <u>capitalized</u>, they are recorded as assets until such time as the acquired services are actually provided.

        2.   Examples: Rent cost for particular month is charged as an expense during the month of occupancy, even though rent payment may be made in previous or subsequent months.

II. **Periodic Adjusting Entries**

    A.   Updating entries

        1.   Some expenses are incurred and some revenues are earned on a continuous basis. Insurance expense for example, is incurred continuously during the period covered by the policy. Since it is impractical to make entries to record such revenues and expenses on

around-the-clock basis, it is necessary to periodically update the accounts.

2. Examples of revenues and expenses which accrue on a continuous basis are interest, rent, insurance, and depreciation. The updating entries affect not only revenue or expense accounts, but related asset or liability account as well. Updating entries <u>do not</u> involve cash, since the mere accounting recognition of the expiration of an asset or the increase in an obligation does not serve to either increase or decrease a firm's cash balance.

B. Correcting entries

1. The need for <u>correcting</u> entries stem from the willingness of firms to permit out-of-date information to remain in the accounts in order to obtain a measure of bookkeeping convenience. Instead of making entry each time they take an action, firms wait until the end of a specified period and then adjust the accounts to bring them up to date.

2. The need for adjusting entries may be illustrated by the way that a magazine publisher accounts for subscription revenue. Subscription revenue should properly be recognized, not when a subscriber orders his magazine, but rather throughout the subscription period, as the magazines are sent to him.

3. The general approach taken in making periodic adjusting entries is to bring either an income or expense account (a "flow" account) and an associated balance sheet account (a "storage" account) into proper relationship. As a rule, the accountant need only determine the correct amount that should be reported in <u>either</u> the balance sheet or the corresponding income statement account. If he makes the proper journal entry to bring that account into line, then the related account will also be increased or decreased to reflect a correct amount.

III. **Errors and Omissions**

A. Some errors are readily detectable. If the sum of the general ledger debits does not equal the sum of the general ledger credits, then the accounts are in error.

B. But other errors are not readily detectable. Many of these errors are self-correcting over time. The overall impact of such errors is to transfer income from one accounting period to another. Income, over the life of the enterprise, will be correctly reported. But that of the individual periods will he misstated. Moreover, since asset and liability accounts represent "stored" revenues or expenses, the balance sheets for all periods between the time that the error was made and that when it was automatically corrected will also be misstated.

IV. **Measures of Financial Performance and Health**

    A. The financial performance and fiscal health of a firm can be described by ratios that relate one aspect of a firm's performance to another. Some ratios are commonly used by investors, creditors, and managers to evaluate both the firm as a whole and its component parts.

    B. There are three primary groups of ratios:

        1. Profitability and activity measures which indicate how well a firm is using its assets. Typical ratios are:

            a. Earnings per share

$$EPS = \frac{\text{Net income}}{\text{Shares of common stock outstanding}}$$

            b. Return on investment

$$ROI = \frac{\text{Net income}}{\text{Owners' Equity}}$$

        2. Liquidity ratios. The Current Ratio is the most widely used measure of liquidity:

$$CR = \frac{\text{Current assets}}{\text{Current liabilities}}$$

        3. Financing ratios. The debt-to-equity ratio measures the extent to which a firm is leveraged:

$$D \text{ to } E = \frac{\text{Total debt}}{\text{Total equity}}$$

KEY ISSUES FOCUSED UPON IN THIS CHAPTER

1. What is the impact of the accrual concept on the recording process? It requires that the effects of transactions be recorded in the accounting records when the have their primary economic impact, regardless of when cash is received or disbursed.

2. What is the basic purpose of making periodic adjusting entries? It is to prepare the accounting record for the determination of net income, the most important step in the accounting process. The adjusting entries attempt to include all the proper revenues and expense of the period in the accounts go the resulting net income calculation will be as accurate as possible.

KEY WORDS AND PHRASES

Accrual Concept	Periodic Inventory Method
Accrued	Perpetual Inventory Method
Capitalize	Realize
Contra Account	Recognize
Control Accounts	Self-Correcting Errors
Correcting Entries	Subsidiary Ledgers
Direct Costs	Updating (Adjusting) Entries
Factory Overhead Costs	
Matching Principle	

ILLUSTRATIONS FOR REVIEW

<u>New Times Magazine</u> began Publication in January 1992. During the year it sold, for cash, 2,000 subscriptions at $12 each. A subscription entitles the subscriber to 12 monthly issues of the magazine. During the year, 14,000 magazines were sent to subscribers. At year-end, a review of subscription records indicated that subscribers had paid for, but not yet received, a total of 10,000 magazine.

Required: Prepare three alternative sets of journal entries to record subscription revenue for 1992.

<u>Alternative A</u>
(1)

    Cash $24,000
         Subscriptions paid for but not yet delivered (liability) $24,000

To record the sale of subscriptions. (The entry summarizes the actual entries to be made each time a subscription is sold.

           Subscriptions paid for but not yet delivered $14,000
                Subscription revenue $14,000

Alternative B

(1)

Cash $24,000
    Subscriptions paid for but not yet delivered $24,000

To record the sale of subscriptions. (This entry summarizes the actual entries to be made each time a subscription is sold).

No entry would be made each month as the firm sends the magazines to its subscribers.

(2)

Subscriptions paid for but not yet delivered $14,000
    Subscription revenue $14,000

To adjust the accounts at year-end to reflect the fact that the firm has an obligation to deliver only 10,000 additional magazines, and at the same time, to recognize revenue from the delivery of 14,000 magazines during the year.

Alternative C

(1)

Cash $24,000
    Subscription revenue $24,000

To record the sale of subscriptions. (This entry summarizes the actual entries to be made each time a subscription is sold.)

No entry would be made each month as the firm sends magazines to its subscribers.

(2)

Subscription revenue $10,000
    Subscriptions paid for but not yet delivered $10,000

To adjust the accounts at year-end to reflect the fact that the firm should properly recognize only $14,000 in subscription revenue and that it still has an obligation to send an additional 10,000 magazines to its subscribers.

EXERCISES

Randall and Joseph Smith, founders of the Elant Corporation, have asked their CPAs, Poole, Jarett and Olden to assist them in maintaining their books and records, and in preparing financial statements after the firm has completed its first month of operation.

The transactions in which the Elant Corporation engaged during July 1991, its first month of operation, are indicated below. You are to put yourself in the position of an associate of the CPA firm of Poole, Jarett and Olden and record the transactions in journal entry form. Use only those accounts that are indicated in the corporation's chart of accounts, which is presented on the following page.

In a section of this exercise, following that in which the financial events are described, the correct entries are presented. These entries have been posted to T-accounts, and a trial balance has been prepared. Based on the trial balance, you are to prepare, In good form. an income statement and a balance sheet. Selected amounts have been provided to assist you in your work.

1. Randall and Joseph Smith formed the Elant Corporation on July 1st to sell automotive parts. The corporation issued to the founders 20,000 shares of $10 par, common stock for $100 per share.

2. July 1st. The company purchased 30 acres of land for $30,000.

3. July 1st. The company purchased an existing warehouse at a total cost of $200,000. The warehouse has an estimated serviceable Life of 40 years. The company borrowed the entire purchase price from the Randall Finance and Loan Company. It issued to the loan company a note which required the payment of interest at an annual rate of 11 percent. The first interest payment is due in 1992; the entire principal is due on July 1, 1998.

4. July 2nd. The company paid the Cox Paving Company $4,000 to install a parking lot (a depreciable asset) near the warehouse. The estimated useful life of the lot is 8 years.

5. July 2nd. The company purchased $10,000 of office furniture and fixtures from the Foxhall Furniture Company. The furniture and fixtures have a useful life of 10 years.

6. July 2nd. The company purchased an 18-month insurance policy from the Gibraltar Insurance Company at a cost of $2,400.

Elant Corporation
Chart of Accounts

Account Number	Account Title
101	Cash in bank
110	Marketable securities
115	Notes receivable
120	Inventory
125	Prepaid insurance
140	Office furniture and fixtures
141	Accumulated depreciation-office furniture and fixtures
150	Deliver trucks
151	Accumulated depreciation-delivery trucks
155	Automobiles
156	Accumulated depreciation-automobiles
160	Warehouse equipment
161	Accumulated depreciation-warehouse equipment
170	Parking lots
171	Accumulated depreciation-parking lots
180	Buildings
181	Accumulated depreciation-buildings
190	Land
201	Accounts payable
210	Accrued interest payable
230	Advanced from customers
250	Notes payable
320	Common stock
321	Contributed capital in excess of par, common stock
350	Dividends
360	Income summary
370	Retained earnings
401	Sales revenue

410	Interest revenue
420	Gain on sale of land
503	Interest expense
504	Depreciation expense
505	Salary expense
506	Utility expense
507	Property tax expense
508	Income tax expense
509	Gas and oil expense
510	Operating supply expense
511	Repair and maintenance expense
512	Cost of goods sold
513	Insurance expense

7. July 3rd. Elant Corporation purchased $100,000 of warehouse equipment from the Delta Equipment Company. It paid $50,000 In cash and financed the balance with a 11 percent note from the Randall Finance and Loan Company (interest is payable on January 1st and July 1st, with the principal due on June 30, 1993). The equipment has a 10-year useful Life.

8. July 3rd. The company purchased 3 delivery trucks for $45,000, and 2 automobiles for $10,000. All vehicles were purchased for cash and have an estimated service life of 5 years.

9. July 5th. The company signed an agreement whit the Johnson Supply Company whereby all auto parts delivered to the Elant Corporation would be paid for within 20 days of delivery to the Elant Corporation's warehouse. In addition, $25,000 worth of auto parts were purchased and delivered.

10. July 8th. Elant Corporation returned $1,000 of damaged auto parts to the Johnson Supply Company.

11. July 20th. The board of directors, at its monthly meeting, declared a $1 per share cash dividend. The dividend was paid on date of declaration.

12. July 25th. The company paid for auto parts purchased on July 5th ($24,000 purchases minus returns of July 8th).

13. July 30th. The company received a $30,000 advance from the Reston's Garage for auto parts that were to be delivered on August 12, 1991.

14. July 30th. The company purchased $50,000 of marketable securities as a temporary investment.

15. July 30th. The company sold 5 acres of land for $15,000 to the Macintosh Trucking Company. It received a $5,000 cash payment and a 60-day, 10 percent note for the remaining $10,000.

16. July 31st. The following additional facts were also brought to the attention of Poole, Jarett and Olden:

    a. Total sales of auto parts for the month were $500,000; all sales were for cash.

    b. Additional purchases of inventories of auto parts, not previously recorded, totaled $172,000.

c. The month-end inventory count revealed that parts which had cost $47,000 were still on hand as of July 31st. The company maintains its inventory on a <u>periodic</u> basis.

d. The following expenses were paid in cash on July 31st:

1. Salary expense	$16,000
2. Utility expense	6,000
3. Property tax	3,000
4. Income tax	15,000
5. Gas and Oil expense	5,000
6. Operating supplies expense	15,000
7. Vehicle and machinery repair and maintenance expense	4,000

17. The accountants were reminded of the need to update the accounts to give recognition to the following:

   a. One month's expiration of the insurance policy purchased on July 2nd.

   b. One month's deprecation on the warehouse, the parking lot, the office furniture and fixtures, the warehouse equipment, the delivery trucks and the automobiles.

   c. One month's interest expense on the notes issued on July 1st and July 3rd.

18. The accountants elected to close the books as of July 31st; it is necessary to make journal entries to close all revenue, expense and dividend accounts.

Compare your journal entries with those drawn up by Mr. Poole, which are presented below. Then notice how the general journal entries are posted to the general ledger accounts.

General Journal

Date	Account Titles and Explanations	Account Number	Debit	Credit
	(1)			
1991 July 1	Cash	101	$2,000,000	
	Common stock	320		$200,000
	Contributed capital in excess of par	321		$1,800,000
	To record the sale of 20,000 shares of $10 par value common stock, at $100 per share			
	(2)			
July 1	Land	190	$30,000	
	Cash	101		$30,000
	To record the purchase of 30-acre tract of land at $1,000 per acre.			
	(3)			
July 1	Buildings	180	$200,000	
	Notes payable	250		$200,000
	To record the purchase of warehouse and issuance of a note.			
	(4)			
July 2	Parking lot	170	$4,000	
	Cash	101		$4,000
	To record the installation of parking lot.			
	(5)			
July 2	Office furniture and fixtures	140	$30,000	
	Cash	101		$30,000
	To record the purchase of furniture and fixtures.			
	(6)			
July 2	Prepaid Insurance	125	$2,400	
	Cash	101		$2,400
	To record the purchase of 18-month insurance policy.			

43

General Journal (Continued)

Date	Account Titles and Explanations	Account Number	Debit	Credit
	(7)			
July 3	Warehouse equipment	160	$ 300,000	
	Notes payable	250		$ 50,000
	Cash	101		50,000
	To record the purchase of warehouse equipment in exchange for cash and a note.			
	(8)			
July 3	Delivery trucks	150	$ 45,000	
	Automobiles	155	10,000	
	Cash	101		$ 55,000
	To record the purchase of company vehicles.			
July 5	No entry required to record signing of contract.			
	(9)			
July 5	Inventory	120	$ 25,000	
	Accounts payable	201		$ 25,000
	To record the purchase of auto parts.			
	(10)			
July 8	Accounts payable	201	$ 1,000	
	Inventory	120		$ 1,000
	To record the return of damaged auto parts to Johnson Supply Company.			
	(11)			
July 20	Dividends	350	$ 20,000	
	Cash	101		$ 20,000
	To record the declaration and payment of a $1 per share cash dividend on 20,000 shares outstanding.			
	(12)			
July 25	Accounts payable	201	$ 24,000	
	Cash	101		$ 24,000
	To record the payment of trade accounts payable.			
	(13)			
July 30	Cash	101	$ 30,000	
	Advances from customers	230		$ 30,000
	To record the receipt of advance payment from Reston's Garage.			

General Journal (Continued)

Date	Account Titles and Explanations	Account Number	Debit	Credit
	(14)			
July 30	Marketable securities	110	$ 50,000	
	Cash	101		$ 50,000
	To record the purchase of marketable securities.			
	(15)			
July 30	Cash	101	$ 5,000	
	Notes receivable	115	10,000	
	Land	190		$ 5,000
	Gain on sale of land	420		10,000
	To record the sale of 5 acres of land (cost of land was $1,000 per acre; 30,000 cost /30 acres) in exchange for cash and a note.			
	(16a)			
July 31	Cash	101	$ 500,000	
	Sales revenue	401		$ 500,000
	To record sales for month of July 1991.			
	(16b)			
July 31	Inventory	120	$ 172,000	
	Accounts payable	201		$ 172,000
	To record the remaining purchases for month of July, 1991.			
	(16c)			
July 31	Cost of goods sold	512	$ 149,000	
	Inventory	120		$ 149,000
	To record the cost of auto parts sold during July, 1991. (Cost of goods sold equals the balance in inventory account—$196,000—less goods actually on hand—$47,000.)			
	(16d)			
July 31	Salary expense	505	$ 16,000	
	Utility expense	506	6,000	
	Property tax expense	507	3,000	
	Income tax expense	508	15,000	
	Gas and oil expense	509	5,000	
	Operating supplies expense	510	15,000	
	Repair and maintenance expense	511	4,000	
	Cash	101		$ 64,000

General Journal (Continued)

Date	Account Titles and Explanations	Account Number	Debit	Credit
	To record the payment of expenses for the month of July, 1991.			
	(17a)			
July 31	Insurance expense	513	$ 133	
	Prepaid insurance	125		$ 133
	To record the expiration of one month's prepaid insurance ($2,400 divided by 18 months.)			
	(17b)			
July 31	Depreciation expense	504	$ 2,292	
	Accumulated depreciation-office furniture and fixtures	141		$ 83
	Accumulated depreciation-trucks	151		750
	Accumulated depreciation-automobiles	156		167
	Accumulated depreciation-warehouse equipment	161		833
	Accumulated depreciation-parking lot	171		42
	Accumulated depreciation-warehouse building	181		417
	To record depreciation expense for month of July, 1991 (cost of asset divided by useful life expressed in terms of months).			
	(17c)			
July 31	Interest expense	503	$ 2,292	
	Accrued interest payable	201		$ 2,292
	To accrue interest on the two notes payable to Randall Finance and Loan Company for the month of July, 1991. (11 percent of total balance of $250,000-$27,500-divided by 12.)			

General Journal (Continued)

Date	Account Titles and Explanations	Account Number	Debit	Credit
	Closing Entries			
	(18a)			
July 31	Income summary	360	$ 217,717	
	Interest expense	503		$ 2,292
	Depreciation expense	504		2,292
	Salary expense	505		16,000
	Utility expense	506		6,000
	Property tax expense	507		3,000
	Income tax expense	508		15,000
	Gas and oil expense	509		5,000
	Operating supply expense	510		15,000
	Repair and maintenance expense	511		4,000
	Cost of goods sold	512		149,000
	Insurance expense	513		133
	To close the expense accounts.			
	(18b)			
July 31	Sales revenue	401	$ 500,000	
	Gain on sale of land	420	10,000	
	Income summary	360		$510,000
	To close the revenue accounts.			
	(18c)			
July 31	Income Summary	360	$ 292,283	
	Retained Earnings	370		$292,283
	(18d)			
July 31	Retained earnings	370	$ 20,000	
	Dividends	350		$ 20,000
	To close the dividends accounts.			

General Ledger Accounts

Cash			101
(1)	2,000,000	30,000	(2)
(13)	30,000	4,000	(4)
(15)	5,000	10,000	(5)
(16a)	500,000	2,400	(6)
		50,000	(7)
		55,000	(8)
		20,000	(11)
		24,000	(12)
		50,000	(14)
		64,000	(16d)
	2,535,000	309,400	
	2,225,600		

Marketable Securities			#110
(14)	50,000		
	50,000		

Notes Receivable			#115
(15)	10,000		
	10,000		

Inventories			#120
(9)	25,000	1,000	(10)
(16b)	172,000	149,000	(16c)
	197,000	150,000	
	47,000		

Prepaid Insurance			125
(6)	2,400	133	(17a)
	2,267		

Office Furniture and Fixtures			#140
(5)	10,000		
	10,000		

Accumulated Depreciation Office Furniture and Fixtures			#141
		83	(17a)
		83	

Delivery Trucks			#150
(8)	45,000		
	45,000		

Accumulated Depreciation Delivery Trucks			#151
		750	(17b)
		750	

Automobiles			#155
(8)	10,000		
	10,000		

Accumulated Depreciation Automobiles			#156
		167	(17b)
		167	

General Ledger Accounts (Cont'd.)

Warehouse Equipment	#160		Accumulated Depreciation Warehouse Equipment	#161
(7) 100,000				833 (17b)
========				========
100,000				833

Parking Lot	#170		Accumulated Depreciation Parking Lot	#171
(4) 4,000				42 (17b)
======				======
4,000				42

Buildings	#180		Accumulated Depreciation Buildings	#181
(3) 200,000				417 (17b)
========				======
200,000				417

Land			#190		Accounts Payable		#201
(2) 30,000	5,000	(15)		(10) 1,000	25,000	(9)
				(12) 24,000	172,000	(16b)
30,000	5,000			25,000	197,000	
======	=====			======	======	
25,000					172,000	

Accrued Interest Payable	#210		Advances from Customers	#230
	2,292 (17c)			30,000 (13)
	======			======
	2,292			30,000

Notes Payable	#250		Common Stock	#320
	200,000 (3)			200,000 (1)
	50,000 (7)			========
	250,000			200,000
	========			
	250,000			

Contributed Capital in Excess of Par	#321		Dividends	#350
	1,800,000 (1)		20,000	20,000 (18c)
	========		======	======
	1,800,000			

Income Summary		#360
(18a) 217,717	510,000	(18b)
(18c) 292,283		

49

Retained Earnings		#370		Sales Revenue		#401
(18d) 20,000	292,283	(18c)	(18b) 500,000	500,000	(16a)

Gain on Sale of Land		#420		Interest Expense		#503
(18b) 10,000	10,000	(15)	2,292	2,292	(18a)

Depreciation Expense		#504		Salary Expense		#505
(17b) 2,292	2,292	(18a)	(16d) 16,000	16,000	(18a)

Utility Expense		#506		Property Tax Expense		#507
(16d) 6,000	6,000	(18a)	(16d) 3,000	3,000	(18a)

Income Tax Expense		#508		Gas and Oil Expense		#509
(16d) 15,000	15,000	(18a)	(16d) 5,000	5,000	(18a)

Operating Supply Expense		#510		Repair and Maintenance Expense		#511
(16d) 15,000	15,000	(18a)	(16d) 4,000	4,000	(18a)

Cost of Goods Sold		#512		Insurance Expense		#513
(16c) 149,000	149,000		(17c) 133	133	(18a)

Based upon the balance in the general ledger accounts, the following trial balance has been prepared:

The Elant Corporation
Trial Balance
July 31, 1991

	Debit	Credit
Cash in Bank	$2,225,600	
Marketable Securities	50,000	
Notes Receivable	10,000	
Inventory	47,000	
Prepaid Insurance	2,267	
Office Furniture and Fixtures	10,000	
Accumulated Depreciation-Office Furniture & Fixtures		$ 83
Delivery Trucks	45,000	
Accumulated Depreciation-Delivery Trucks		750
Automobiles	10,000	
Accumulated Depreciation-Automobiles		167
Warehouse Equipment	100,000	
Accumulated Depreciation-Warehouse Equipment		833
Parking Lot	4,000	
Accumulated Depreciation-Parking Lot		42
Building	200,000	
Accumulated Depreciation-Building		417
Land	25,000	
Accounts Payable		172,000
Accrued Interest Payable		2,292
Advances from Customers		30,000
Notes Payable		250,000
Common Stock		200,000
Contributed Capital in Excess of Par		1,800,000
Dividends	20,000	
Sales Revenue		500,000
Gain on Sale of Land		10,000
Interest Expense	2,292	
Depreciation Expense	2,292	
Salary Expense	16,000	
Utility Expense	6,000	
Property Tax Expense	3,000	
Income Tax Expense	15,000	
Gas and Oil Expense	5,000	
Operating Supply Expense	15,000	
Repair and Maintenance Expense	4,000	
Cost of Goods Sold	149,000	
Insurance Expense	133	
Totals	$2,966,584	$2,966,584

Using the trial balance presented on page 47, complete the income statement and balance sheet of the Elant Corporation, presented below.

The Elant Corporation
Income Statement
For the Month of July, 1991

Revenues:

Less: Expenses

Total Expenses	$ 217,717
Net Income From Operations	$ 292,283

The Elant Corporation
Balance Sheet
As of July 31, 1991

Assets

Total Assets $2,726,575

Liabilities and Owners' Equity

Total Liabilities $ 454,292

Total Liabilities and Owners' Equity $2,726,575

Now, compare your statements with those presented on the following pages.

SOLUTIONS TO CHAPTER FOUR EXERCISES

The Elant Corporation
Income Statement
For the Month of July, 1991

Revenues:
  From Sales $ 500,000
  From Gain on Sale of Land   10,000 $ 510,000

Less: Expenses
  Cost of Goods Sold $ 149,000
  Salaries   16,000
  Income Taxes   15,000
  Operating Supplies   15,000
  Utilities   6,000
  Gas and Oil   5,000
  Repair and Maintenance   4,000
  Property Taxes   3,000
  Interest   2,292
  Depreciation   2,292
  Insurance   133 $ 217,717

Net Income (Loss) from Operations $ 292,283

The Elant Corporation
Balance Sheet
As of July 31, 1991

Assets

Current Assets:
  Cash in Bank $2,225,600
  Marketable Securities   50,000
  Notes Receivable   10,000
  Inventory   47,000
  Prepaid Insurance   1,600
    Total Current Assets $2,334,200

Non-Current Assets:
  Prepaid Insurance $ 667
  Office Furniture and Fixtures $ 10,000
  Less Accumulated Depreciation   83   9,917
  Delivery Trucks   45,000
  Less: Accumulated Depreciation   750   44,250
  Automobiles   10,000
  Less: Accumulated Depreciation   167   9,833
  Warehouse Equipment   100,000
  Less: Accumulated Depreciation   833   99,167
  Parking Lot   4,000
  Less: Accumulated Depreciation   42   3,958
  Building   200,000
  Less: Accumulated Depreciation   417   199,583
  Land   25,000
    Total Non-Current Assets $ 392,375
Total Assets $2,726,575

Liabilities and Owners' Equity

Current Liabilities:
  Accounts Payable $ 172,000
  Accrued Interest Payable   2,292
  Advances from Customers   30,000
    Total Current Liabilities $ 204,292
  Non-Current Liabilities:
    Notes Payable   250,000

Owners' Equity:
  Common Stock $ 200,000
  Contributed Capital in Excess of Par   1,800,000
  Retained Earnings*   272,283
    Total Owners' Equity   2,272,283
Total Liabilities and Owners' Equity   2,726,575

*Net Income - Dividends Paid=Balance in Retained Earnings
$292,283 - 20,000=$272,283

{Chapter 5}

MEASURING AND REPORTING REVENUES

As a general rule, revenues should be given accounting recognition when they are "earned". Costs should be matched to the revenues that they help to generate and should thereby be charged as expenses in the same period as the revenues are recognized it is not always easy, however, to determine when revenues have, in fact, been earned and to which revenues costs can most logically be associated. The methods by which revenues and expenses are recognized have a direct bearing on the values assigned to related assets and liabilities. Indeed, almost all important accounting issues revolve around questions of revenue and expense recognition.

KEY POINTS

I. **Statement of the Problem**

   A. The accounting questions with respect to income determination arise because owners and other parties who are concerned about the financial health of an enterprise, desire <u>periodic</u> reports of earnings. It is necessary, therefore, for accountants to assign both revenues and expenses to particular periods-and to develop appropriate criteria for making such assignments.

   B. Most commonly, revenue is recognized at the point of sale. But point of sale may not be a suitable time for all companies to recognize revenue.

   C. Expenses, it is said, should be <u>matched</u> to revenues. But it is not always clear to which revenue a certain cost should be matched.

   D. The issues of revenue recognition are inherently related to those of asset valuation. Revenue has been defined as an inflow of cash or other assets attributable to the goods or services provided by the firm. Any time recognition is given to revenue, so also must it be given to the increase in net assets.

   1. In those periods in which revenue is recognized, the firm must record an increase in assets (or, of course, a decrease in liabilities) <u>and</u> a corresponding increase in owners' equity.

2. In those periods in which revenue is not recognized, the firm should not record an increase in net assets. Instead (assuming that productive activity takes place), it should only record an exchange of some assets for other assets of equal value.

E. Similarly, expense has been defined as an outflow of cash or other assets (or, of course, an increase in liabilities) which serves to generate revenues. When recognition is given to expenses, so also must it be given to the decrease in net assets.

1. In those periods in which a cost is charged as an expense, the firm should record a decrease in net assets (that is, a decrease in assets or an increase in liabilities) and a corresponding decrease in owners' equity.

2. In those periods in which an expense is not recognized, the firm should not record a decrease in net assets. Instead, it should capitalize all cost Incurred and thereby "store" them in asset accounts until such time as it is appropriate to charge the costs as expenses.

II. **Criteria for Revenue Recognition.** Revenue from a productive or service activity should be recognized as soon as:

A. The firm has exerted a substantial portion of its production and sales effort, the major portion of costs have been incurred and the remaining costs can be estimated with reasonable reliability and precision;

B. The revenue can be objectively measured, eventual collection of cash can reasonably be assured;

C. For most firms, revenue is recognized at the time of sale. when the goods are transferred to the customer.

III. **Recognition of Revenue During Production**

A. Recognition of revenue during the entire period of production is associated primarily with firms that engage in long-term construction projects-projects that take more than one accounting period to complete. Recognition of revenue during the periods in which production efforts take place enables the firm to avoid the distortions of income that would result if the entire amount of revenue were recognized only in the period of sale.

B. The most widely used means of recognizing revenue throughout the entire production process is known as the percentage of completion method. On any given contract, the proportion of total contract price to be recognized as revenue in a particular accounting period is the percentage of the total project completed during that period. Thus, If 30 percent of a project is completed, then 30 percent of the sales price would be recognized as revenue and 30 percent of costs would be charged as expenses.

The percentage of completion method is appropriate only when total costs of completing a project can be estimated with reasonable reliability and precision, the contract price is fixed and certain to be collected, and there can be no doubt about the ability of the firm to complete the project and have it accepted by the other party to the contract.

IV. **Recognition of Revenue at Completion of Production**

    A. Recognition of revenue at <u>completion of production</u> is associated with those companies that face a ready and stable market for their products. Whenever a firm is certain that it will be able to sell all the goods that it produces at a known price, then by the time the production process is completed, it has satisfied the four criteria for revenue recognition.

    B. If a firm recognizes revenue upon completion of production, then it must, in the same period in which the revenue is recognized, charge as expenses <u>all</u> costs that can reasonably be related to the products completed.

V. **Recognition of Revenue Subsequent to Sale**

The cash (or <u>installment</u>) basis of recognizing revenue is appropriate when there is unusual uncertainty as to whether the company will actually be able to collect the selling price of the property sold. It should be used when losses on bad debts cannot primarily be reasonably estimated.

VI. **Conservatism**

    A. <u>Conservatism</u>, as it relates to accounting, means that it is generally preferable that any possible errors in measurement be in the direction of under-statement rather than overstatement of net income and net assets. in matters of doubt the Recognition of favorable events should be delayed, while that of unfavorable occurrences should be hastened.

    B. The convention of conservatism is one that must be applied judiciously. Insofar as accounting measurements are taken from a perspective of pessimism, they can easily be distorted. And to the extent that similar transactions (such as those which happen to result in gains rather than losses) are accounted for differently, the resulting financial statements may be internally inconsistent.

KEY ISSUES FOCUSED UPON IN THIS CHAPTER

1. When should revenues be recognized?

    Although there are established criteria as to when revenues should be recognized, it is not always clear as to when the criteria are actually satisfied. When, for example, can it be said that the firm has exerted a substantial portion production and sales efforts? When can it be said that the collection reasonably assured? In some cases, these questions must be answered with industry practices in mind.

2. When should costs be charged as expenses?

    As a general rule costs should be charged as expenses in the same account period as the revenues with which they are associated are recognized. It is not always obvious which costs should be matched with which revenues. A cause effect relationship between expenses and revenues is not always apparent.

KEY WORDS AND PHRASES

Arm's Length Transaction

Closely-Held Corporation

Completed Contract Method

Conservatism

Exchange Prices

Installment Method

Liquidation Value

Percentage of Completion Method

ILLUSTRATION FOR REVIEW

The Hull Construction Company agrees to construct 3 parking lots for the township of Grevin at a total contract price of $600,000. The company estimates that it will cost $400,000 to construct the lots. The township will take possession of all lots only upon the completion of the entire project but will make periodic cash advance to the company.

The following schedule indicates the firm's projection (which turns out to be correct) of cash receipts, construction costs incurred and parking lots completed. All construction costs are paid in cash as incurred.

	1991	1992	Total
Cash receipts	$250,000	$350,000	$600,010
Construction costs incurred	150,000	250,000	400,000
Parking lots completed	1	2	3

Presented below are examples of journal entries to record the construction of the parking lot and the collection of cash assuming three different criteria of revenue recognition:

1. Percentage of completion a measured by costs incurred.
2. Percentage of completion as measured by lots completed.
3. Entire project completed.

1. Percentage of completion as measured by costs incurred.

<u>1991</u>

    Construction in process at cost $150,000
       Cash $150,000

To record costs incurred in construction of parking lots.

    Construction in process at contract value $225,000
       Revenue from construction $225,000

To recognize revenue based upon a percentage of project completed (150,000/400,000-37.5 percent-of expected total revenue).

    Expenses relating to revenue from construction $150,000
       Construction in process at cost $150,000

To record expenses pertaining to construction (150,000/400,000-37.5 percent-of expected total costs).

    Completed parking lots at contract value $200,000
       Construction in process at contract value $200,000

To record the completion of one parking lot.

    Cash $250,000
       Cash advances $250,000

To record the receipt of a partial payment on the contract price.

<u>1992</u>

    Construction in process at cost $250,000
       Cash $250,000

To record costs pertaining to construction of parking lots.

    Construction in process at contract value $375,000
       Revenue from construction $375,000

To record expenses pertaining to construction (250 000/400,000-62.5 percent-of expected total costs).

Expenses relating to revenue from construction	$250,000	
Construction in process at cost		$250,000

To record expenses pertaining to construction (250,000/400,000-62.5 percent-of expected total costs).

Completed parking lots at contract value	$400,000	
Construction in process at contract value		$400,000

To record the completion of two parking lots.

Cash	$350,000	
Cash advances	250,000	
Completed parking lots at contract value		$600,000

To record the receipt of the remaining balance due on the contract and the delivery of the parking lots to the township.

2. Percentage of completion as measured by lots completed.

1991

Construction in process at cost	$150,000	
Cash		$150,000

To record costs pertaining to construction.

Completed parking lots at contract value	$200,000	
Revenue from construction		$200,000

To recognize revenue based upon completion of one parking lot (1/3-33 percent-of expected total revenue).

Expenses relating to revenue from construction	$133,000	
Construction in process at cost		$133,000

To record expenses pertaining to construction (1.3-33 percent-of expected total costs).

Cash	$250,000	
Cash advances		$250,000

To record the receipt of a partial payment on the contract price.

1992

Construction in process at cost	$250,000	
Cash		$250,000

To record costs pertaining to construction.

    Completed parking lots at contract value $400,000
        Revenue from construction $400,000

To recognize revenue based upon completion of production of remaining two parking lots (2/3-6) percent-of total expected revenue).

    Expenses relating to revenue from
    construction $267,000
        Construction in process at cost $267,000

To record expense pertaining to construction (2/3-67) percent-of expected total costs).

    Cash $350,000
    Cash advances   250,000
        Completed parking lots at contract value $600,000

To record receipt of the remaining balance due on the contract and the delivery of the parking lots to the township.

3. Entire project completed

<u>1991</u>

    Construction in process at cost $150,000
        Cash $150,000

To record costs pertaining to construction.

    Completed parking lots at cost $133,000
        Construction in process at cost $133,000

To record completion of one parking lot.

    Cash $250,000
        Cash advances $250,000

To record receipt of a partial payment on the contract price.

<u>1992</u>

    Construction in process at cost $250,000
        Cash $250,000

To record costs pertaining to construction.

    Completed parking lots at cost $267,000
        Construction in process   at cost $267,000

To record completion of two parking lots.

  Completed parking lot at contract value $600,000
   Revenue from construction $600,000

To recognize revenue upon completion of all parking lots.

  Expenses relating to revenue from
   construction $400,000
   Completed parking lot at cost $400,000

To record the expense pertaining to construction.

  Cash $350,000
  Cash advance $250,000
   Completed parking lots at contract value $600,000

To record receipt of the remaining balance due on the contract and the delivery of the parking lot to the township.

EXERCISES

1. The Peterson Cement Company is a medium-sized manufacturer of cement block machines. Each cement block machine costs the company $500,000 to produce and can be sold for $750,000. The company sells one of its machines in 1992, and collects the full sale price from the purchaser.

  A. Prepare the necessary journal entries to record the sale of the machine and to recognize the related costs.

B. Each machine carries a one-year warranty against defects. The cost of making repairs on machines under the warranty has, in the past, averaged one percent of sales price. Record the warranty liability attributable to the sale of one machine.

C. Prior to the expiration of the warranty, the Peterson Cement Company incurs $7,500 in repair costs on the machine sold in 1992. Assuming that all costs are paid in cash, prepare a journal entry to record the costs of making the required repairs.

2. Digitronics Incorporated is a small manufacturer of electronic calculators. The company receives a contract for 500 calculators from one of its customers, a major retailer of office products. The customer agrees to pay $100 per calculator, but under the terms of the contract, Digitronics is to store the calculators until they are needed by the purchaser. The customer is to be billed for the goods upon delivery. It costs Digitronics $60 to manufacture each calculator. The company produces all 500 calculators during the year, but ships only 350 of them to its customer.

Digitronics recognizes revenues and expenses on a completion of production basis.

A. Prepare a journal entry to record the payment of production costs. Production costs are to be included in work in process.

B. Prepare a journal entry to record the transfer of goods in process to finished goods.

C. Prepare journal entries to give recognition to revenues and expenses upon completion of production.

D. Prepare a journal entry to record the delivery to its customer of the 350 calculators.

3. On January 31, 1991, the Weston Rail Corporation signed a contract with the Baltimore and Pacific Railroad Company to manufacture two diesel locomotives at a sales price of $1,000,000 per locomotive. The chief engineer of the Weston Rail Corporation estimates that his firm can manufacture the two locomotives over a period of two years at a total cost of $1,500,000.

The following schedule indicates anticipated cash payments, cash receipts and production costs over the two-year period during which the locomotives will be manufactured.

	1991	1992	Total
Cash receipts	$500,000	$1,500,000	$2,000,000
Manufacturing costs to be incurred	900,000	600,000	1,500,000

All cash was received and costs incurred as predicted.

A. Assume that the Weston Rail Corporation recognizes revenues and expenses on a percentage of completion basis.

1. Prepare a journal entry to record the cash received in 1991. Assume that the cash is not contractually due until the locomotives are delivered.

2. Prepare a journal entry to record the manufacturing costs of 1991. All costs were paid in cash and are to be included in work in process.

3. What percentage of total project was completed in 1991?

4. Prepare journal entries to give recognition to revenues and expenses in 1991.

B. Assume instead that Weston Corporation elects to recognize revenue and expenses on a completed contract basis.

1. What portion of the total revenues and expenses should be recognized in 1991?

2. Prepare a journal entry to record the cash received in 1991 from the Baltimore and Pacific Railroad Company. Assume that the cash is not contractually due until the locomotives are delivered.

3. Prepare a journal entry to record the manufacturing costs of 1991. All costs were paid in cash and are to be included in work in process.

4. What portion of total revenues and expenses should be recognized in 1992?

5. Prepare a journal entry to record the manufacturing costs of 1992. All costs were paid in cash and are to be included in work in process.

6. Prepare a journal entry to record the completion of the locomotives.

7. Prepare journal entries to recognize revenues and expenses in 1992.

8. Prepare a journal entry to record the cash received in 1992 from the Baltimore and Pacific Railroad Company and the delivery of the locomotives.

SOLUTIONS TO CHAPTER FIVE EXERCISES

1. A.

    Cash $750,000
        Sales Revenue $750,000

    To record the sale of equipment

    Cost of goods sold $500,000
        Merchandise inventory $500,000

    To record the expenses associated with the revenue recognized.

B.

    Warranty expense $7,500
        Warranty liability $7,500

    To record the warranty expenses associated with the revenue recognized.

C.

    Warranty Liability $7,500
        Cash $7,500

    To record costs incurred to fulfill the warranty obligation.

2. A.

    Work in process, electronic calculators $ 30,000
        Cash $30,000

    To record costs of production.

B.
    Finished goods at cost $ 30,000
       Work in process, electronic calculators $30,000

To record transfer of good completed to finished goods.

C.
    Finished goods at market value $ 50,000
       Manufacturing revenue $50,000

To recognize revenues upon completion of goods manufactured.

    Cost of goods manufactured $ 30 000
       Finished goods at cost $30,000

To record the expenses pertaining to the manufacture of the goods.

D.
    Accounts receivable $ 35,000
       Finished goods at market value $ 35,000

To record delivery of goods.

3. A.1.
    Cash $500,000
       Cash advances $500,000

To record the receipt of a partial payment on the contract price.

2.
    Work in process at cost $900,000
       Cash $900,000

To record costs pertaining to manufacture of locomotives.

3.
The percentage completed should be based upon the ratio of the total costs incurred to date to the total expected costs to complete the project.

The percentage of the project completed would be calculated as follows:

Percent of project completed   =

$$\text{Percent of project completed} = \frac{\text{Total costs incurred to date}}{\text{Total expected costs to complete the project}}$$

Percent of project completed = $\dfrac{900,000}{1,500,000}$ = 60%

4.
    Work in process at contract value $1,200,000
       Revenue from manufacturing $1,200,000

To recognize revenue based upon a percentage of the project completed (900,000/1,500,000-60 percent-of expected total revenue of $2,000,000).

Expenses relating to revenue from manufacturing $ 900,000
   Work in process at cost $ 900,000

To record expenses pertaining to manufacturing (900,000/1,500,000-60 percent-of expected total costs).

B.1.
None. Since the company is using the completed contract method of recognizing revenues and expenses, no revenues or expenses should be recognized until the entire project is completed.

2.
Cash $500,000
   Cash advances $500,000

To record receipt of a partial payment on the contract price.

3.
Work in progress at cost $900,000
   Cash $900,000

To record costs pertaining to manufacturing of locomotives.

4.
Since the project is finished in the second year, all of the revenues and expenses would be given accounting recognition in that period. Thus, the portion to be recognized is 100 percent.

5.
Work in process at cost $ 600,000
   Cash $600,000

To record costs pertaining to manufacturing of locomotives.

6.
Completed locomotives at cost $1,500,000
   Work in progress at cost $1,500,000

To record the completion of the locomotives.

7.
Completed locomotives at contract value $2,000,000
   Revenue from manufacturing $2,000,000

To recognize revenues upon completion of contract.

Expenses relating to revenues from manufacturing $1,500,000
   Completed locomotives at cost $1,500,000

To record expenses pertaining to manufacturing of locomotives.

8.
Cash $1,500,000
Cash advances 500,000
   Completed locomotives at contract value $2,000,000

To record receipt of remaining balance due on contract and the delivery of the locomotives to the Baltimore and Pacific Railroad Company.

{Chapter 6}

VALUATION OF ASSETS; CASH AND MARKETABLE SECURITIES

The issue of asset valuation is central to financial accounting. In Part I of Chapter 6 we describe and evaluate three alternative concepts of asset valuation, each of which has important implications for current accounting practice. It is important to keep in mind that questions of asset valuation are directly related to those of revenue and expense recognition. The value assigned to an asset is a direct determinant of how much revenue or expense is recorded in a particular accounting period.

In part I, we also provide an introduction to the principles of compound interest and present value-principles that will be applied in several subsequent chapters. In Part II, we concentrate on two particular current assets, <u>cash</u> and <u>marketable securities</u>, and highlight the key accounting issues associated with each.

KEY POINTS

I. **Three Concepts of Value**

    A. Value may be defined in at least three different ways.

        1. An <u>assigned</u> or calculated numerical quality.

        2. The <u>worth</u> of something sold or exchanged; is fair market price.

        3. Worth in <u>usefulness</u> or importance to the possessor, utility or merit.

    B. Each of the three definitions suggests an approach to asset valuation different from the others.

II. **Historical Cost**

    A. The historical cost approach to asset valuation in consistent with the first definition (an assigned or calculated number). Assets are initially assigned the amounts paid for them. Subsequent to time of purchase, assets are usually reported at either the initial amount paid for them or the initial amount less accumulated depreciations or amortization.

B. Historical cost values are different in that they provide no indication of either the prices at which assets could be sold or of the worth of the services they will provide.

C. But values based on historical cost are reasonably objective, they are based on actual exchange transactions between independent parties. They are consistent with accepted concepts of income determination by which the cost of an asset is spread over its useful life. The reported value of an asset at any given time represents the initial cost of an asset less that portion of its cost assigned to the services which it has already provided. The balance sheet may be viewed as a statement of residuals-costs which have not yet been charged-off as expenses and must, therefore, be carried forward to future accounting periods.

D. <u>Current accounting practice is based primarily upon historical costs.</u>

III. **Market Values**

A. The market value approach to asset valuation is consistent with the second definition of value-worth in terms of the amount for which an asset can be bought or sold.

B. Several arguments have been advanced in favor of the market price approach to asset valuation. Among them are:

1. It would provide investors its information that is more relevant to the decisions that they ordinarily have to make.

2. It would indicate the amount for which an asset could be sold or which would have to be paid to replace it.

3. It would facilitate the determination of the opportunity cost of using an asset-the amount that might be earned if the asset were sold and the proceeds used in the best alternative capacity.

C. The market value of an asset may be interpreted as either a current <u>output</u> or a current <u>input price</u>.

D. There are disadvantages to the current value of reporting assets. For example, the current market prices of an asset may be less that its value to a particular user. Even though the replacement cost of an asset may decline (perhaps because newer models become available), its utility and its value to its current owner may remain the same or even increase.

IV. **Value to User**

   A. The value of an asset to its user can generally be expressed in terms of the value of the value of the total future benefits that it will provide. The ultimate benefit associated with an asset is the cash that it will provide.

   B. The value to user approach has appeal to theoreticians because it expresses the value of an asset with respect to its particular owner. But the approach is difficult to implement in practice because it requires that the future benefits of an asset be specifically identified and measure-an especially difficult task in as much as many assets have value only when used in conjunction with others.

   C. Because the benefits of an asset take into account the <u>time value of money</u> in assessing their value.

V. **The Time Value of Money**

   A. A payment received today is of greater value to the recipient than one to be received in the future. The amount received today can be deposited in an interest-bearing account or otherwise invested in income-producing endeavors. It can be used, therefore, to provide additional returns to its holder while an identical amount to be received in the future will provide no such additional returns.

   B. In considering the time value of money, four basic questions are frequently asked:

   1. If a single payment were received today and invested as to earn compounded interest each period at a specific rate, to what amount would such payment accumulate after a given number of periods? The answer to this question may be determined with reference to Table I in the text, Future Value of $1.

   2. If a fixed amount is to be received some time in the future, what is the equivalent amount that need be received today for it to accumulate to the amount of the future payment, assuming that it could be invested as to earn interest compounded each period at a specified rate? The answer to this question may be determined with reference to Table 2, Present Value of $1.

   3. If a series of equal payments were received at the end of each of several periods and invested so as to earn interest compounded each period at a specified rate, to what amount would these payments accumulate when the last payment is received? The answer to this question may be found with reference to Table 3, Future Value of an Annuity of $1. An annuity is a series of equal payments at fixed intervals.

4. If a series of equal payments is to be received at the end of each of several periods in the future, what is the amount that need be deposited today to allow for periodic withdrawals equal in amounts to the expected payments, assuming that the deposit could be invested so as to earn interest compounded which period at a specific rate? The answer to this question may be determined with reference to Table 4, Present Value of an Annuity of $1.

C. The value to a particular firm of wither a single asset or a group of assets may ba determined by calculating the present value of anticipated cash flows-that is by identifying all of the expected cash receipts and disbursements associated with the asset and <u>discounting</u> them back to the present.

VI. **Cash**

A. <u>Cash</u> represents both currency on hand and funds on deposit in banks that are subject to immediate and unconditional withdrawal. It includes balances in checking accounts less any checks which have been written but have not yet "cleared" the bank plus any deposits in transit.

B. Cash is the most liquid of assets and is the common medium of exchange in our society. As such, it must be the subject of especially tight safeguards and controls.

C. Since cash is the accepted medium of paying bills and satisfying obligations, it is essential that a firm have an adequate amount of cash available to meet its debts as they come due and make the day-to-day payments required of it. But cash is basically an unproductive asset. Cash on hand or on deposit in a checking account earns no interest.

D. Cash in the bank is generally reported on the balance sheet at the amount indicated by the records of the firm. But such amount may differ from that indicated on the books of the bank because the records of either the bank or the firm may not be up to date. For example, checks written by the firm may not yet have been recorded by the bank. As a consequence, it is necessary to reconcile periodically the balance per the company's books with that indicated on the statement of the bank.

E. Cash is ordinarily classified as a current asset. If, however, there are restrictions on its withdrawal-either by contract or by management intent - which prevent it from being used within one year or one operating cycle of the business, if greater than one year, then it should properly be classified as a non-current asset.

VII. **Marketable Securities**

    A. Marketable securities are composed of stocks, bonds, or commercial paper, which the company has purchased as a temporary investment.

    B. Marketable securities are generally reported on the balance sheet at their initial cost of acquisition.

    C. Gains or losses resulting from changes in the market prices of the securities are ordinarily recognized only upon their sale.

    D. The one critical exception to the general rule that marketable securities be reported at acquisition cost and that gains and losses be recognized only upon their sale is that whatever the market price of an entire portfolio is less than its cost, the carrying value of the portfolio should be reduced to the market value and the corresponding loss should be recognized.

KEY ISSUES FOCUSED UPON IN THIS CHAPTER

1. What values should be assigned to assets?

Three primary means of reporting asset were described in this chapter: valuation at historical cost (adjusted to take into account depreciation or amortization); valuation at current market values at current market values (either the amount that would have to be paid to replace an asset or the amount for which it could be sold); the present value of anticipated cash flows associated with an asset.

2. Should marketable securities be reported at their original costs or at their market prices? Should gains or losses attributable to fluctuations in market prices be recognized only upon sale of the securities or in the periods in which the changes in prices take place?

These questions are, of course, specific applications of the more general question posed in #1. Current practice dictates that (with the exception noted in the outline) marketable securities be recorded at their initial cost that gains or losses be recognized only upon sale. In light of the ease by which market price of many types of securities can be obtained from published sources-and their resultant objectivity-many accountants have urged that marketable securities be reported at market value rather than historical cost and that gains or losses from price fluctuations be recognized as soon as they occur.

KEY WORDS AND PHRASES

Annuity	Lower of Cost or Market Rule
Annuity Due	Marketable Securities
Annuity in Arrears	Opportunity Cost
Bank Reconciliation	Ordinary Annuity
Depreciated Cost	Output Price
Discount Rate	Petty Cash
Future Value	Present Value
Imprest Basis	Prime Rate
Input Price	Sinking Fund
	Time Value of Money

ILLUSTRATIONS FOR REVIEW

1. If an individual were to place $1,000 in a savings account which earned interest at the rate of 8 percent compounded annually, to how much would the balance in the account accumulate at the end of 5 years?

```
$1,000.00    $1,080.00    $1,166.40    $1,259.70    $1,360.50    $1,469.30
----+------------+------------+------------+------------+------------+----
    0            1            2            3            4            5
 Initial                                                      Balance after
 Deposit                                                         5 years
```

As indicated in Table 1, the value after 5 years of $1, invested so as to earn interest at a rate of 8 percent compounded annually would be $1.4693. Thus the value of $1,000 would be

$1,000 x 1.4693 = $1,4693.30

2. If an individual requires $1,000 at the end of six years, how much must he deposit in a savings account which earns interest at the rate of 6 percent compounded semi-annually? Because interest is compounded semi-annually, to compute the relevant number of periods and the rate of return, the number of years must be multiplied by two, and the annual interest rate must be divided by two.

Number of periods = 2 x 6 = 12
Periodic interest rate = .06 / 2 = .03 per semi-annual period

```
701.40     722.40     744.10     766.40     789.40     813.10
  0                      1                     2                   year
--+----------+----------+----------+----------+----------+--------------
  0          1          2          3          4          5       payment
Required                                              Future
Deposit                                          Amount Required


837.50     862.60     888.50     915.10     942.60     970.90    1,000.00
  3                      4                     5                   6  year
--+----------+----------+----------+----------+----------+----------+------
  6          7          8          9         10         11        12 payment

Required                                              Future
Deposit                                          Amount Required
```

As indicated in Table 2, the present value of $1, <u>discounted</u> at a rate of 3 percent per period for 12 periods, is $.7014. The present value of $1,000, the amount that has to be deposited for today is

$$\$1{,}000 \times .7014 = \$701.40$$

3. To what amount would a fund accumulate if an individual were to make three annual payments (at year-end) of $1,000 each, assuming that the amount in the fund earns interest at an annual rate of 5 percent?

```
   0              1           years                    2                      3
                $1,000.00─────────────────────────→$1,050.00─────────→$1,102.50
                                                    1,000.00 ───────→  1,050.00
                                                                       1,000.00
              ─────────────                       ─────────          ──────────
              Amount $1,000.00                    $2,050.00          $3,152.50
              Available
```

As indicated in Table 3, an annuity of $1 per period compounded at an annual rate of 5 percent would accumulate at the end of three periods to $3.1525. An annuity of $1,000 per year compounded at an annual rate of 5 percent would accumulate at the end of 3 years to:

$$\$1{,}000 \times 3.1525 = \$3{,}152.50$$

4. What amount should an individual accept today so as to be equally well off as he would be if he were to receive an annuity of $1,000 for 8 years? Assume that the individual could invest the money that he receives so as to earn a return of 10 percent compounded annually.

```
        --+-----+-----+-----+-----+-----+-----+-----+-----+--
          0     1     2     3     4     5     6     7     8
```

$ 909.09<----1,000
  826.45<----------1,000   Present Value of
  751.31<---------------1,000   Annuity Payments
  683.00<---------------------1,000
  620.92<---------------------------1,000
  564.47<---------------------------------1,000
  513.16<---------------------------------------1,000
  466.50<---1,000
$5,334.90

As indicated in Table 4, the present value of an annuity (a series of equal payments) of $1 for 8 periods discounted at an annual rate of 10 percent is $5.3349. The present value of an annuity of $1,000 for 8 years discounted at a rate of 10 percent is

$$\$1{,}000 \times \$4.3349 = \$5{,}334.90$$

$5,334.90 also represents the sum of the present values of each of the individual payments of $1,000 discounted at a rate of 10 percent for an appropriate number of years.

EXERCISES

1. A company deposits $2,500 in a fund which earns interest at an annual rate of 6 percent. To what amount will the initial deposit accumulate after 4 years? In other words, what is the value, 4 years in the future, of $2,500 deposited in an account today?

2. A company wants to deposit an amount in a bank today so that at the end of 5 years it would have $100,000 on hand. The bank pays interest at an annual rate of 8 percent compounded semi-annually. How much should the company deposit today so that it will have the require $100,000 at the end of the fifth year? In other words, what is the present value of $100,000 to be received after semi-annual periods, assuming that interest is earned at a rate of 4 percent per semi-annual period?

3. An executive is to receive $10,000 at the end of each 5 years. He expects to deposit the entire amount of each payment in a savings bank as he receives it. The savings bank pays interest at a rate of 6 percent compounded annually. To how much will the payments accumulate by the end of the fifth year? On other words, what is the future value of a series of 5 payments of $10,000 compounded at an annual interest rate of 6 percent.

4. A company has agreed to pay a retired executive $10,000 at the end of each of 5 years. It wants to deposit in a fund today an amount to satisfy completely its obligation to the executive. The fund will earn interest at a rate of 6 percent per year. How much should the company deposit? On other words, what is the present value of a series of 5 equal payments of $10,000 discounted at an annual rate of 6 percent?

5. The Simpson Corporation is planning to acquire a new plant in five years. The cost of the new plant will be $100,000. The company wants to "save" for the new plant by making semi-annual payments of an equal amount into a sinking fund. Amounts on deposit will earn interest at a rate of 8 percent, compounded semi-annually (that is, 4 percent every six months). What should be the amount of each of the 10 payments if the company is to have accumulated $100,000 at the end of five years.

6. An individual decides to establish a savings account so that he will have sufficient funds available to pay his child's college tuition fees for 5 years of education at the time the child enters college. He estimates that by the time his child enters college, tuition charges will be $4,000 per year. His child will enter college in 10 years, and the savings account will earn interest at an annual rate of 6 percent. The payments to the savings account will be made at the end of each of the ten years. It may be assumed that the tuition payments will be paid at the conclusion of each year in which

the child is in college. Withdrawals from the savings account will be made only as required, no deposits to the fund will be made once the child enters college.

a. How much money must be made available in the savings account at the time the child enters college in order to make five annual payments of $4,000 each? That is, what is the present value, at the time the child enters college, of the five annual payments of $4,000 each, assuming that funds earn interest at a rate of 6 percent compounded annually?

b. How much must be deposited at the end of each of ten years to have the amount required per the computation above? That is, an annuity of what amount will accumulate in value (in the future) to the amount computed above. Or, in other words, the amount computed above is the future value of an annuity of how much per year for ten years?

7. The Cunningham Company has just received from its bank a statement of its account as of June 30, 1992. The statement indicates that the balance in the account of the company is $3,684.38. By contrast, the books and records of the Cunningham Company indicate that the firm has $11,297.00 on deposit in the bank.

The following information may help to account for the discrepancy:

a. The company had deposited $2,000 on June 29th and $6,830 on June 30th. Neither of these deposits is recorded on the statement from the bank.

b. Included with the bank statement is a <u>debit memo</u> indicating that the bank had charged the account of the company with its normal monthly service fee of $4.62.

c. The bank statement also indicates that the account of the company had been reduced by $278 to take into account a check which the company had deposited in its account. The check was given to the company by a customer. Upon attempting to collect the amount of the check, the bank learned that the customer had insufficient funds in his account to cover the amount of the check. The bank returned the check to the Cunningham Company marked N.S.F. (not sufficient funds), but the company has not yet made an entry to record the return of the check.

d. The bank statement reveals that the bank had collected a note due the company from a customer. The note was in the amount of $1,000. The company had not yet recorded the note.

e. As of June 30th, the company had written several checks which have not yet cleared the bank:

#201	$107.30
#206	205.50
#207	100.00
#210	87.20
Total Outstanding Checks	$500.00

Prepare a bank reconciliation for the Cunningham Company following the format given in Exhibit 6-5 in the text.

The Cunningham Company
Bank Reconciliation
As of June 30, 1992

	Per Firm's Own Books	Per Bank Statement
Balance, June 30, 1992	$11,297.00	$ 3,684.38

SOLUTIONS TO CHAPTER SIX EXERCISES

1. Per Table (6 percent column, 4 period row), the future value of $1 is $1.2625. The future value of $2,500 is $2,500 x 1.2625 + $3,156.25

   The initial deposit will accumulate to $3,156.25.

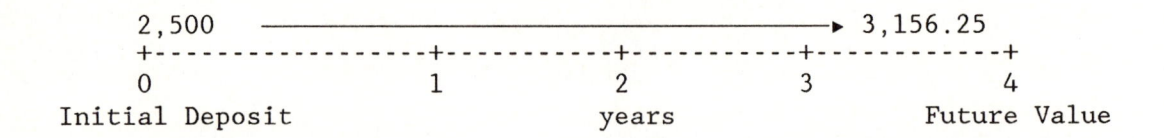

   ```
   2,500  ─────────────────────────►  3,156.25
   +------------------+----------+----------+------------+
   0                  1          2          3            4
   Initial Deposit              years               Future Value
   ```

2. Per Table 2, the represent value of $1 to be received after 10 periods in the future, discounted at a rate of 4 percent, is $.6756. The present value of $100,000 is therefore 100,000 x .6765 = $67,560.

   The company would have to deposit $67,560 if it expects to have $100,000 on hand at the end of five years.

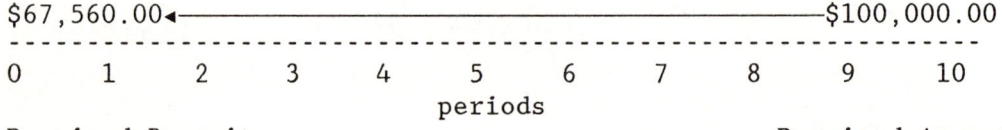

   ```
   $67,560.00◄─────────────────────────────────$100,000.00
   --------------------------------------------------------
   0   1   2   3   4   5   6   7   8   9   10
                       periods
   Required Deposit                    Required Amount
   ```

3. Per Table 3, the future value of an annuity of $1 for 5 periods, compounded at a rate of 6 percent, is $5.6371. The future value of an annuity of $10,000 is $10,000 x .6371 = $56,371.

   The payments will accumulate to $56,371.

   ```
                              Years
   ───────────────────────────────────────────────────────────
   0        1         2         3         4         5
           10,000──►10,600──►11,236──►11,910──►12,625
                    10,000──►10,600──►11,236──►11,910
                             10,000──►10,600──►11,236
                                      10,000   10,600
   Amount Available                            10,000
          $10,000   $20,600   $31,836   $43,746   $56,371
   ```

4. Per Table 4, the present value of an annuity of $1 for 5 periods, discounted at an annual rate of 6 percent, is $4.2124. The present value of an annuity of $10,000 is $1000 x 4.124 = $42,124.

   The company would have to deposit $42,124.

```
                    0           1            2           3           4           5
    Present      9,434<———————10,000
    Value of     8,900<————————————————10,000
    Annuity      8,396<—————————————————————————10,000
    Payment      7,921<——————————————————————————————————10,000
                 7,473<————————————————————————————————————————————10,000
                $42,124
```

5. Per Table 3, the amount to which an annuity of $1 for ten periods, at a rate of 4 percent per period, will accumulate is $12.0061. That is $1 x 12.0061 = $12.0061.

    The amount of the annuity required to accumulate $100,000 can therefore be determined as follows:

    $$\$100,000 = A \times 12.0061 \text{ or}$$
    $$\frac{100,000}{12.0061} = A \text{ or}$$
    $$A = \$8,239.10$$

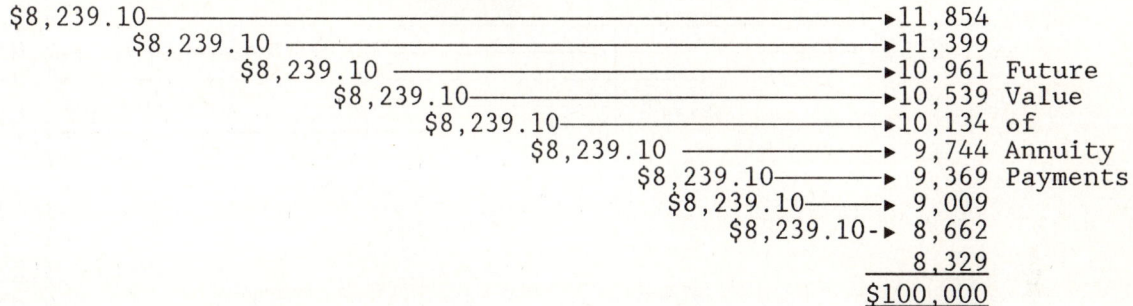

```
    0        1          2         3         4          5
    0    1   2    3    4    5    6    7    8    9    10
                        Periods
    $8,239.10————————————————————————————————————►11,854
       $8,239.10  ———————————————————————————————►11,399
          $8,239.10 ————————————————————————————►10,961  Future
             $8,239.10————————————————————————►10,539   Value
                $8,239.10—————————————————————►10,134   of
                   $8,239.10 ———————————————► 9,744 Annuity
                      $8,239.10————————————► 9,369 Payments
                         $8,239.10————————► 9,009
                            $8,239.10-► 8,662
                                          8,329
                                       $100,000
```

The company would have to deposit $8,329.10 at the end of each of ten periods if it is to have $100,000 at the end of the tenth period.

6.a. Per Table 4, the present value of an annuity of $1 for 5 periods, discounted at annual rate of 6 percent, is $4.2124. The present value of an annuity of $4,000 is $4,000 x 4.2124 = $16,850.

The individual will have to have $16,850 in the savings account at the end of the year so that he will be able to withdraw $4,000 per year for 5 years.

```
----+---------+---------+---------+---------+---------+-
    10        11        12        13        14        15
```

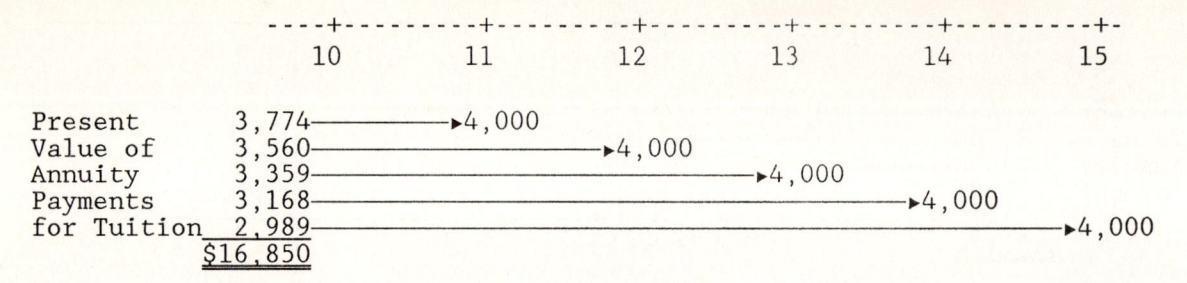

Present	3,774──────▶4,000	
Value of	3,560───────────────▶4,000	
Annuity	3,359────────────────────────▶4,000	
Payments	3,168─────────────────────────────────▶4,000	
for Tuition	2,989──▶4,000	
	$16,850	

b. Per Table 3, the amount which an annuity of $1 for ten periods at a rate of 6 percent per period, will accumulate is $13.1808. That is $1 x 13.1808 = $13.1808.

The amount of the annuity required to accumulate $16,850 can therefore be determined as follows:

$$\$16,850 = A \times 13.1808$$
$$\frac{16,850}{13.1808} = A$$

$$A = \$1,278$$

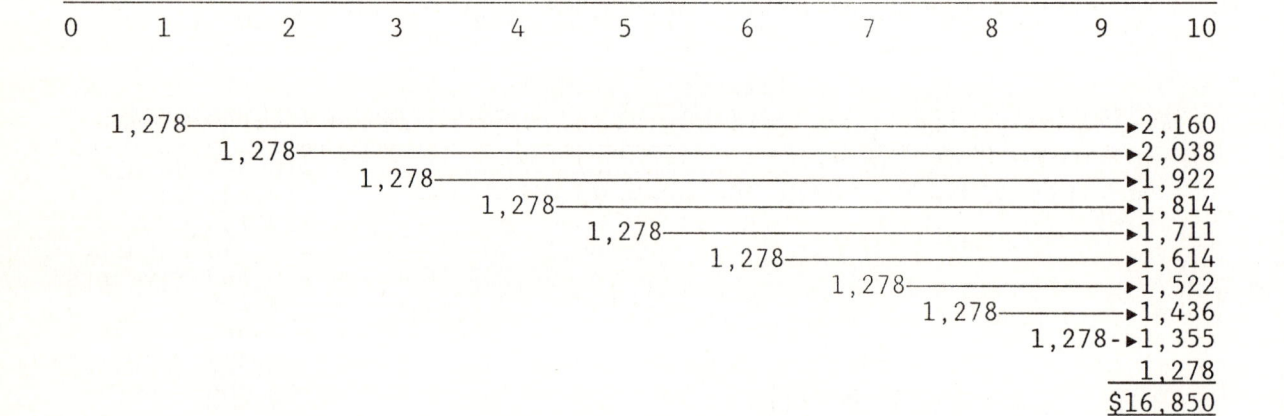

```
0    1    2    3    4    5    6    7    8    9    10
```

1,278──────────────────────────────────────▶2,160	
1,278─────────────────────────────────▶2,038	
1,278──────────────────────────────▶1,922	
1,278───────────────────────────▶1,814	
1,278────────────────────────▶1,711	
1,278─────────────────────▶1,614	
1,278──────────────────▶1,522	
1,278───────────────▶1,436	
1,278-▶1,355	
1,278	
$16,850	

The Cunningham Corporation
Bank Reconciliation
June 30, 1992

	Per Firm's Own Books	Per Bank Statement
Balance, June 30, 1992	$ 11,297.00	$ 3,684.38
Reconciling Items:		
Add: Deposits in Transit (note a)*		8,830.00
Subtract: Outstanding Checks (note e)		(500.00)
" Bank Service Charge (note b)	(4.62)	
" N.S.F. Check (note c)	(278.00)	
Add: Note Collected by Bank (note d)	1,000.00	
Adjusted Balance, June 30, 1992	$12,014.38	$12,014.38

* Refers to information given in the problem.

{Chapter 7}

RECEIVABLES AND PAYABLES

Accounts or notes receivable represent claims of a firm arising from the sale of goods, the performance of services, the lending of funds or some other type of transaction which establishes a relationship whereby one party is indebted to another. Claims are usually stated in terms of a fixed number of dollars. However, the amount at which a receivable should be reported on the balance sheet is not always equal to the stated amount of the claim. First, all or a portion of the claims may prove to be uncollectible. And second, the stated amount of the claim may include an element of unearned interest. Since interest revenue on a claim is not commonly recognized until it is actually earned, the amount of unearned interest included in the stated value of the claim must be excluded from the reported value of the receivable.

Accounts or notes payable represent claims <u>against</u> the firm. In general, the accounting issues presented by payable are similar to those related to receivables. Thus, the major emphasis in this chapter will be on accounting for receivables.

KEY POINTS

I. **Uncollectible Accounts Receivable**

   For the vast majority of firms, the most common receivable arises from sales of products or services on credit, resulting in Accounts Receivable. A major accounting problem, because of the matching process, is accounting for uncollectible accounts receivable.

   A. There are two basic ways of accounting for uncollectible accounts receivable.

      1. Under the <u>direct write-off</u> method an account is written off to expense as soon as it is concluded that it will not be collected. At that time the asset (accounts receivable) is reduced and an expense (bad debt expense) is charged. But the method is unacceptable for at least one major reason: It leads to an overstatement of income in the year in which sales are made and revenues are recognized. The error of a company in selling to a party that will prove unable to pay its debts is made at the time of the sale. The bad debt expense should be recognized in that period-not that in which the account is finally

determined to be uncollectible.

  2. Under the <u>indirect write-off</u> or <u>allowance</u> method an estimate of anticipated credit losses is made at the end of each accounting period. As part of the year-end adjusting entries, the asset (accounts receivable) is reduced and an expense (bad debt expense) is charged. Since it is not known at the time the asset is reduced which particular accounts will prove uncollectible, it is customary to credit a contra account (accounts receivable-allowance for uncollectibles) are reduced by the amount to be written off. At that time no charge is made to an expense account. The effect of the uncollectible account on income would have been recognized previously in the year in which the related sales were made.

 B. There are two widely used methods of determining the amount to be added each year to the contra account, accounts receivable-allowance for uncollectibles.

  1. Under the first method the company determines the amount to be added by applying to credit sales of the year an established percentage. Such percentage should be representative of the bad debt losses of previous years.

  2. Under the second method, the company estimates the actual dollar amount of the balance in accounts receivable that will prove uncollectible. It does so by classifying the receivables by "age" - the number of days that they have been outstanding. It applies to each category of receivables (that is, those that are current, 0 to 30 days past due, 30 to 60 days past due, etc.) a percentage based on previous experience. The sum of the amounts in each category that are estimated to be uncollectible represents the required balance in the accounts receivable-allowance for uncollectible contra account. The required addition is the difference between the present balance and the required balance.

 C. Sales returns are similar to bad debts and are accounted for in much the same way. If merchandise that has been sold is expected to be returned in a later accounting period, the firm should recognize the potential returns in the same period as the sales.

II. **Cash Discounts**

 A. Cash discounts must be accounted for so as to give recognition to the substance of a transaction rather than its form. If a customer is permitted a cash discount for prompt payment, such discount can usually be interpreted as a reduction in the price the goods. The amount of any discount lost may be viewed as a penalty for not paying promptly.

B. There are two basic ways in which discounts may be accounted for.

1. The net method gives direct recognition to substance over form. Under the net method (from the standpoint of the purchaser) both goods acquired and the related payable are recorded into the net amount, as if the discount will be taken. If the discount is not taken, then the discount lost is recorded as an expense.

2. Under the gross method, both goods acquired and the related payable are recorded at the gross amount. As a consequence, inventory is overstated by the amount of the allowable discount. To correct the overstatement, inventory (or cost of goods sold insofar as the goods have already been sold) should be reduced by the amount of the discount and, if the firm fails to take advantage of the discount, the discount lost should be classified as an expense.

III. Promissory Notes

A. A promissory note is a legal document indicating the obligation of a debtor to make payment to a creditor.

B. A promissory note is conventionally reported on the balance sheet as its principle or face amount. Such amount should exclude the interest expected to be received by the creditor but not yet earned. Interest should be recognized as revenue-and thereby added to the reported value of the note-only as it is earned with the passage of time.

IV. Notes with Interest Included in Face Value

Sometimes the face or stated value of a note will include not only the amount borrowed but the applicable interest charges as well. The effective receivable to be reported on the balance sheet should exclude unearned interest. It is necessary to deduct the unearned interest from the stated value of the note. Ordinarily such a deduction is reported in an account contra to the note itself. Thus, for example:

```
Notes Receivable-face value    $1,000
Less:  Discount on Notes
         (unearned interest)       30    $970
```

Over time, the balance in the contra account should be reduced by the amount of interest earned, the reported effective amount of the note will thereby be increased.

V. Non-Interest Bearing Notes

A. Occasionally a company will accept from a customer a note that does not require the payment of interest. Since a dollar to be received in the future is worth less than one to be received today, such notes should be viewed critically by the accountant. In substance, if not in form, almost all notes require the payment of interest.

B. Where a note does not explicitly require payment of interest (or in those instances in which the stated rate of interest is unreasonably low), a determination must be made as to what a fair rate of interest would be. But the face value of the note must be divided between the principal and unearned interest and the two elements of the note accounted for separately. The principal should be recorded as an asset immediately. The interest to be received should be recognized as an asset (either as part of the note or as interest receivable) only as it is actually earned with the passage of time.

C. Correspondingly, if a note that does not explicitly bear a reasonable rate of interest is received as part of the sales transaction, then the face value of the note cannot be accepted as being indicative of the real price of goods sold and the amount to be recognized as sales revenue. The face value will include an element of interest which should properly be recognized as revenue only as it is earned over time. The apparent selling price (the face amount of the note) should be divided into its component parts-the true selling price and the interest. The sales revenue (based on the true selling price) should be recognized in the period of sale; the interest revenue should be recognized over the period in which the note is outstanding and the interest is actually earned.

VI. Payroll Transactions

The accounting for payroll transactions is characterized by the fact that the wage or salary expense pertaining to an employee may be considerably greater than might be indicated by his wage or salary rate, and that the amount that will actually be paid to him may be considerably less. The business firm must pay payroll taxes that are specifically levied on the employer and must provide for "fringe" benefits in addition to regular wage and salary payments. Moreover, the employer must withhold from each employee's wage or salary the employee's share of payroll taxes as well as amounts for other designated purposes such as union dues or savings bond purchases. The entries to record payroll costs must reflect the actual expense to the employer and give recognition to any liabilities to third parties for any amounts withheld from the wages or salaries of employees.

VII. Accounts Receivable Ratios

There are two ratios that are useful in the control and evaluation of accounts receivable:

The accounts receivable turnover ratio is an activity ratio:

$$ART = \frac{Sales}{Average\ accounts\ receivable}$$

The quick ratio is a liquidity ratio:

$$QR = \frac{Cash,\ cash\ equivalents\ and\ accounts\ receivable}{Current\ Liabilities}$$

KEY ISSUES FOCUSED UPON IN THIS CHAPTER

1. How should anticipated customer defaults be provided for?

   In most industries it is likely that a portion of outstanding receivables will prove to be uncollectible. In this chapter we have examined several means of accounting for "bad debts" and have emphasized the importance of making adequate provision for those accounts that will, in all probability, be uncollectible.

2. How should notes that are "interest-free" or which bear unusually low rates of interest be accounted for?

   In Chapter 7 we have emphasized the importance of accounting for substance over form. Only in most unusual circumstances would a firm allow a customer to delay payment for more than a short period of time without demanding compensation (i.e., interest) for the use of its money. As a consequence, "interest free" notes or those which bear an unusually low rate of interest must be viewed with suspicion. Often, an element of interest may be included in the face amount of a note. Since interest revenue should be accounted for only as earned over time, it is important that interest be "broken-out" and accounted for apart from revenue from other sources, such as sales.

3. When should revenue be recognized?

   The issues associated with accounts and notes receivable are subsets or broader questions pertaining to the timing of revenue recognition. Increases in the recorded value of accounts and notes receivable are commonly associated with realization of sales or other forms of revenue. The example in the text pertaining to the franchise industry was designed to highlight this relationship. As long as there is a question as to whether the amount for a franchise is sold will be fully collectible, there is also a question as to whether the entire amount of the sales price should be recognized as revenue.

KEY WORDS AND PHRASES

Accounts Receivable	Notes Receivable
Aging Schedule	Payee
Discount	Payor
Discounted Note	Principal
Factor	Promissory Note
Negotiable Note	

ILLUSTRATIONS FOR REVIEW

1. The Bustle Company receives a $100,000 "interest free" note on December 31, 1991 in exchange for a parcel of land. The note is payable in one year. If the purchaser of the land had to borrow the cost of the land from a bank, he would have had to pay interest at an annual rate of 10 percent.

    a. What would you regard to be the fair market value of the land sold?

    The face value of the note ($100,000) includes both the fair market value of the land (x) and one year's interest charges a s well (.10x). Thus the fair market value of the land can be calculated as follows:

    $$x + .10x = \$100,000$$
    $$1.10x = \$100,000$$
    $$x = \$ 90,909 = \text{Fair market value of the land.}$$

    b. Prepare a journal entry by which the Bustle Company could record the sale of the land on December 31, 1991.

```
            Notes receivable                  $100,000
               Land                                          $90,909
               Notes receivable-discounted                    9,091
```

To record the receipt of a note in exchange for land.

c. Prepare a journal entry by which the Bustle Company could record the collection of the note and the recognition of interest revenue on December 3, 1991.

```
            Notes receivable-discount         $  9,091
               Interest revenue                              $  9,091
```

To record interest revenue for the year.

```
            Cash                              $100,000
               Notes receivable                              $100,000
```

To record the collection of the note.

2. In the following series of situations, determine the interest revenue that will be earned on each note held for the period indicated.

   a. A $5,000 note, to be held for 180 days, which earns interest at an annual rate of 8 percent.

$$\text{Interest revenue} = \text{Principal} \times \text{Rate} \times \frac{\text{Days of Loan}}{\text{Total Days in one year}}$$

$$\text{Interest revenue} = \$5{,}000 \times .08 \times \frac{180}{360}$$

Interest revenue = $200

   b. A $10,000 note, to be held for 60 days, which earns interest at an annual rate of 6 percent.

$$\text{Interest revenue} = \$10{,}000 \times .06 \times \frac{60}{360}$$

Interest revenue = $100

c. A $15,000 note, to be held for 540 days, which earns interest at an annual rate of 9 percent.

$$\text{Interest revenue} = \$15{,}000 \times .09 \times \frac{540}{360}$$

Interest revenue = $ 2,025.

3. For each of the following <u>discounted</u> notes, calculate the amount actually borrowed-- the amount to be received by the borrower. The following relationship should serve as a basis for your computation.

Face amount of note = Amount actually borrowed (x) + Interest to be earned (amount actually borrowed times the rate of interest).

To apply the relationship, it is necessary, however, to express the annual rate of interest in terms of the actual period of the loan:

$$\text{Rate for the period of loan} = \text{Annual interest rate} \times \frac{\text{Days of Loan}}{\text{Total days in one year}}$$

a. A $5,000, 90-day note when the prevailing rate of interest is 12 percent per year.

Rate for period of loan = Annual interest rate x $\dfrac{\text{Days of Loan}}{\text{Total days in one year}}$

Rate for period of loan = .12 x $\dfrac{90}{360}$ = .03

Let x = Amount to be received by the borrower.

$$x + .03x = \$5{,}000$$
$$1.03x = \$5{,}000$$
$$x = \$4{,}854 = \text{Amount to be received by the borrower.}$$

b. A $14,000, 180-day note when the prevailing rate of interest is 14 percent per year.

Rate for period of loan = .14 x $\dfrac{180}{360}$ = .07

Let x = Amount to be received by borrower.

$$x + .07x = \$14{,}000$$
$$1.07x = \$14{,}000$$
$$x = \$13{,}084 = \text{Amount to be received by the borrower.}$$

c. A $20,000, one-year note when the prevailing rate of interest is 8 percent per year.

There is no need to adjust the rate of interest, since the period is for one year and the rate is expressed as an annual percentage.

Let x = Amount to be received by borrower.

$$x + .08x = \$20,000$$
$$1.08x = \$20,000$$
$$x = \$18,519 = \text{Amount to be received by the borrower}$$

EXERCISES

1. The Monckton Company has received a 12-month, $10,00 note receivable from a customer, Ronald Howard, in settlement of a 10,000 debt owed to the company. The note bears interest at an annual rate of 6 percent.

   a. How much cash, both principal and interest, can the Monckton Company expect to collect at the end of one year?

   b. Suppose, that instead of holding the note to maturity (for one year) the Monckton Company elects to discount the note immediately at the First National Bank. The bank will discount the note at an annual rate of 8 percent.

      1. How much cash would the bank expect to collect at the end of one year from Ronald Howard?

      2. How much cash would the bank be willing to give the Monckton Company for the note? The amount to be received by the company (x), when multiplied times 1.08 (to add the interest charged by the bank) will equal the amount that the bank expects to collect from Ronald Howard.

      3. Prepare a journal entry to record, on the books of the Monckton

Company, the discounting of the note at the First National Bank. Assume that any of the difference between the cash received from the bank and the <u>face</u> value of the note will be recognized as discount revenue or expense.

2. The Kenon Company purchases $200,000 of merchandise from its supplier on terms of 2/15, n/30.

    a. If the company were to pay for the purchases within 15 days, what amount of discount may it deduct from the sales price?

    b. What would be the effective annual rate of interest paid by the Kenon Company if it did not avail itself of the discount?

    c. Assume that the company uses the net method to record its purchases of merchandise.

        1. Prepare a journal entry to record the purchase of the merchandise.

        2. Prepare a journal entry to record payment for the inventories, if payment were made after the discount period had expired.

d. Now assume that the company uses the gross method to record its purchases of merchandise.

    1. Prepare a journal entry to record the purchase of the merchandise.

    2. Prepare a journal entry that the company could use to record the payment for the merchandise within the discount period.

3. The Caldwell Company's accountants have asked you to assist in the determination of their company's allowance for uncollectibles and bad debt expense for the year ended December 31, 1991. They have provided you with the following information.

Balance in accounts receivable as of December 31, 1991-$549,300

Balance in allowance for uncollectibles as of December 31 1991-$12,00.

Credit sales for year ending December 31, 1991-$2,000,000. An aging schedule prepared by the accountants indicated the following totals.

Number of Days Past Due

Total Balance	Current	1-30	31-60	61-90	Over 90
$549,300	300,000	160,000	65,200	14,100	10,000

The company's accountants estimate that approximately 4 percent of all credit sales made during the year will prove to be uncollectible.

The accountants also estimate that the following percentages of the accounts receivable balance at any date will prove to be uncollectible:

Number of days past due	Percent likely to be uncollectible
Current	2
1-30	6
31-60	10
61-90	20
over 90	50

a. Using the information provided, calculate the balance required in the allowance for uncollectibles account. Assume that the Caldwell Company uses the aging <u>schedule</u> method to determine the balance.

b. Prepare a journal entry to adjust the balance in the allowance for uncollectibles so that it will contain the required amount at year-end.

c. Assume instead that the company determines the addition to the allowance for uncollectibles using the <u>percentage of sales</u> method. What would be the required addition to the allowance for uncollectibles as of December 31, 1991?

d. Prepare the required journal entry to reflect the adjustment to the allowance for uncollectibles account calculated in part c above.

e. Assume that the Caldwell Company receives information from its attorneys that the account of John Dudley, $1,000, is going to be uncollectible. Prepare the required journal entry to write off John Dudley's account.

4. Mr. Larry Ralston wishes to borrow some money to take a short vacation. He plans to borrow the $1,000 he needs from one of three banks he has contacted. Calculate the interest expense associated with each of the following $1,000 face value notes.

    a. A 180-day note with the First National Bank, which charges interest at an annual rate of 10 percent.

    b. A one-year discount note with the Second National Bank. The current discount rate charged by the bank is 7 percent annually.

    c. A 180-day discount note with the Second National Bank. The current discount rate charged by the bank is 7 percent annually.

    d. A 270-day note with the Anson Street Bank, which charges interest at an annual rate of 12 percent.

SOLUTIONS TO CHAPTER SEVEN EXERCISES

1. a. The company will earn $600 interest revenue ($10,000 x .06) in one year. When the interest is added to the principal of $10,000, the company can expect to receive 10,600 at the end of one year.

   b. 1. The bank will now collect the proceeds of the note. Thus it will collect the principal ($10,000) plus the interest ($600) - a total of $10,600.

      2. $10,600 = x + .08x
         $10,600 = 1.08x
         x = $9,814.81 = Amount that bank will pay for the note.

      3. Cash $9,814.81
         Discounting cost (expense)   185.19
            Note receivable-discounted $10,000.00

2. a. The company would calculate the discount by multiplying the discount rate, 2 percent, by the sales price, $100,000. Thus the discount available would equal .02 x $200,00 = $4,000.

   b. The effective interest rate = $\frac{360 \text{ days}}{15 \text{ days}*} \times \frac{\$4,000}{\$196,000} = 48.98\%$

   * Maximum period of loan-that between latest payment date regardless of whether company takes advantage of discount (30 days after sale) and latest payment date if company does take advantage of discount (15 days).

   In effect the company borrowed the cost of the fair market value of the merchandise, $196,000 and paid interest of $4,000.

   c. 1. Inventory $196,000
         Accounts payable $196,000

      To record the purchase of merchandise.

      2. Accounts payable $196,000
         Purchase discounts lose   4,000
            Cash $200,000

      To record the payment after the discount period.

   d. 1. Inventory $200,000
         Accounts Payable $200,000

101

To record the purchase of merchandise.

    2.   Accounts payable $200,000
            Cash $196,000
            Purchase discounts   4,000

To record the payment within the discount period.

3.   a.

Number of days past due	Amount	Percent likely to be uncollectible	Required provision
Current	$300,000	2	$ 6,000
1-30	160,000	6	9,600
31-60	65,200	10	6,520
61-90	14,100	20	2,280
over 90	10,000	50	5,000
	$549,300		$ 29,940

The balance in the allowance for uncollectibles should be $29,940.

    b.   Since the current balance in the allowance for uncollectibles account is $12,000, the required addition is $29,940 less $12,000 = $17,940.

          Bad debt expense $17,940
             Allowance for uncollectibles $17,940

To record bad debt expenses for 1991 and to adjust the allowance for uncollectibles account.

    c.   To determine the addition, the credit sales for the year must be multiplied by the percentage estimate of the credit sales that will prove uncollectible. Thus, $2,000,000 x .04 = $80,000.

    d.   Bad debt expense $80,000
            Allowance for uncollectibles $80,000

To record bad debt expenses for 1991 and to adjust the allowance for uncollectibles account.

    e.   Allowance for uncollectibles $ 1,000
            Accounts receivable $ 1,000

To write-off as uncollectible the account of John Dudley.

4.   a.   Interest expense = Principal x Rate x $\dfrac{\text{Days of Loan}}{\text{Total Days in one year}}$

        Interest expense = $1,000 x .10 x $\dfrac{180}{360}$
        Interest expense = $50

    b.   Rate for period of loan =
            Annual interest rate x $\dfrac{\text{Days of Loan}}{\text{Total Days in one year}}$

Since the loan is for one year, there is no need to adjust the 7 percent annual rate.

Let x = Amount to be received by borrower.

Face amount of note = Amount actually borrowed (x) + interest to be earned (amount actually borrowed times the rate of interest).

$$x + .07x = \$1,000.00$$
$$1.07x = \$1,000.00$$
$$x = 934.58$$

The interest expense is $1,000 - 934.58 = $65.42

c. Rate for period of loan = $.07 \times \frac{180}{360} = .035$

$$x + .035x = \$1,000.00$$
$$1.035x = \$1,000.00$$
$$x = \$\ 966.18$$

Therefore, the interest expense is $1,000 - 966.18 = $33.82.

d. Interest expense = $\$1,000 \times .12 \times \frac{270}{360}$

   Interest expense = $90

{Chapter 8}

INVENTORIES AND COST OF GOODS SOLD

Inventory represents the goods of a firm that are in various stages of production or are awaiting sale. Inventory includes supplies, raw materials, work in process and finished goods.

Issues of inventory measurement and valuation are particularly important. The values assigned to the goods on hand and the balance sheet as assets represent an important component of the Current Asset section of the Balance Sheet and these values eventually flow into the Income Statement as cost of goods sold (an expense) when the inventory is sold.

Cost of goods sold is the single largest expense of many business enterprises and in recent years, an inventory method (LIFO), has been adopted as a partial solution to the problem of inflation.

KEY POINTS

I. **Objectives of Inventory Measurement and Valuation**

    A. The overriding objective of inventory accounting is to match the costs of acquiring or producing goods with the revenues that they generate. In some firms, goods are acquired or produced in one accounting period, but sold in another, The cost of acquiring or producing the goods cannot properly be considered an expense until such goods are actually sold-until they can be matched with specific revenues.

    B. Costs representing goods that have not yet been sold are "stored" in asset accounts and are reported on the balance sheet; Those representing goods sold during the period covered by the financial statement are reported on the income statement as expenses.

II. **Cost Included in Inventory**

    A. Inventories are conventionally stated at their historical cost-that of acquiring or producing them. Cost, as applied to inventories includes the sum of both direct and indirect costs incurred in bringing an article to its existing condition and location. Cost would include not only the price paid for the goods acquired but also the amounts paid for packaging and transporting them. Trade, cash or other special discounts would ordinarily be deducted from the stated price.

    B.   If goods are produced by the company itself, cost would include charges for labor and materials that can be associated directly with the product as well as <u>overhead</u> costs such as rent, maintenance, and utilities that may be common to several products manufactured in the same plant. The company may have to allocate, on a rational basis, such common charges among its various products.

III. Accounting for Quantities on Hand

    A.   Under the <u>perpetual</u> method of accounting for inventories, immediate accounting recognition is given to all changes in inventory at the time goods are added to or withdrawn from inventory. The inventory account keeps track of the amount of inventory on hand. When goods are purchased, their cost is added to this account; when goods are sold, their cost is taken from the inventory account and added to the cost of goods sold account.

    B.   Under the <u>periodic</u> method immediate recognition is given to increase in inventory (such as those arising from purchases or production) but not to decreases. Recognition is given to decreases only periodically-usually once a year. At that time, a physical count is made of goods actually on hand and the accounting records are adjusted to reflect such count. It is assumed that the difference between amounts indicated by the records (the sum of goods on hand at the beginning of the period and the purchases during the period) and the amounts actually on hand, per the count, represent the quantities sold or used during the accounting period. Under the periodic method the accounts are continually out of date, they misstate the quantity and cost of goods on hand. Only at the end of the accounting period (when financial statements have to be prepared) are the records updated to indicate the amount of inventory actually on hand and the cost of goods sold or used in the course of business during the period.

IV. Flow of Costs

    A.   Because the cost of producing or acquiring goods does not remain constant and because it is not always possible (or desirable) to keep track of the specific units which have been sold or used, it is necessary to make assumptions as to the cost of those goods that have been sold or used and those that remain on hand.

    B.   Under the <u>specific identification</u> method the enterprise does, in fact, keep track of the case of each individual item bought and sold. The costs associated with goods sold are charged as an expense, <u>cost of goods sold</u>, those associated with the goods remaining are "stored" in asset accounts (inventory).

    1.   The specific identification method is most appropriate for enterprises that sell relatively few items of large cost (those that are easy to keep track of), such as automobiles, appliances, or heavy equipment.

    2.   The advantage of the specific identification method is that it assures that the amounts charged as expenses are the actual cost of the specific goods sold.

    3.   The disadvantage is that it provides management with an opportunity to manipulate income. Cost of goods sold by selecting for sale either high cost or low cost units of inventory can be regulated.

C.   Under the <u>first-in, first-out</u> (FIFO) method, the enterprise <u>assumes</u> that those goods which are produced or acquired first are sold first. The first costs incurred are assigned to the first goods sold. Those items on hand at the end of the accounting period are <u>assumed</u> to be those that were acquired last.

    1.   The advantage of the FIFO method is that in most instances the flow of costs follow the actual physical flow of goods (that is, in most businesses the goods acquired first are, in fact, sold first). Moreover, it results in a balance sheet composed of the cost of those items acquired most recently, which are thereby more representative of current replacement cost.

    2.   The disadvantage of the FIFO method is that the cost assigned to the goods sold are often not representative of their current replacement costs. In the view of some, the FIFO method, in a period of rising prices, tends to understate cost of goods sold and thereby overstate reported income.

D.   Under the <u>weighted average</u> method the enterprise assumes that all costs can be aggregated and that the cost to be assigned to any particular unit should be the weighted average of the costs of all the units held for sale during the accounting period.

    1.   The advantage of the weighted average method is that it is convenient. If applied on a periodic basis (as it generally is), then all goods sold during the period or that remain on hand at the end of the period can be assigned identical costs. Moreover, the weighted average method can be set forth as representing the physical flow of goods when all goods available for sale are mixed with one another.

    2.   The disadvantage of the weighted average method is that the average cost is based on the sum of the cost of all goods on hand at the beginning of the year and those purchased during the year. As a

consequence, cost of goods sold (assuming that the method is applied a periodic basis) may be distorted by the inclusion in the average cost of goods purchased after the last sale of the year has been made. Such goods could not possibly have been mixed in with those that were actually sold during the year.

E. Under the last-in, first-out (LIFO) method the enterprise assumes that those goods which have been acquired most recently were sold first. The latest costs incurred are assigned to the goods that are sold first. Those items on hand at the end of the accounting period are assumed to be those that were acquired first. The earliest costs incurred are assigned to the goods that are sold last or those that remain in inventory.

1. The advantage of LIFO is that it tends to reduce distortions in reported income attributable to inflation. Cost of goods sold is determined on the basis of the latest prices paid and, hence, is usually a better measure of the cost related to the revenues from sales.

2. The disadvantage of LIFO is that it results in a reported inventory value on the balance sheet which is composed of amounts that may be long out of date. The reported inventory value may represent prices paid several years earlier. Moreover, to the extent that the firm has to dip into its inventory "base" (the minimum stock of goods that it maintains), then the costs assigned to the goods sold will be those of the previous periods-costs that may be hopelessly out of date. In such event, reported costs of goods sold-and hence reported income-will be of little relevance to any decisions ordinarily made by users of financial statements.

V. **Lower of Cost or Market Rule**

A. The "lower of cost or market rule" requires that inventory should be stated at the lower of the amount paid to acquire the inventory (cost) or that which would have to be paid to replace the inventory (market).

B. The lower of cost or market rule is rooted in the attitude of conservatism. A decline in the utility of goods on hand (such as that resulting from physical damage, obsolescence, or a general decline in the level of prices) should be recognized as soon as possible.

C. The lower of cost or market rule may be applied on an item by item basis or on a group basis. If applied on an individual item basis, then a write-down of inventory is required whenever the cost of any individual item exceeds its market value. If applied on a group basis, then a write-down is required only if the total cost of all items combined exceeds their combined total market value.

VI. **Proposed Alternative: Use of Current Values**

   A. Many accountants have proposed that inventories should be stated at their current values as opposed to their historical costs. They propose that accounting recognition be given to increases in market value rather than just decreases (as under current practice). Current value is most commonly used to indicate the amount that would have to be paid to replace a particular item that is, its replacement cost.

   B. If inventories were to be stated at current values, then it would be possible to separate the gains arising from the sale of goods into their component elements-the gains arising from holding merchandise during a period of time in which the market price of the goods increases and those arising from the normal trading activities of the firm. Holding gains could be recognized in the period in which they take place; there would be no need to wait until the period of sale to recognize the entire gain.

   C. In the view of many accountants current value accounting would result in a more meaningful balance sheet, in that all inventories would be stated at their current market values (and hence there would be no need to make assumptions regarding which goods are sold at a particular time) as well as a more meaningful income statement, in that gains from holding inventories would be recognized in the period in which they actually take place.

VII. **Inventory Turnover**

A common activity ratio for the evaluation of inventory is the inventory turnover:

$$IT = \frac{\text{Cost of Goods Sold}}{\text{Average Inventory}}$$

KEY ISSUES FOCUSED UPON IN THIS CHAPTER

1. How should the costs of acquiring and producing goods intended for sale be divided among those goods that have been sold (cost of goods sold) and those that remain on hand (inventory)?

In some situations it may be both possible and advantageous to identify specific costs with specific goods. In most instances, however, it is necessary to make assumptions as to the flow of goods and the cost to be assigned to such goods. It may be assumed, for example, that goods which are purchased first are sold first, that all goods are mixed together and the goods which are sold are drawn from a common pool or that goods purchased last are sold first. Each of the assumptions leads to a different cost of goods sold and inventory values.

2. Should inventories be stated at <u>historical cost</u> as required by conventional practice (with the exception that inventories are "written-down" in accord with the lower of cost or market rule) or should they be stated at current value?

Many accountants believe that if inventories were to be stated at current value, then both the balance sheet and the income statement would provide more relevant information for those who use financial statements. The balance sheet would reflect the market values of the assets (the amounts for which they could be bought or sold). The income statement would reflect gains or losses from holding inventories in the periods in which such gains or losses occur, it would be necessary to wait until the goods were actually sold only to recognize the trading gains, not the holding gains.

KEY WORDS AND PHRASES

Cost Accounting

Cost of Goods Sold

Dollar-Value LIFO

First-in, First-out (FIFO) Method

Holding Gain (Loss)

Inventory

Last-in, First-out (LIFO) Method

Specific Identification Method

Weighted Average Method

ILLUSTRATION FOR REVIEW

1. The following information was taken from the inventory records of the Crystal Glass Company.

Item #603

Date	Purchases No. Units	Cost per Unit	Unit Sales	Balance in Units
1-1-91*	200	$ 6		200
1-14-91	400	8		600
3-15-91			200	400
6-17-91	200	10		600
11-25-91			300	300
12-21-91	100	11		400

* Beginning Balance

    a. Indicate the total number of units to be accounted for-those to be divided between cost of goods sold and year-end inventory.

The total number of units to be accounted for is the sum of the beginning balance and the purchases during the year-900 units.

b. Indicate the total costs to be accounted for-those to be divided between the cost of goods sold and the year-end inventory.

The total costs to be accounted for are the sum of the costs of the beginning balance and the purchases during the year:

```
        200 x $  6 = $1,200
        400 x    8 =  3,200
        200 x   10 =  2,000
        100 x   11 =  1,100
Total Costs           $7,500
```

c. Suppose that the Crystal Company maintains its inventory on a first-in, first-out (FIFO) basis determined periodically.

1. What value should be assigned to the 400 units on hand at year-end?

The goods on hand at year-end would be assigned the costs of those items purchased most recently. Thus:

```
Purchase of                  12-21-91    100 x $11    $1,100
Purchase of                   6-17-91    200 x  10     2,000
Portion of purchase of        1-14-91    100 x   8       800
       Year-end inventory                             $3,900
```

2. What value should be assigned to the 500 units that were sold during the year?

The value to be assigned to the goods that have been sold would be the total costs to be accounted for less those costs that have been assigned to the ending inventory. Thus, $7,500 less $3,900 = $3,600.

Such value can be determined directly by assigning to cost of goods sold the costs of the items acquired earliest. Thus:

```
Beginning balance           1-1-91    200 x $6    $1,200
Portion of purchase of      1-14-91   300 x  8     2,400
        Cost of goods sold                        $3,600
```

3. Would it make a difference if the company maintained its inventory records on a perpetual rather than a periodic basis?

No. When the FIFO method if inventory calculation is used it makes no difference whether inventories are maintained on a periodic or a perpetual basis.

d. Suppose the company maintained its inventory on a last-in, fist-out (LIFO) basis determined periodically.

1. What value should be assigned to the 400 units on hand at year-end?

The goods on hand at year-end would be assigned the cost of those items purchased earliest. Thus:

```
Beginning balance           1-1-91    200 x $6    $1,200
Portion of purchase of      1-14-91   200 x  8     1,600
        Year-end inventory                        $2,800
```

2. What value would be assigned to the 500 units that were sold during the year?

The value to be assigned to the goods that have been sold would be the total costs to be accounted for less those that have been assigned to the ending inventory. Thus, $7,500 less $2,800 = $4,700.

112

Such value can be determined directly by assigning to cost of goods sold the cost of the items acquired most recently. Thus:

Purchase of	12-21-91	100 x $11	$1,100
Purchase of	6-17-91	200 x 10	2,000
Portion of purchase of 1-14-91		200 x 8	1,600
Cost of goods sold			$4,700

3. Would it make a difference if the company maintained its inventory records on a perpetual rather than a periodic basis?

Yes. Cost of goods sold and ending inventory would be determined as indicated in the following table:

Date	Units	Purchases Unit Cost	Total Costs	Units	Sales Unit Cost	Total Costs	Units	Inventory Balance Unit Cost	Total Costs
1-1-91							200	$ 6	$1,200
1-14-91	400	$ 8	$3,200				200	6	1,200
							400	8	3,200
3-15-91				200	$ 8	$1,600	200	6	1,200
							200	8	1,600
6-17-91	200	10	2,000				200	6	1,200
							200	8	1,600
							200	10	2,000
11-25-91				200	10	2,000	200	6	1,200
				100	8	800	100	8	800
12-21-91	100	11	1,100				200	6	1,200
							100	8	800
							100	11	1,100
						$4,400			$3,100

Total cost of goods sold would be $4,400; total balance in inventory at year-end would be $3,100.

e. Suppose the company maintained its inventory on a weighted average basis determined periodically.

1. What value should be assigned to the 400 units on hand?

There are a total of 900 units and total costs of $7,500 to be accounted for. Weighted average per unit would be $7,500 divided by 900 units = $8.33.

Therefore, the total value of year-end inventory would be 400 units times $8.33 = $3,332.

2. What value should be assigned to the 500 units that were sold during the year?

The value to be assigned to the units sold during the year would be:

500 units times $8.33 = $4,165.

(The total of ending inventory and cost of goods sold would sum to $7,500 were it not for a rounding discrepancy.)

3. Would it make a difference if the company maintained its inventory on a perpetual rather than a periodic basis?

Yes. The cost of goods sold and those that remain on hand would have to be determined after each transaction as shown in the following table:

		Purchases			Sales			Inventory Balance	
Date	Units	Unit Cost	Total Costs	Units	Unit Cost	Total Costs	Units	Unit Cost	Total Costs
1-1-91							200	$ 6	$1,200
1-14-91	400	$ 8	$3,200				600	7.33*	4,400
3-15-91				200	$7.33	$1,467	400	7.33	2,933
6-17-91	200	10	2,000				600	8.22*	4,933
11-15-91				300	8.22	2,466	300	8.22	2,467
12-21-91	100	11	1,100				400	8.92*	3,567
						$3,933			

* The average cost is recalculated following each purchase.

EXERCISE

The following information is taken from the inventory records of the J.B. Stoppard Company:

Item 401B

Date	Type of Transaction	Units	Cost Per Unit	Sales Price Per Unit
1-1-91	Beginning inventory	1,000	$6	
3-4-91	Sale	500		$10
8-10-91	Purchase	1,500	8	
10-18-91	Sale	1,000		11
12-23-91	Purchase	500	9	
12-30-91	Sale	500		11

a. Determine the total cost of goods available for sale during the year, that is, the total costs to be accounted for.

b. Determine the number of units sold during the year.

c. Determine the number of units in inventory as of December 31, 1991.

d. Suppose the company maintains its records on a first-in, first-out (FIFO) basis.

1. Determine the value that should be assigned to inventory at year-end.

2. Determine the value to be assigned to the goods sold during the year.

3. Determine the gross margin or gross profit (sales revenue less cost of goods sold) for the year.

e. Suppose the company maintains its inventory records on a last-in, first-out (LIFO) basis determined periodically.

1. What value should be assigned to the goods on hand as of 12-31-85?

2. What value should be assigned to the goods that were sold during the year?

f. Assume the company maintains its inventory records using the weighted average method determined on a periodic basis.

1. What value should be assigned to the goods on hand as of 12-31-85?

2. What value should be assigned to the goods that were sold during the year?

g. Assume the firm used the last-in, first-out (LIFO) inventory method applied on a perpetual basis. What values should be assigned to both ending inventory and cost of goods sold?

h.   Assume that the firm used the weighted average method applied on a perpetual basis. What values should be assigned to both ending inventory and cost of goods sold?

SOLUTIONS TO CHAPTER EIGHT EXERCISES

a. Balance   1-1-91   1,000 units x $6 $ 6,000
    Purchase of   9-10-91   1,500 units x $8   12,000
    Purchase of   11-23-91   500 units x 9   4,500
              Cost of goods available for sale $22,500

b. Units sold:

	Units
3-4-91	500
10-18-91	1,000
12-30-91	500
Total units sold	2,000

c. Inventory, 1-1-91   1,000
    Plus: purchases   2,000
    Units available for sale   3,000
    Less: units sold   2,000
    Inventory, 12-31-91   1,000

d. 1. Under the FIFO method, the ending inventory represents those goods that have been acquired most recently.

   The 1,000 units ending inventory would be valued as follows:

   Purchases of 11-23-91   500 units x $9 $4,500
   Purchases of 8-10-91   500 units x 8   4,000
              Ending inventory $8,500

2. Cost of goods available for sale $22,500
        Less: Cost assigned to ending inventory   8,500
                  Cost of good sold $14,000

3. Sales Revenue (50 x 10) + [(1,500 x 11)] $21,500
   Less: Cost of goods sold   14,000
              Gross profit on sales $ 7,500

117

e. 1. Under the LIFO method, the items in inventory are assumed to be those acquired at the earliest date. Therefore, the 1,000 units on hand at year-end would be assigned a value of

   1,000 x $6 = $6,000 Value of ending inventory.

  2.
Cost of goods available for sale	$22,500
Less: Costs assigned to ending inventory	6,000
Cost of goods sold	$16,500

f. 1. Under the periodic weighted average method, the ending inventory value is determined by multiplying the average cost per unit by the number of units on hand at year-end.

   $$\text{Average cost per unit} = \frac{\text{Cost of goods available for sale}}{\text{Total number of units available for sale}}$$

   $$\text{Average cost per unit} = \frac{\$22,5000}{3,000} = \$7.50$$

   Value of ending inventory = $7.50 x 1,000 = $7,500

  2.
Cost of goods available for sale	$22,500
Less: Costs assigned to ending inventory	7,500
Cost of goods sold	$15,000

g. The values to be assigned to ending inventory and cost of goods sold, assuming a perpetual method, would be determined as follows:

	Purchases			Sales			Inventory Balance		
Date	Units	Unit Cost	Total Costs	Units	Unit Cost	Total Costs	Units	Unit Cost	Total Costs
1-1-91							1,000	6	$ 6,000
3-4-91				500	$6	$3,000	500	6	3,000
8-10-91	1,500	$8	$ 12,000				500	6	3,000
							1,500	8	12,000
10-18-91				1,000	8	8,000	500	6	3,000
							500	8	4,000
11-23-91	500	9	4,500				500	6	3,000
							500	8	4,000
							500	9	4,500
12-30-91				500	9	4,500	500	6	3,000
							500	8	4,000
						$15,500			$7,000

The value of the ending inventory would be: $7,000

The cost of goods sold would be: $15,500

h. The values to be assigned to ending inventory and cost of goods sold, assuming a perpetual method, would be determined as follows:

		Purchases			Sales			Inventory Balance	
Date	Units	Unit Cost	Total Costs	Units	Unit Cost	Total Costs	Units	Unit Cost	Total Costs
1-1-91							1,000	$6	$ 6,000
3-4-91				500	$6	$ 3,000	500	6	3,000
8-10-91	1,500	$8	$12,000				2,000	7.50	15,000
10-18-91				1,000	7.50	7,500	1,000	7.50	7,500
11-23-91	500	9	4,500				1,500	8	12,000
12-30-91				500	8	4,000	1,000	8	8,000
						$14,500			$ 8,000

The value of ending inventory would be: $8,000

The cost of goods sold would be: $14,500

The depreciation charge for each year would be calculated in the following manner:

Net depreciable amount = Original cost($15,000)-Residual value ($3,000)
Net depreciable amount = $17,000

The sum of the years' digit (the denominator of the depreciation fraction) may be calculated as follows:

$$\frac{n(n+1)^*}{2} = \frac{3(3+1)}{2} = \frac{12}{2} = 6 \qquad \text{*where n, number of years} = 3$$

Year	Net Depreciable Amount	X	Depreciation Fraction**	=	Depreciation Charge
1	$12,000	X	3/6	=	$ 6,000
2	12,000	X	2/6	=	4,000
3	12,000	X	1/6	=	2,000
			6/6		$12,000

**Depreciation fraction = $\dfrac{\text{The remaining life in years at start of year}}{\text{Sum of the years of life}}$

C. Assume that the company elects to compute depreciation charges using the double-declining balance method. Compute the depreciation charges for each of the three years.

The depreciation charges for each year would be calculated in the following manner:

The straight-line rate of depreciation is 33 1/3 percent-that is, 1/3 of the asset would be depreciated during each of the three years of useful life.

Twice the straight-line rate = 67 percent.

Each year's depreciation charges would be determined as indicated in the table below.

Year	Cost less accumulation depreciation (book value)	X	Depreciation rate	=	Depreciation charge	Remaining book value
1	$15,000	X	.67	=	$10,000	$5,000
2	5,000	X	.67	=	2,000*	3,000
3	3,000	X	.67	=	-0-**	3,000

*The depreciation charge in any year cannot serve to reduce the book value below the residual value of the asset. Thus, in year two, the depreciation expense cannot exceed $2,000-book value at the end of year 1 ($5,000) less salvage value ($3,000).

**There is no value remaining to be depreciated in year three, since the book value at the end of year 2 ($3,000) equals the residual value of the machine ($3,000).

D. Assume that the company elects to compute depreciation charges using the unit of output method. The firm estimates that it will make approximately 300,000 copies during the first year of operation, 200,000 copies during the second year, and 100,000 copies during the third year. Compute the depreciation charges for each of the three years.

The firm plans to make a total of 600,000 copies (300,000 in year 1, plus 200,000 in year 2, and 100,000 in year 3). Depreciation charges for each of the three years would be determined by multiplying total depreciable cost of $12,000 ($15,000 cost less $3,000 residual value) by the fraction of total copies to be made in any one year.

Each year's depreciation charges would be determined as indicated in the table below:

Year	Copies Made	Copies made as a Percent of 600,000	Net depreciable amount	Depreciation charge
1	300,000	50	$12,000	$ 6,000
2	200,000	33	12,000	4,000
3	100,000	17	12,000	2,000
	600,000	100		$12,000

EXERCISES

1. The Tower Print Company acquires a new printing press on January 1, 1991. The press costs $100,000 and has a useful life of four years, after which It can be sold for approximately $20,000. It is estimated that the printing press will be used in the production of a total of 40,000 books; 15,000 books in each of the first two years of useful life; 5,000 books in each of the last two years.

   A. In the matrix below, indicate the depreciation charges for each of the four years. Show your calculations in the space provided below the matrix.

Depreciation Method

Year	Straight-Line	Sum-of-the-Year's Digits	Double-Declining Balance	Unit of Output
1				
2				
3				
4				

B. Assume that the Tower Print Company has used a straight-line method to calculate its depreciation charges. At the end of the third year the company sells the printing press for $50,000. Prepare the journal entry needed to record the sale.

C. Following the sale of the old press, the company purchases a new printing press for $120,000. Prepare an appropriate journal entry to record the purchase.

2. The Fenton Mining Company has just purchased a coal mine for $125,000. The company's engineers estimate that the company will be able to extract 2,500,000 tons of coal from the mine.

   A. Determine the depletion charge per ton of coal that is extracted.

   B. In its first year of operations, the company extracted 750,000 tons of coal. Prepare a journal entry to record depletion charges for the first year of operations.

C. The management of the Fenton Mining Company has decided to sell the mine after extracting 1,500,000 tons of coal. Prepare a journal entry to record the sale of the mine for $75,000,000 cash.

SOLUTIONS TO CHAPTER NINE EXERCISES

1.A

Depreciation Method

Year	Straight-Line	Sum-of-the-Year's Digits	Double Declining Balance	Unit of Output
1	$20,000	$32,000	$50,000	$30,000
2	$20,000	$24,000	$25,000	$30,000
3	$20,000	$16,000	$ 5,000	$10,000
4	$20,000	$ 8,000	-0-	$10,000

<u>Straight-line method</u>:

Depreciation cost for each year =

$$\frac{\text{(Original cost - Residual value) net depreciable amount}}{\text{Useful life}}$$

Depreciation cost for each year =

$$\frac{\$100,000 - \$20,000}{4 \text{ years}} = \$20,000$$

<u>Sum-of-the-years' digits method</u>:

The denominator for the depreciation fraction would be calculated as follows:

$$\frac{n(n+1)*}{2} = \frac{4(4+1)}{2} = 10 \quad \text{*where n, the number of years, equals 4}$$

Each year's depreciation charge calculation is shown in the following table:

Year	Net depreciable amount	X	Depreciation fraction	=	Depreciation charge
1	$80,000	X	4/10	=	$32,000
2	80,000	X	3/10	=	24,000
3	80,000	X	2/10	=	16,000
4	80,000	X	1/10	=	8,000
			10/10		$80,000

Double-declining balance method:

The straight-line rate of depreciation is 25 percent--that is, 1/4 of the asset's net depreciable costs would be depreciated during each of the four years of useful life.

Twice the straight-line rate = 25 x 2 = 50 percent.

Each year's depreciation charge calculation is shown in the following table:

Year	Book Value	X	Depreciation rate	=	Depreciation charge	Remaining book value
1	$100,000	X	.50	=	$50,000	$50,000
2	50,000	X	.50	=	25,000	25,000
3	25,000	X	.50	=	5,000*	20,000
4	20,000	X	.50	=	-0-	20,000

*Book value cannot be reduced below the expected residual value of the asset, $20,000.

Unit of output method:

Depreciation charge per book = Net depreciable costs / Total book output expected

Depreciation charge per book = $80,000 / 40,000 units = $2 per book

Year	Units Produced	Units produced as a Percent of 40,000	X	Net depreciable Amount	=	Depreciation charge
1	15,000	37.5	X	$80,000	=	$30,000
2	15,000	37.5	X	80,000	=	30,000
3	5,000	12.5	X	80,000	=	10,000
4	5,000	12.5	x	80,000	=	10,000
	40,000	100				$80,000

These values can also be determined by multiplying units produced by $2 charge per unit.

B. Accumulated depreciation-printing press $60,000*
    Cash   50,000
        Printing press $100,000
        Gain on sale of printing press   10,000

    To record sale of old printing press.
    *Three years depreciation charge @ $20,000 per year.

C. Printing press $120,000
        Cash $120,000

    To record the purchase of the new printing press.

2.A.

   Depletion charge per ton = $\dfrac{\text{Total costs of mine}}{\text{Total tons of coal expected to be extracted}}$

   Depletion charge per ton = $\dfrac{\$125,000,000}{2,500,000 \text{ tons}}$ = $50 per ton

B. Depletion charge = Cost per ton X tons mined during the year

    Depletion charge = $50 X 750,000 = $37,500,000

    Depletion expense $37,500,000
        Accumulated depletion - coal mine $37,500,000

    To record first year's depletion expense.

C. Total depletion to date - $50 X 1,500,000 = $75,000,000

    Cash $75,000,000
    Accumulated depletion - coal mine   75,000,000
        Coal mine $125,000,000
        Gain on sale of coal mine   25,000

    To record sale of coal mine.

{Chapter 10}

LIABILITIES

AND RELATED EXPENSES

Chapter 10 presents some of the most complicated issues to develop in financial accounting within recent times. They are related to the measurement and reporting of non-current liabilities and associated expenses. This chapter gives consideration to the accounting questions associated with bonds, income tax liabilities, and pension liabilities. In addition, it examines issues pertaining to obligations arising from lease agreements-obligations that until recently were not even considered to be liabilities.

KEY POINTS

I. **Bonds**

    A. A bond is a formal certificate of indebtedness, conventionally issued in connection with the long-term (five years or more) borrowings of an enterprise.

    B. A bond conventionally contains promise to make two types of payments: periodic payments of interest (generally twice a year) and a payment of principal upon its maturity, the amount of which is indicated by its face value.

        1. Although the issuer of the bond conventionally sets the <u>coupon</u> rate of interest (the dollar amount of annual interest payments expressed as a percent of the face value of the bond), the effective interest rate is determined by the amount that lenders are willing to lend the issuer (i.e., to pay for the bond). Insofar as lenders are willing to pay for a bond an amount greater than its face value (the principal payment to be received upon maturity), then the effective interest rate is <u>less</u> than that stated in the bond agreement. However, if the lenders are willing to pay for a bond an amount less than its face value, then the effective interest rate is <u>greater</u> than that stated in the bond agreement. The interest rate stated in the bond agreement is referred to as the coupon rate; the effective interest rate is referred to as the <u>yield</u> rate.

        2. If an enterprise issues bonds at an amount greater than their face value (that is, at an amount which results in a yield rate less than the coupon

rate), then the difference between the actual issue price and the face value is referred to as a <u>premium</u>. If it issues bonds at an amount less than their face value (at an amount which results in a yield rate greater than the coupon rate), then the difference between the face value and the actual issue price is referred to as a <u>discount</u>.

    3.   A lender would be willing to pay a premium for a bond (an amount above face value) when the prevailing rate of interest on similar bonds is less than the coupon rate on the particular bond.' He could acquire a bond at a discount when the prevailing rate is greater than the coupon rate on the particular bond.

C.   Determination of the total amount that an investor would be willing to pay for a bond requires an analysis of the promise (to make payments of principal and interest) inherent in it. Such amount would be equal to the <u>present</u> value, using an appropriate discount rate, of the actual interest and principal payments to be received. The appropriate discount rate would be the rate which similar securities are yielding--the prevailing rate at the time the purchase is to be made.

D.   Alternatively, the amount of any premium or discount to be added to or subtracted from the face value of a bond in determining purchase price may be calculated directly by answering four questions:

    1.   How much interest per period (based on <u>coupon rate</u>) is a purchaser of the bond actually going to receive?

    2.   How much interest would he like to receive (i.e., what is the <u>yield</u> or prevailing rate?)

    3.   What is the difference between the two amounts?

    4.   What is the present value, discounted at the <u>yield rate</u>, of such difference?

E.   The bond premium or discount represents an addition to or deduction from the amount of interest that the issuer of the bond will be required to pay over the entire life of the bond. If, for example, a company issued a $1,000 face value bond for $980-a discount of $20-then it has effectively borrowed (received the use of) $980. It will be required to repay $1,000. The $20 represents an additional interest expense, and it should be accounted for as such.

    1.   Bonds should be reported on the balance sheet in such a way as to indicate the effective liability--that is, face amounts of bonds plus or minus the unamortized portion of the premium or discount.

    2.   The premium or discount should be amortized over the life of the bond; the interest expense to be reported each period should be the

actual interest payments made plus or minus the portion of the discount or premium amortized in the period.

  3. Alternatively, the interest expense for a period may be determined directly by multiplying the effective liability at the start of the accounting period the face value of the bond plus or minus the unamortized premium or discount) by the yield rate (the effective interest rate at the time the bonds were first issued). The difference between the interest expense and the amount of interest actually required to be paid--the amount indicated on the coupon--represents the amount of premium or discount to be amortized during the period.

F. When a firm redeems a bond before maturity, it would often reacquire the bond--and thereby satisfy its outstanding liability--for an amount greater than or less than its book value the face value plus or minus the unamortized premium or discount). If the amount paid to retire the bond is different from its book value, the company would recognize a gain or loss on retirement of an amount which is equal to the difference between the amount paid and the book value of the bond.

G. Starting in the mid-1980's, a new wave of corporate takeovers were funded with debt rather than equity capital. The term leveraged buyout (LBO) was used to describe these debt financing transactions. Some bonds issued as part of these takeovers were called junk bonds because they had high interest rates and high risk.

II. **Leases**

A. In a strict sense, a lease involves the right to use land, buildings, equipment or other property for a specified period of time in return for rent or other compensation. In practice, however, many lease arrangements are the equivalent of installment purchases or other forms of buy--borrow arrangements. Leases should be accounted for in a manner that recognizes their substance rather than merely their legal form.

B. If a firm acquired property under a lease arrangement, which is in substance an installment purchase, then the property acquired should be recorded as an asset. The asset should be recorded initially at the <u>present value</u> of the contractually required lease payments. The required lease payments should be discounted at an interest rate equal to that which the company would have had to pay had it elected to buy the equipment outright and borrow the necessary funds. At the same time, the firm should record a corresponding liability of an equal amount.

C. Over its useful life, the asset should be depreciated in a rational and systematic manner--just as if the company had purchased the property outright.

D. Each lease payment should be considered in part a reduction of the principal balance of the recorded liability and in part a payment of interest. The portion of the payment representing interest could be computed by multiplying the outstanding balance in the liability account by the applicable rate of interest; that representing principal would be the remainder of the payment. The portion representing interest should be charged as an expense; that representing principal should be accounted for as a reduction in the recorded liability.

E. Under present practice, not all property acquired under lease agreements need be capitalized as assets--only those acquired under lease arrangements which are in substance installment purchases.

III. **Accounting for Income Taxes**

A. As a general rule, corporate earnings for tax purposes are determined in the same manner as for general financial reporting. There are, however, a number of exceptions. The exceptions fall into two categories; permanent differences and timing differences. A _permanent difference_ is one, which, because of special legislative considerations, particular revenues or expenses are omitted from computation of taxable income. A _timing difference_ is one in which an item is includable in or deductible from income in one period for tax purposes but in a different period for general reporting purposes. Because of the magnitude of the tax, financial statements could easily be distorted if the tax associated with a particular revenue or expense were reported in a period other than that in which the revenue or expense were recorded. Suppose, for example, that a major item of revenue were included in the computation of income for financial reporting purposes in period 1, but in the computation of taxable income in period 2. Since the tax obligation in period 1 would be relatively low, after-tax income would be misleadingly high. Correspondingly, in period 2, when the tax had to be paid and there was no related revenue to be recognized for purposes of financial reporting, after-tax income would be deceptively low.

B. In order to avoid distortions in reported after-tax income, it is necessary to _allocate_ taxes among accounting periods. In essence, tax allocation requires that the reported income tax expense be based on _pretax_ financial reporting income. Reported tax expense would be determined by multiplying the pretax financial reporting income by the applicable tax rate.

C. The reported tax liability for a particular year would be divided into two parts; that which is currently payable (per the tax return), and that which can be deferred until future periods (the difference between the reported tax expense and the amount that is currently payable). In years in which the firm is able to postpone taxes, an account for the deferred portion of the liability would ordinarily be credited that is, increased); in years in which the firm must "repay" the taxes that had been postponed the deferred liability account would be debited (and thereby decreased). In summary, under tax allocation procedures, the reported tax expense follows <u>the financial reporting income</u>.

IV. **Accounting for Pensions**

    A. Pensions represent periodic payments to retired or disabled employees owing to their years of employment. Most pension plans require that a company make fixed monthly payments to an employee from the time of his retirement to the date of either his death or that of his surviving spouse.

    B. The accounting issues pertaining to pensions arise from the fact that payments to an employee do not have to be made until he retires. Yet the cost to the company arises from the service that he provides during his years of employment.

    C. Some (but not all) companies make periodic payments to pension funds during the working years of their employees. But, regardless of whether they do make such payments, and regardless of the pattern of those payments, pension costs must be charged as expenses in the period in which the employees provide their services.

    D. The amount that should be charged as an expense is indicated by the "required" payments to the fund as determined by the actuarial cost method that the firm elects to use. The reported expense would be the same regardless of whether the firm actually makes those payments. The difference between the required payment for a period and the amount that a company actually pays into the fund should be added to or subtracted from a liability account, <u>accrued pension liability</u>. The pension liability, as reported on the balance sheet would thereby be increased each year by the recorded pension expense (the required payments to the fund) and decreased by the actual payments to the fund. An <u>actuarial cost method</u> is a means of determining the required payments to a fund, taking into account the life expectancy of employees, employee turnover, rate of return that the company will earn on investments purchased with cash paid into the fund and the benefits to which the employee will be entitled.

KEY ISSUES FOCUSED UPON IN THIS CHAPTER

1. Should the value of all property rights acquired under lease agreements be capitalized and reported as assets on the balance sheet? Should the required payments under such lease arrangements be recorded and reported as liabilities?

Under current practice, acquisitions of property under lease arrangements that are in economic substance installment purchases must be accorded balance sheet recognition. Some accountants argue that <u>all</u> lease arrangements create property rights and corresponding obligations that should be reported on the balance sheet.

2. Should income taxes be allocated among accounting periods?

Inter-period allocation of income taxes is presently required by pronouncements set forth by the rule-making bodies of the accounting profession. Some accountants contend, however, that tax allocation results in financial statements in which both the tax liability and the tax expense are materially overstated. They assert that often, especially in the case of an expanding company, the deferred tax obligation never, in fact, has to be paid; instead it is deferred indefinitely.

KEY WORDS AND PHRASES

Accrued Pension Expense (Liability)	Debentures
Actuarial Cost Method	Inter-period Tax Allocation
Actuary	Lease
Bond Discount	Par Value
Bond Premium	Pensions
Bonds	Redemption
Call Premium	Yield Rate
Coupon Bonds	
Coupon Rate	

ILLUSTRATIONS FOR REVIEW

1. The Sungate Company plans to issue 8 percent, 10 year bonds, each with a face value of $1,000, to finance an expansion of its plant facilities. The bonds will pay interest semi-annually and are to be sold at a time when the prevailing rate of interest is 10 percent.

    A. For how many semi-annual periods will the bonds be outstanding--that is, how many payments of interest will the company be required to make?

The number of semi-annual periods over the life of the bond may be calculated by multiplying the life of the bond, in years, by two--10 years X 2 = 20 semi-annual interest payments.

B. What is the amount of each of the semi-annual interest payments on each bond?

The amount of each semi-annual interest payment may be determined by multiplying the principal amount of each bond--$1,000--by the stated rate of interest for one-half year - 8 percent ÷ 2 = 4 percent. Thus, the amount of each interest payment would be calculated as follows:

$1,000 X .04 = $40

C. How much will the company have to pay upon the maturity of each bond--that is, what is the required principal payment upon maturity?

The company will have to repay the face or principal amount of each bond. Thus, the company will have to repay $1,000 per bond, upon maturity.

D. What is the present value of the principal amount of the bond to be received, upon the maturity of the bond, in ten years (20 periods), based on the prevailing rate of interest of 5 percent per period?

The present value (per Table 2) of $11 to be received in 20 periods, discounted at a rate of 5 percent, is $.3769. Thus, the present value of $1,000 is

$1,000 X .3769 = $376.90

E. What is the present value of the 20 payments of interest to be received each six months, based on the prevailing rate of interest of 5 percent per period?

Each payment of interest will be $40. The present value (per Table 4) of 20 payments of $1, discounted at a rate of 5 percent, is 12.4622. Thus, the present value of 20 payments of $40 is

$$\$40 \times 12.4622 = \$498.89$$

F. For how much will the Sungate Company be able to issue each bond--that is, what is the effective liability to be incurred?

The amount to be received for each bond will be the sum of the present values of the required principal and interest payments. Thus, the amount to be received for each bond would be

$$\$376.90 + \$498.49 = \$875.39$$

G. What would be the amount of the discount on each bond?

The amount of the discount on each bond may be calculated by subtracting the amount received for each bond from its face value. Thus:

$$\$1,000 - \$875.39 = \$124.61$$

H. Prepare a journal entry to record the issuance of one bond.

Cash	$875.39	
Discount on bonds payable	124.61	
Bonds payable		$1,000.00

To record the issuance of one bond.

I. What is the effective interest expense on each bond--that based on the actual amount borrowed and the rate of interest prevailing at the time of the sale--during the first one-half year in which the bond is outstanding?

142

The effective interest expense may be determined by multiplying the effective rate at the time of the bond's issuance by the effective liability at the start of the interest period--the face amount of a bond ($1,000) minus the unamortized discount ($124.61). Thus the effective interest expense may be calculated as follows:

Effective interest expense = ($1,000 - $124.61) X .05
Effective interest expense = $875.39 X .05 = $43.77

J. What is the actual periodic interest payment required; that is, how much cash must the company pay on one bond each six months?

As determined in part B, the amount of cash to be paid every six months is $40 per bond.

K. What is the difference between the effective interest expense and the required cash payment--by how much should the discount account be amortized?

The difference between the effective interest expense ($3.77) and the required cash payment ($40.00) is $3.77. That is the amount by which the bond discount must be amortized (reduced) at the time of the first payment of interest.

L. Prepare a journal entry to record the first payment of interest on one bond.

Interest expense	$43.77	
Cash		$40.00
Discount on bonds payable		3.77

To record the payment of interest.

M. After the payment of interest for the first one-half year, what is the effective liability of the company for one bond (the face value less the unamortized discount)?

As a result of the journal entry in Part L, the unamortized portion of the bond discount has been reduced from $124.61 to $120.84 - by the $3.77 discount amortized.

Thus, the effective liability on one bond would be its face value less the unamortized discount.

Effective liability - $1,000 - $120.84 = $879.16

N. Prepare the journal entry that would be required to record the second payment of interest on one bond.

The effective interest expense may be calculated by multiplying the effective liability at the start of the second interest period ($879,16) by the <u>yield</u> rate --the rate of interest that prevailed at the time the bond was first issued (5 percent). Thus:

$879.16 X .05 - $43.96

The required cash payment is unchanged -$40. The amount by which the bond discount will be amortized is the difference between the effective interest expense and the required payment - $3.96.

Interest expense	$43.96	
Cash		$40.00
Discount on bonds payable		3.96

2. On January 1, 1992, the Monitor Corporation purchased radio-monitoring equipment for $14,000. The equipment has a useful life of three years and salvage value of $2,000. Monitor plans to depreciate the equipment using the straight-line method of depreciation for financial-reporting purposes, and the sum-of-the-years' digits method for tax-reporting purposes.

In 1992 the firm had income before depreciation and taxes of $15,000. The company pays taxes at a rate of 40 percent.

A. What is the depreciation expense, using the sum-of-the-years' digits method, to be reported by Monitor for tax purposes in 1992?

Net depreciable cost of equipment = $14,000 - $2,000 = $12,000

The sum-of-the-years' digits is 3 + 2 + 1 = 6. In 1992, depreciation expense for tax purposes will be

3/6 X $12,000 = $6,000

B. What is the taxable income of the company in 1992?

Taxable income may be calculated by subtracting the depreciation charges ($6,000) from the company's income before depreciation and taxes ($15,000). Thus:

Taxable income = $15,000 - $6,000 = $9,000

C. What is Monitor's tax liability for 1992--that is, what is the required amount of the company's tax payment for 1992?

The required tax payment may be calculated by multiplying the taxable income by the appropriate tax rate--40 percent. Thus:

Required tax payment = $9,000 X .40 = $3,600

D. What is the depreciation expense to be reported by Monitor on its 1992 financial reports--that calculated by the straight-line method?

Depreciation expense = $12,000 X 1/3 = $4,000

E. What is the amount of reported income on which the company should calculate the tax expense to be reported on its financial statements?

The reported income in 1992 may be calculated by subtracting the depreciation charged ($4,000) from the company's income before depreciation and taxes ($15,000). Thus:

Reported income = $15,000 - $4,000 = $11,000

F. What is the tax expense that the company should report in 1992, assuming that the reported tax expense is to be based on reported income?

The reported tax expense is calculated by multiplying the reported income by the appropriate tax rate. Thus:

Reported tax expense = $11,000 X .40 = $4,400

G. What is the difference between the reported tax expense and the required tax payment--that is, how much should be reported as a deferred tax liability?

The difference may be calculated by subtracting the required tax payment ($3,600) from the reported tax expense ($4,400). Thus:

Amount to be reported as a deferred tax liability =

$4,400 = $3,600 = $800

H. Prepare a journal entry to record Monitor Company's 1992 tax expense.

Tax expense	$4,400	
Taxes deferred until future years		$ 800
Taxes payable-in current year		3,600

To record tax expense for 1992.

EXERCISES

1. The Prolon Company plans to issue $100,000 of 10-year, 10 percent bonds to finance a generator for its plant. The bonds will pay interest semi-annually and are to be issued at a time when the prevailing rate of interest is 8 percent.

   A. What is the required amount of each semi-annual interest payment?

   B. What is the present value of the required payment of principal upon the maturity of the bonds, based on the prevailing rate of interest (the yield rate) of 4 percent per semi-annual period?

   C. What is the present value of the 20 payments of interest--that is, what is the present value of an annuity of $5,000, for 20 periods, discounted at a rate of 4 percent?

   D. What is the amount for which the Prolon Company could issue the $100,000 bonds--that is, what is the amount that the company could expect to actually receive?

   E. What is the amount of the premium or discount on the bond issue?

F. Prepare a journal entry to record the issuance of the bond issue.

G. What is the first period's effective interest expense on the bond issue-that based on the actual amount borrowed and the rate of interest prevailing at the time of the sale (the yield rate)?

H. What is the difference between the effective interest expense and the required cash payment on the bonds for the first period--that is, by how much should the premium be amortized?

I. Prepare a journal entry to record the first payment of interest on the bond issue.

J. Prepare a journal entry to record the second payment of interest on the bond issue.

2. A company wishes to issue a 10-year, 6 percent, $100,000 bond. The bond requires interest to be paid annually and is to be issued when the prevailing rate of interest is 8 percent.

   A. How much interest per year (based on the coupon rate) is a purchaser of the bond actually going to receive?

B. How much interest, based on the prevailing rate of interest, would the purchaser "like" to receive?

C. What is the difference between the actual interest payment and the desired interest payment?

D. What is the present value, discounted at the prevailing rate of interest (8 percent for 10 years), of an annuity of such a difference; that is, what is the amount of discount or premium at which the company will be required to sell its bonds?

E. What is the price for which the company could issue its bonds?

F. Prepare a journal entry to record the issuance of the bonds.

3. The Frontier Oil Company purchased a tank truck to transport its product. The truck cost the oil company $20,000 and has an estimated useful life of 4 years, after which the company plans to sell the truck for $4,000.

The truck was purchased on January 2, 1991, and the company uses the double-declining balance method to calculate depreciation charges for tax purposes and the straight-line method for financial reporting purposes. In 1991 the firm had an income before taxes and depreciation of $25,000. The company pays taxes at a rate of 40 percent.

A. What is the depreciation expense to be reported by Frontier for tax purposes in 1991, assuming that the firm uses the double-declining balance method to compute depreciation?

B. What would be the amount of Frontier Company's required tax payment in 1991?

C. What is the depreciation expense to be reported by Frontier on its financial statements in 1991, assuming that the firm uses the straight-line method?

D. How much tax expense should the company report in 1991?

E. Prepare a journal entry to record Frontier Company's 1991 tax expense.

4. A company wishes to issue a 5-year, 8 percent, $10,000 bond. The bond requires semi-annual interest payments and is to be issued at a time when the prevailing rate of interest is 6 percent.

A. How much interest (based on the coupon rate) is a purchaser of the bond actually going to receive every six months?

B. How much interest would the purchaser "like" to receive every six months, based on the prevailing rate of interest?

C. What is the difference between the actual interest payment and the desired interest payment?

D. What is the present value, discounted at the prevailing rate of interest of 3 percent per semi-annual period, for 10 periods of an annuity of such a difference?

E. Prepare a journal entry to record the issuance of the bond.

F. What is the effective interest expense for the first six-month period, based on the actual amount borrowed and the rate of interest prevailing at the time of the sale (the yield rate)?

G. Prepare a journal entry to record the first payment of interest.

SOLUTIONS TO CHAPTER TEN EXERCISES

1. A. The required interest payment is 5 percent (the per period coupon rate) of $100,000-$5,000.

   B. The present value of $1 discounted at a rate of 4 percent per period for 20 periods is (per Table 2) $.4564. The present value of $100,000 is

   $100,000 X .4564 = $45,640

   C. The present value of an annuity of $1 per period for 20 periods, discounted at a rate of 4 percent per period, is (per Table 4) $13.5903. The present value of an annuity of $5,000 is

   $5,000 X 13.5903 - $67,951.50

   D. The amount to be received for the bond issue is the sum of the present values of the expected principal and interest payments. Thus:

   $45,640.00 + $67,951.50 = $113,591.50

   E. The amount of premium may be determined by subtracting the face value of the bonds ($100,000) from the issue price ($113,591.50). Thus:

   $113,591.50 - $100,000.00 = $13,591.50

   F. Cash $113,591.50
        Bonds payable $100,000.00
        Premium on bonds payable   13,591.50

   To record the issuance of the bonds.

   G. The effective interest expense may be calculated by multiplying the effective rate, at the time the bonds are issued, by the effective liability at the start of the first interest period. Thus:

   $113,591.50 X .04 - $4,543.66

   H. Amount of premium amortization = $5,000 - $4,543.66 = $456.34.

   I. Interest expense $4,543.66
      Premium on bonds payable   456.34
         Cash $5,000.00

   To record the payment of interest.

J.   Interest expense* $4,525.41
     Premium on bonds payable   474.59
        Cash $5,000.00

To record the payment of interest.

*Effective interest expense = ($113,591.50 - $456.34) X .04
Effective interest expense = $4,525.41

2. A.   The annual interest to be received by the purchaser may be calculated by multiplying the face amount of the bond ($400,000) by the coupon rate of interest (6 percent). Thus:

$100,000 X .06 = $6,000

B.   The purchaser would like to receive a return of 8 percent. Thus:

$100,000 X .08 = $8,000

C.   Desired annual interest payment - actual annual interest payment =

$8,000 - $6,000 = $2,000

D.   The present value of a $2,000 annuity, discounted at a rate of 8 percent per period, for 10 periods, is (per Table 4)

$2,000 X 6.7101 = $13,420.20 (discount)

E.   The price may be calculated by subtracting the discount of $132,420.20 from the face value of $100,000. Thus:

Sale price of bonds = $100,000.00 - $13,420.20 = $86,579.80

F.   Cash $86,579.80
     Discount on bonds payable   13,420.20
        Bonds payable $100,000.00

To record the issuance of the bonds.

3. A.   The depreciation expense to be reported in 1991 may be calculated as follows:

Depreciation charge = Cost less accumulated   X   Depreciation rate (twice
                     depreciation   straight-line rate of
                     (book value)   25 percent)

Depreciation charge = $10,000 X .50 = $10,000

B. The required tax payment is calculated by multiplying taxable income by the appropriate tax rate - 40 percent.

Required tax payment =

[$25.000(income) - $10,000(depreciation expense X-40)] = $15,000 X .40 = $6,000

C. Net depreciable cost = $20,000 - $4,000 = $16,000

Depreciation charge = $16,000 X .25 = $4,000

D. The reported tax expense is calculated by multiplying the reported net taxable income by the appropriate tax rate. Thus:

Reported tax expense =

[$25,000(income) - $4,000(depreciation expense)] X .40 = $21,000 X .40 = $8,400

E. Tax expense $8,400
   Taxes deferred until future years $2,400
   Taxes payable--in current year   6,000

To record tax expense for 1991.

4. A. The semi-annual interest to be received by the purchaser may be calculated by multiplying the face amount of the bond ($10,000) by the semi-annual coupon rate of 4 percent (8 percent X 1/2). Thus:

$10,000 X .04 = $400

B. The purchaser would like to receive, each six months, a return of 3 percent 1/2 of the prevailing annual rate of 6 percent. Thus:

$10,000 X .03 = $300

C. Actual semi-annual - Desired semi-annual = $400-$300 = $100
   interest payment   interest payment

D. The present value of $100, discounted at a rate of 3 percent per period, for 10 periods, is (per Table 4)

$100 X 8.5302 = $853.02

E. Cash $10,853.02
      Bonds payable $10,000.00
      Premium on bonds payable   853.02

   To record the issuance of the bond.

F. Effective interest expense = $10,853.02 X .03 = $325.59

G. Interest expense $325.59
    Premium on bonds payable   74.41
      Cash $400.00

   To record the payment of interest.

{Chapter 11}

TRANSACTIONS BETWEEN A FIRM AND ITS OWNERS

Up to this point little distinction has been made between the accounting concerns of the various legal forms of business in the United States: proprietorships, partnerships, and corporations. Chapter 11 identifies the accounting practices that are unique to partnerships and proprietorships, compares them to corporations, and examines a number of accounting issues pertaining to the capital stock of corporations. The latter subject, and, especially, its recent complexities are continued in the next chapter.

KEY POINTS

I. **Characteristics of Proprietorships and Partnerships**

   A. A proprietorship is a business owned by one person. A partnership is one owned by two or more parties.

   B. Proprietorships and partnerships are, in a legal sense, extensions of their owners. One or more parties simply establish a business; no formal charter or state certificate is required.

   C. A proprietor, as well as each partner of a partnership, is usually individually responsible for all obligations of his business. If the enterprise suffers losses, the owners are jointly and severally responsible for all debts incurred. A partner will generally be held liable not only for his share of partnership debts but for those of his partner as well in the event that they are unable to satisfy their shares of partnership obligations.

   D. Neither the proprietorship nor the partnership form of organization provides for the ready transfer of interest from one owner to another. Partners do not individually own or have a share in the ownership of <u>specific</u> partnership assets. Instead each partner owns a share in <u>all</u> partnership property. Generally a partner can sell or transfer his interest to an outsider only with permission of the remaining partners.

   E. Neither the proprietorship nor the partnership is subject to federal or state taxes or income. Instead, the tax is assessed on the individual owners. Each partner is taxed on his share of partnership earnings.

II. **Characteristics of Corporations**

   A. A corporation is a legal entity separate and distinct from its owners and its managers. Being a legal "person" created by the state, it has the right to own property in its own name, and it can sue or be sued.

   B. The single most significant distinction between corporations and other forms of business organizations is that <u>the liability of a corporation's stockholders is limited to the amount of their initial investment in the company</u>, whereas that of the owners of proprietorships or partnerships is unlimited. With few exceptions, the maximum loss that a stockholder can sustain on a purchase of an interest in a corporation is the amount of his initial investment. Should the Corporation fail, creditors can avail themselves only of the assets of the corporation; they cannot, except in rare circumstances, seek redress against the personal assets of the owners.

   C. Corporations, like other legal persons, are subject to both federal and state income taxes. Earnings of a corporation are taxed irrespective of whether they are actually distributed in the form of dividends to the individual stockholders.

   D. Shares of stock can usually be freely transferred. Those of larger corporations are traded on stock exchanges, such as the New York Stock Exchange.

III. **Distinctive Features of Partnership Accounting**

   A. The owner's equity section of a partnership balance sheet usually consists of one capital account for each partner. Each capital account is credited (increased) by a partner's contributions to the firm and by his share of partnership profits. It is debited (decreased) by a partner's drawings from the firm and by his share of partnership losses.

   B. When a partner contributes property, be it cash or other assets, to a partnership the increase in his capital account is determined by the fair market value of the property contributed.

   C. The difficult conceptual questions pertaining to partnership accounting relate to the sale of partnership interests and the admission of new partners. The key issue is whether such events demand an overall revaluation of partnership assets. Suppose, for example, a new partner has paid for an interest in a partnership an amount greater than the book value of such interest. The transaction indicates that the partnership taken as a whole is worth more than its book value. Should the partnership "write-up" its assets to reflect its fair market value as indicated by the amount that the new partner is willing to pay for a partial interest or should it account for the "excess" payment as a bonus paid by the new partner to the old partners?

1. The <u>revaluation approach</u> is based on the contention that the transfer of the partnership interest in an arms length transaction provides an objective means of determining the fair market value of partnership assets. It is objectionable, however, in that it is inconsistent with the historical cost basis of accounting, which provides that assets are stated on the balance sheet at original cost less any accumulated depreciation regardless of changes in market values.

2. The <u>bonus approach</u> requires that any excess of the price paid by the new partner over the book value of the proportionate interest he has acquired be credited to the capital accounts of the existing partners. Recorded total assets of the partnership are increased only to the extent that the amount paid by the new partner exceeds the book value of the interest with which he will be credited.

IV. **Corporate Capital Accounts-Common Stock and Preferred Stock**

A. Common Stock is the "usual" type of stock; when only one class of stock is issued it is almost certain to be common stock.

1. Common stockholders share in the earnings of the corporation only when dividends are declared by its board of directors.

2. Common stockholders also have a <u>residual</u> interest in their company. Upon dissolution of the corporation, they have the right to share in the assets of the old company which remain after all claimants, including preferred stockholders, have been satisfied.

3. Common stockholders ordinarily possess the right to vote on a one vote per share basis. They can elect members of the board of directors and can vote on such matters of corporate policy as are specifically set forth in the corporate by-laws.

4. Often a company will issue more than one class of common stock. The alternative classes are typically restricted in certain rights, such as voting rights, granted to the shareholders of the other classes.

B. Preferred stock is a hybrid between common stock and bonds; it combines the benefits and limitations of both.

1. Preferred stock ordinarily stipulates that a fixed dividend will be paid to the stockholder each year. The dividend may be stated as a dollar amount (e.g. $3 per share) or as a percentage of par value (e.g. 3 percent of par value of $100).

2. The specific features of preferred stock vary from issue to issue. Generally, preferred stockholders do not have voting rights, except

when the company has failed to pay preferred dividends for a specified number of periods. Preferred stock, unlike bonds, does not mature on a particular date; usually, however, the corporation has the option to <u>call</u> (redeem) the stock at a stipulated price after a specified number of years has elapsed since its date of issue. Often shares of preferred stock are convertible into shares of common stock; the conversion ratio is established at the time the preferred stock is first issued.

    3.   Preferred stock has one critical disadvantage over bonds or other pure debt securities. The dividends on preferred stock (like those on common stock) are not deductible from corporate income for tax purposes, whereas interest payments are. The effective after-tax cost of acquiring capital by issuing preferred stock rather than bonds is, therefore, comparatively greater.

V. Formation of a Corporation and Issuance of Common Stock

A. A corporation is ordinarily formed by one or more individuals known as <u>promoters</u>. The promoters organize the corporation, apply for a charter and establish the by-laws under which the corporation will initially operate.

B. Common stock traditionally bears an indication of <u>par value</u> per share. The requirement that common stock be assigned a par value was initially designed to protect creditors of the corporation. Today, the par value of a stock is usually an arbitrarily assigned amount, which has little economic significance. Nevertheless, when a company issues stock, it is customary to account for the increase in corporate owners' equity in two parts: the par value of the shares issued; any amount in excess of par.

C. When a corporation issues stock in exchange for assets other than cash or for services rendered, it is essential that the assets or services received are recorded at their fair market value and that the number of shares issued be based on such values.

D. The amount that an investor is willing to pay for a share of common stock is likely to be influenced, in large measure, by his expectation as to the future earnings of the company.

VI. Issuance of Preferred Stock

A. Preferred stock has many of the characteristics of bonds. The preferred stockholder is less concerned with the future earnings of the company than is the common stockholder, since the dividend rate on preferred stock is fixed; it does not vary with the earnings of the company. His primary concern in selecting an issue of preferred stock is how the yield that he will obtain compares to that available from other investments with similar risk characteristics. If an issue of preferred stock pays dividends at a percentage rate (dividends as a percentage of par value) less than that which the investor could obtain elsewhere, then the investor would be willing to purchase the stock only at a discount--an amount less than its par value. If it pays dividends at a percentage rate greater than that which he could obtain elsewhere, then he would be willing to pay a premium to acquire it.

B. When preferred stock is issued, it is customary to record in one capital account the par value of the shares issued and in another the difference between the amount received and the par value of the issued stock.

VII. **Transactions in a Corporation's Own Shares**

A. Companies may purchase their own outstanding shares of stock for a number of reasons. They may wish to reissue the shares to executives or other employees in connection with stock option or related compensation plans, to "invest" temporarily in their own shares, or to reduce the scale of their operations and return to stockholders a share of the capital they had previously contributed.

B. Stock which is acquired and retained by the issuing corporation is known as treasury stock. Treasury shares may not be voted, they do not receive dividends and they carry none of the usual rights of ownership.

C. There are two primary methods of accounting for treasury stock.

1. Under the cost method treasury stock is accounted for in a separate account, treasury stock. The treasury stock account would be reported contra to the other equity accounts. It should not be reported as an asset. As the company purchases treasury stock, the account is debited (increased) in the amount of the actual price paid for the shares. If the company subsequently sells the stock the account is credited (decreased) for the amount at which the shares had been carried (the amount for which they had been purchased). Should the company sell the shares for an amount other than what was paid for them, then the difference would be added to or subtracted from contributed capital in excess of par.

2. Under the par value method, the shares acquired are accounted for as if they were being retired. First, both the common stock, par value and the contributed capital in excess of par accounts would be debited (reduced) by an amount which corresponds to the percentage of shares being retired. Then, retained earnings would also be debited (reduced) by any amount paid for the shares in excess of the amounts debited to the other accounts. If the company subsequently reissues the shares retired, then the reissue would be accounted for in the same general manner as if the shares were being issued for the first time.

3. The choice between the two methods should ordinarily be governed by the <u>intent</u> of the company's management. If the corporation expects to resell or reissue the shares within a short period of time, then the cost method would be preferable. If it does not, then the par value method would be preferable.

VIII. **Convertible Securities**

A. Convertible securities are true hybrids; they have characteristics of both debt and equity financial instruments. For example, convertible bonds can, at the holder's option, be exchanged (at a specified conversion ration) into shares of the issuer's common stock.

B. Convertible securities offer advantages to both the issuer and investor. For example, with convertible bonds, the issuer usually pays a lower rate of interest and the investor can benefit from appreciation in the market value of the issuer's stock

C. The issuance of convertible bonds is recorded the same as the issuance of conventional bonds. Although the conversion rights are an important element in the issuance of a convertible bond, as a practical matter, they are not separately valued or recorded.

D. When the exchange occurs, the conversion may be accounted for on the basis of either the book value of the bonds or market values.

1. When historical costs are used, the new stock to be issued is recorded at the book value of the bonds they replace and no gain or loss is recorded.

2. When market values are used, the market value of the stock is used and a gain or loss (measured by the difference between the market value of the stock issued and the book value of the bonds retired) recognized.

IX. **Financial Ratio**

The debt-to-equity, a financing ratio, compares the claims of creditors with the equity of the stockholders. The ratio is:

$$\text{D-to-E} = \frac{\text{Total debt}}{\text{Stockholders' equity}}$$

KEY ISSUES FOCUSED UPON IN THIS CHAPTER

1. Should the admission of a new partner be considered sufficient cause for a partnership to revalue its assets?

    The price paid in an arm's length transaction for an interest in a partnership can serve as an objective basis by which to determine the overall market value of the enterprise. Some accountants believe a partnership should be restated to reflect their fair market values each time a new partner is admitted to the partnership. Other accountants maintain that such revaluation would be inconsistent with the historical cost basis of accounting and argue instead that any amounts paid by a new partner in excess of the "book" value of the interest he is to receive should be accounted for as a "bonus" to the existing partners.

2. How should treasury stock be accounted for?

    Treasury stock may be accounted for by either the cost method or the par value method. Under the cost method, shares held for redistribution are recorded in a separate account. Under the par value method, the shares are treated as if they were to be permanently retired. Although the issue of which method is preferable is not considered a critical one by most accountants, the two methods do result in differing balances in the various owners' equity accounts.

3. Is interest really an expense?

    Some accountants would take exception to the practice of classifying interest as an expense. They argue that interest has more of the characteristics of dividends than it does of other expenses. In essence, they assert, interest, like dividends, represents a return to the parties who have supplied capital to the enterprise and should be accounted for as such.

4. When a firm needs more capital, how should it decide whether to issue bonds, common stock, or preferred stock?

    The choice among issuing common stock, preferred stock and bonds is usually made using earnings per share (after taxes) as the primary criterion--how would the earnings per share of existing common stockholders be affected if one type of security as opposed to another were issued.

    The sale of either bonds or preferred stock enables existing shareholders to <u>leverage</u> their investment. Since bonds and preferred stock carry a fixed return, any earnings above the required interest or dividend payment would accrue entirely to the common stockholders. The excess earnings need not be shared with the holders of the other types of securities. Conversely, any deficiency between the earnings of the company and the required payment must be made up entirely by the common stockholders. The payments must be made regardless of the actual earnings of the company.

The relative advantages of issuing the three types of securities depend on the anticipated earnings of the company, the prevailing interest and dividend rates and the market price of common stock, which affects the number of shares of stock that must be issued to acquire a given amount of capital.

KEY WORDS AND PHRASES

Authorized Shares	Leverage
Call	Outstanding Shares
Corporation	Participating Preferred Stock
Issued Shares	Promoters

ILLUSTRATIONS FOR REVIEW

1. The balance sheet of the Davis and Hudson Salvage Company as of June 30, 1992 is presented on the next page.

   John Davis and William Hudson, the two owners of the firm, have determined that the firm is in need of additional capital to expand its operations. To acquire the needed funds, the owners have decided to admit a third partner.

   On July 1, 1992, Lewis Shanter offers to purchase a one-third interest in the partnership for $400,000 cash. His offer is accepted by the existing partners.

   The partnership's accountant is considering the most appropriate means of recording the transaction. He wishes to compare the effects on recorded assets and equities of (A) revaluing the partnership assets based on the amount paid by Mr. Shanter and (B) considering the excess of the price paid by Mr. Shanter over the book value of his interest to be a bonus to the existing partners.

Davis and Hudson Salvage Company
Balance Sheet
As of June 30, 1992

Assets

Current Assets:		
Cash		$ 45,000
Supplies Inventory		20,000
Total Current Assets		$ 65,000
Non-Current Assets:		
Office Furniture	$ 12,000	
Less: Accumulated Depreciation	2,000	10,000
Operating Vehicles	$150,000	
Less: Accumulated Depreciation	30,000	120,000
Salvage Equipment	$400,000	
Less: Accumulated Depreciation	50,000	350,000
Buildings	$125,000	
Less: Accumulated Depreciation	25,000	100,000
Land		118,000
Total Non-Current Assets		$698,000
Total Assets		$763,000

Liabilities and Partners' Equity

Current Liabilities:	
Accounts Payable	$ 43,000
Non-Current Liabilities:	
Notes' Payable	120,000
Total Liabilities	$163,000
Partners' Equity:	
Capital, Davis	300,000
Capital, Hudson	300,000
Total Partners' Equity	$600,000
Total Liabilities and Partners' Equity	$763,000

A. <u>The Revaluation Approach</u>

    1.   What is the book value of the partners' equity (assets minus liabilities) as of June 30, 1992?

        The total equity of the partners is $600,000 (assets of $763,000 minus liabilities of $163,000).

2. After the partnership receives $400,000 cash from Mr. Shanter, what will be the total value of the assets owned by the partners? What will be the total equity of the partners?

The total assets of the partnership will now be $1,163,000. Since the liabilities of the partnership will remain unchanged, total equity of the partners (now three partners) will be $1,000,000.

3. If Mr. Shanter is willing to pay $400,000 for a one-third interest in the partnership, what is the implied fair market value of the entire partnership?

If one-third of the partnership is worth $400,000 (based on the arms length transaction), then three-thirds must be worth

$400,000 X 3 = $1,200,000

4. By how much does the implied (fair market) value of the partnership exceed the total book value (equity of the partners) after the admission of the new partner? If the assets are to be revalued to reflect the fair market value of the partnership, by how much must the value of the partnership assets be increased?

The fair market value of the partnership ($1,200,000) exceeds the book value ($1,000,000) by $200,000; therefore, the assets must be increased in value by $200,000.

5. If the fair market value of the partnership is $1,200,000, and the liabilities of the company are $163,000 what value should be assigned to total partnership assets? What value should be assigned to total partners' equity?

Since the liabilities of the partnership are $163,000, the fair market value of the assets must be $1,363,000. The total value to be assigned to the partners' equity must be $1,200,000.

6. If Mr. Shanter is to receive a capital credit of $400,000, the capital accounts of Mr. Davis and Mr. Hudson each have a balance of $300,000, and the total value to be assigned to the capital accounts of all three partners is $1,200,000, then how much must be added to the existing capital accounts of Mr. Davis and Mr. Hudson.

The balances in the capital accounts of each of the three partners must be $400,000, since they are to have an equal interest in a partnership with a total book value of $1,200,000. Therefore, $100,000 must be added to each of the capital accounts of Mr. Davis and Mr. Hudson.

7. Prepare a journal entry to record the cash contribution of Mr. Shanter, the revaluation of the assets of the company, and the adjustment of the capital account balances. Assume that the amount by which the assets are to be revalued represents an intangible assets, goodwill.

Cash	$400,000	
Goodwill	200,000	
Capital, Davis		$100,000
Capital, Hudson		100,000
Capital, Shanter		400,000

To record the admission of the new partner.

B. The Bonus Approach

1. After the partnership receives $400,000 cash from Mr. Shanter, what will be the total value of the assets owned by the partners? What will be the total equity of the partners?

The total assets of the partnership will now be $1,163,000. Since the liabilities of the partnership will remain unchanged, total equity of the partners will be $1,000,000.

2. If total partnership equity is $1,000,000, and Mr. Shanter is to have a one-third interest in the partnership, what is the amount of the capital credit that he should receive?

Mr. Shanter should receive a capital credit of $333,334 ($1,000,000 ÷ 3).

3. By how much does the contribution of Mr. Shanter exceed the capital credit that he is to receive? How much of a <u>bonus</u>, to be shared equally between the existing partners, is Mr. Shanter paying to join the partnership?

Mr. Shanter is apparently willing to pay a bonus of $66,666, the excess of his cash contribution over the capital credit he will receive, to join the partnership.

4. Prepare a journal entry to record the cash contribution of Mr. Shanter and the related adjustment to the capital accounts.

Cash	$400,000	
Capital, Davis		$ 33,333
Capital, Hudson		33,333
Capital, Shanter		333,334

To record the admission of the new partner.

5. Following the admission of Mr. Shanter into the partnership, Mr. Hudson decides to sell his interest in the partnership to Mr. Jones for $333,333, an amount equal to the balance in his capital account. Prepare a journal entry to record the sale of the partnership interest to Mr. Jones. No entry of substance is required. All that is necessary is to transfer the balance in the capital account of Mr. Hudson to a new capital account established for Mr. Jones. Thus:

Capital, Hudson	$333,333	
Capital, Jones		$333,333

To record the sale of a partner's interest.

2. The management of the Holzman Corporation believed that the market price of their stock on the exchange was too low. They had some extra cash in the company and decided it was time to buy their own stock for future issuance in an employee stock option plan. They purchased 100 shares of their own company's stock ($1 par) for $10 per share.

   A. What entry would be made to record the acquisition of this stock, assuming that the Holzman Corporation used the cost method of accounting for treasury stock?

       Treasury stock $1,000
         Cash $1,000

   The account, Treasury stock, would be debited for the total cost of the reacquired shares.

   B. Assume that later on, the firm changed its mind about using the stock in the employee option plan and sold it for $15 per share. What entry would they make to record the reissuance of this stock (100 shares) at $15 each using the cost method?

       Cash $1,500
         Treasury stock $1,000
         Contributed capital
           in excess of par   500

   When the shares are reissued, any differences between the reacquisition cost and the reissuance price ($10 and $15) should be credited to the account, Contributed Capital in Excess of Par.

3. The Dooright Manufacturing Company reacquired 100 shares of the company's own stock (par value of $2 per share) for $12 per share. What entry would be required on the books of the Dooright Company to record the acquisition of this stock, assuming that they used the par value method of accounting for treasury stock, and that these shares were originally issued at $4 per share?

```
            Common stock            $ 200
            Contributed capital
              in excess of par        200
            Retained earnings         800
                Cash                          $1,200
```

Under the par value method, the entry to record the reacquisition of stock must reverse the original entry to record the first issuance of this stock. Any amounts paid above this to acquire the stock are debited to the Retained Earnings account. What entry would be required later if they reissued this stock for $11 per share?

```
            Cash                   $1,100
                Common stock               $ 200
                Contributed capital
                  in excess of par            900
```

The subsequent reissuance of this stock is treated as a normal sale. The amount of the proceeds representing par value is credited to the stock account and any excess credited to Contributed Capital in Excess of Par.

EXERCISES

1. The Newberry Corporation received its charter from the state of Texas on July 14, 1992. At its first meeting on July 15th, the board of directors decides to issue 25,000 shares of $3 par value common stock at a price of $15 per share and 15,000 shares of $100 par value preferred stock "at par".

    A. Prepare a journal entry to record the sale of the common stock for $15 per share.

    B. Prepare a journal entry to record the sale of the preferred stock for $100 per share.

C. Several weeks later, the board of directors agrees to issue 5,000 shares of common stock to the Dalton Machine Company in exchange for machinery for the company's shop and 40 shares to the company's lawyer, Charles Stidham, in return for his efforts in organizing the corporation. Prepare a journal entry to record the issuance of the additional shares of common stock. Assume that the machinery has a fair market value of $80,000 and the legal services are to be valued at $640.

2. The Loumas Company plans to issue 20,000 shares of $100 par value preferred stock, which will pay dividends of $9 per share each year. On the day of issue, July 1, 1992, the prevailing yield on similar types of securities is 8 percent.

A. For how much is each share of preferred stock likely to be sold?

B. Assuming that the shares are in fact sold for $112.50 per share, prepare a journal entry to record the sale of the 20,000 shares of preferred stock.

C. Prepare a journal entry to record the payment of a semi-annual dividend of $4.50 per share on December 31, 1992.

D. On June 10, 1991, the company decides to repurchase and retire 10,000 shares of its preferred stock. It is able to acquire the stock at a price of $102 per share. Prepare a journal entry to record the repurchase and retirement of the 10,000 shares of preferred stock.

3. The Wottle Company has decided to purchase, in the open market, 4,000 shares of its $5 par value common stock for $15 per share. The shares were originally sold for $8 per share.

    A. Which method would yo recommend that the company use to record the purchase of the shares of treasury stock if the company plans to reissue the shares of stock in connection with an employee stock purchase plan?

        1. Assume that at the time the firm purchases the shares, the balance in its retained earnings account is $1,000,000. The company decides to use the cost method to record the transaction. Prepare a journal entry to record the purchase of the 4,000 shares.

        2. Assume that the company sells the 4,000 shares of stock to its employees for $10 per share, the price at which employees are permitted to acquire the stock as set forth in the employee stock purchase agreement.

            a. How should the company give accounting recognition to the $5 per share "loss" when the company resells the stock to its employees?

b. Prepare a journal entry to record the sale of the 4,000 shares to the employees for $10 per share.

B. Which method should the company use to record the purchase of the shares of treasury stock if it plans to hold the shares for an indefinite period of time?

1. Assume that the company uses the <u>par value</u> method to record the purchase. Since the stock has a par value of $5 and was sold initially for $8 per share, how much was credited, at the time of sale, to the Contributed Capital in Excess of Par account in connection with the issuance of the 4,000 shares?

2. How much should be removed from (debited to) the Contributed Capital in Excess of Par account upon the retirement of the 4,000 shares?

3. To what account should the excess of the amount paid to reacquire the stock over the amount received when the stock was issued be debited?

4. Assume that the balance in the retained earnings account is $1,000,000. Prepare a journal entry to record the reacquisition of the 4,000 shares of common stock.

5. Assume that the company subsequently reissues the 4,000 shares held in the treasury at a price of $11 per share. Prepare a journal entry to record the sale.

4. On January 1, 1992, Ragtop Corporation issued $1,000,000 of 8% convertible bonds at a premium of $30,000. Each bond had a face value of $1,000 and is convertible into the firm's common stock ($10 par value) at a conversion ration of 5 to 1. The market price of the common stock on January 1, 1992 is $150.

   A. Into how many total shares of common stock can this bond issue be converted?

   B. Prepare the journal entry to record the issuance of these bonds.

   C. Assume that five years have passed and on January 1, 1991, the market value of the common stock is $225 per share and the bond premium has been amortized down to $20,000. What is the book value of these bonds?

   D. If the bondholders exercise their option to exchange their bonds for common stock on January 1, 1991, prepare the journal entry to record conversion and issuance of the new common stock, assuming that the conversion is accounted for on the basis of book value.

E. Repeat step D. assuming that the conversion is accounted for on the basis of market value.

F. What is the book value per bond immediately prior to conversion?

G. What is the market value of the common stock that can be obtained by the conversion of one bond on January 1, 1991, just prior to conversion?

SOLUTIONS TO CHAPTER ELEVEN EXERCISES

1. A. Cash $ 375,000
    Common stock $ 75,000
    Contributed capital in excess
      of par, common stock   300,000

To record the sale of 25,000 shares of common stock.

B. Cash $1,500,000
    Preferred stock $1,500,000

To record the sale of 15,000 shares of preferred stock.

C. Machinery $ 80,000
   Organizational costs (asset)   640
    Common stock $ 15,120
    Contributed capital in excess
      of par, common stock   65,520

To record the exchange of common stock for shop machinery and organizational legal costs.

2. A. If a share of preferred stock, which pays dividends of $9 per year, is to be sold to yield 8 percent; then, the anticipated selling price may be determined by dividing the annual interest payment per share by the required yield rate. Thus:

$$\text{Sales price*} = \$9/.08 = \$112.50$$

*Since the preferred stock has no maturity date, the return can be assumed to be a perpetuity; hence, there is no need to refer to the present value to determine the sales price.

B.
Cash	$2,250,000	
Preferred stock		$2,000,000
Contributed capital in excess of par,		
preferred stock		250,000

To record the sale of preferred stock.

C.
Dividends, preferred stock	$ 90,000	
Cash		$ 90,000

To record the payment of semi-annual preferred stock dividends.

*Since the issue of preferred stock is assumed to have an infinitely long life, there is no need to amortize the capital contributed in excess of par.

D.
Preferred stock	$1,000,000	
Contributed capital in excess of		
par, preferred stock*	20,000	
Cash		$1,020,000

To record the purchase and retirement of preferred stock.

*Amount paid per share ($102) less par value per share ($100) times number of shares acquired (10,000).

3. A. The company should use the cost method to record the purchase, since its intent is to reissue the shares within a short period of time.

1.
Treasury stock	$ 60,000	
Cash		$ 60,000

To record the purchase of treasury stock.

2. a. The difference between the fair market value of the stock ($15 per share--the amount the company had to pay to acquire the stock) and the price that the employees would pay for the stock ($10 per share) is accounted for as additional employee compensation.

    b.
Cash	$ 40,000	
Employee compensation (expense)	20,000	
Treasury stock		$ 60,000

    To record the sale of treasury stock to employees under stock purchase plan.

B. Since the company intends to hold the 4,000 shares of its own stock for an indefinite period, it should use the <u>par value</u> method to record the purchase.

   1. The sales price of $8 was $3 greater than the par value of $5 per share; thus, $12,000 was originally credited to contributed capital in excess of par when the 4,000 shares were sold.

   2. The entire $12,000 originally credited to the account would be removed (debited).

   3. $7 per share (the amount paid per share, $15, less the original sales price, $8) should be recorded as a reduction of retained earnings.

   4.
Common stock	$ 20,000	
Contributed capital in excess of par, common stock	12,000	
Retained earnings	28,000	
Cash		$ 60,000

   To record the purchase of treasury stock.

   5. The sale should be treated as an entirely new issue of common stock. Thus:

Cash	$ 44,000	
Common stock		$ 20,000
Contributed capital in excess of par value, common stock		24,000

   To record the sale of common shares.

4. A. The bonds can be converted into a total of 5,000 shares of common stock:

   $1,000,000/1,000 = 1,000$ bonds X 5 shares = 5,000 shares of stock

B. The journal entry would be

    Cash $1,030,000
        Bonds payable $1,000,000
        Premium on Bonds Payable   30,000

C. The book value is $1,020,000:

    $1,000,000 + ($30,000-$10,000) = $1,020,000

D. The conversion would be recorded:

    Bonds Payable $1,000,000
    Premium on Bonds Payable   20,000
        Common Stock, Par Value
        (5,000 shares @ $10) $ 50,000
        Capital Contributed in
          Excess of Par
        ($1,020,000-50,000)   970,000

E. The entry to record the conversion on the basis of market value:

    Bonds Payable $1,000,000
    Premium on Bonds Payable   20,000
    Loss on Conversion   105,000
        Common Stock, Par Value $ 50,000
        Contributed Capital in Excess
          of Par ($1,125,000-50,000) $1,075,000

F. The book value per bond is $1,020:

$$\frac{\$1,000,000 + \$20,000}{1,000 \text{ bonds}} =$$

G. Each convertible bond can be exchanged for $1,125 of stock at market value:

    1 bond = 5 shares of common stock

    1 bond - 5 X $225

    1 bond = $1,125 of common stock

{Chapter 12}

SPECIAL PROBLEMS OF MEASURING AND REPORTING DIVIDENDS AND EARNINGS

Chapter 12 is directed toward additional transactions that affect the owners' equity accounts of the corporation. Among the topics discussed are stock rights and options, and dividends. Also considered in this chapter are two important problems with respect to reports of earnings: calculation of earnings per share and determination of earnings for an interim period.

The chapter presents some complicated and often misunderstood aspects of the accounting for the capital structure of the modern corporation.

KEY POINTS

I. **Retained Earnings and Cash Dividends**

    A. Retained earnings represent the total accumulated earnings of a corporation less amounts distributed to stockholders as dividends and amounts transferred to other capital accounts.

    B. Dividends are distributions of assets. They are charged (debited) to retained earnings, and are paid in cash or other tangible assets.

    C. It does not follow that merely because a company has a balance in retained earnings it has the means to make dividend payments. Retained earnings are a part of owners' equity. Owners' equity corresponds to the excess of assets over liabilities. Retained earnings cannot be associated with specific assets or groups of assets to which stockholders have claim. Decisions as to when and how much of a dividend to declare are normally made primarily with reference, not to the balance in retained earnings, but to the amount of cash that is available for distribution to stockholders.

II. **Dividends in Kind**

   A. Dividends in kind are those for which property other than cash is distributed to stockholders.

   B. When a company declares a dividend in kind, the debit to retained earnings should be of an amount equal to the market value of the property distributed. A firm should recognize gains and losses on the declaration of dividends in kind when the fair market value of the property distributed differs from the original cost to the firm.

III. **Stock Splits**

   A. When a corporation splits its stock, it issues additional shares of stock for each share outstanding at the time. Stock splits are ordinarily intended to reduce the market price per share, to obtain a wider distribution of corporate ownership, and to improve the marketability of the outstanding shares.

   B. As a consequence of a stock split, each stockholder would end up with more shares of stock, but his proportionate interest in the company would remain unchanged. The book value of each share would be proportionately reduced; the total book value represented by the shares held by each stockholder would remain unchanged.

   C. A stock split neither increases nor decreases the corporation's assets, liabilities, total par value of the stock outstanding (although after the split there will be a greater number of shares each with a reduced par value), capital contributed in excess of par or retained earnings. <u>No special journal entries are required to record a stock split.</u>

IV. **Stock Dividends**

   A. A stock dividend is one form of stock split. A corporation will distribute to each shareholder, on a <u>pro rata</u> basis, additional shares of its own stock. Ordinarily the ratio of new shares to be issued to outstanding shares is lower than that of other types of stock splits; usually the number of new shares would be less than (25) percent of previously outstanding shares. The purpose of a stock dividend is to provide shareholders with tangible evidence of an increase in their ownership interest. Stock dividends are commonly issued as a substitute for a dividend in cash or other property.

   B. A stock dividend, like other types of stock splits, has no effect on the intrinsic worth of either the corporation or the shareholder's investment. Nevertheless it is usually accounted for differently. According to pronouncements of the rule-making authorities of the accounting profession, a corporation should transfer from retained earnings to "permanent" capital (i.e., common stock, par value and capital contributed in excess of par) an amount equal to the fair market value of the additional shares to be issued. The company would transfer to the par value account an amount reflective of the par value of the new shares to be issued and to the capital contributed in excess of par account the difference between the fair market value of the shares and the amount transferred to the par value account.

V. **Employee Stock Options**

- A. Employee stock options are a form of employee compensation. They permit the employee to purchase a specified number of shares of his employer's stock at a fixed price, usually after he has continued to be employed for an established length of time.

- B. The accounting issues with respect to employee options are related to the measurement of both the value of the options granted and the compensation paid. A problem arises because the number of shares to be issued in the event the employee exercises his option cannot be known at the time the option be granted.

- C. As recommended by the Accounting Principles Board, the value of an option and the related compensation should be measured as of the date the option is first granted (as opposed, for example, to that when the option is exercised). Such date is generally within the accounting period in which the employee has performed the services for which the option was granted and in which both parties have measured the value of such services. The value of the option and the related compensation would be indicated by the number of shares required to be issued times the excess(assuming that the option exercise price is <u>less</u> than the prevailing market price of the shares) of the prevailing market price of the shares over the price at which the option may be exercised. If the exercise price is <u>equal to or greater than</u> the prevailing market price, then both the option and the related compensation would be assumed to have a value of <u>zero</u>. Notice that for purposes of recording the option, the prevailing market price of the shares at the time of exercise is irrelevant.

VI. **Earnings Per Share**

- A. In its simplest form earnings per share (EPS) can be calculated as follows:

$$\frac{\text{Net Earnings-Preferred Stock Dividends}}{\text{Number of Shares of Common Stock Outstanding}}$$

Net earnings would be those after taxes. * Preferred stock dividends are deducted from net earnings because the ratio is generally used to provide a measure of earnings available to common stockholders. Number of shares outstanding would be the <u>average</u> number of shares outstanding during the year.

B. If a firm has a complex capital structure the ratio, unless adjusted, may be misleading since the firm may have an obligation to issue additional shares in the future. Such obligation may stem from outstanding stock rights, warrants, options, convertible bonds and preferred stock. The additional shares to be issued may dilute earnings per share

C. Current pronouncements of the APB require that a firm with a complex capital structure present two types of earnings per share computations. The first would indicate <u>primary</u> earnings per share; the second, <u>fully diluted</u> earnings per share.

D. In calculating <u>primary earnings</u> per share the denominator shares outstanding) should be based on common stock presently outstanding plus those other types of securities that are considered to be <u>common stock equivalents</u>.

 1. A common stock equivalent is a security that is not, in form, common stock but which is convertible to common stock. It is a security that derives its value from the common stock in that it may eventually be exchanged for common stock. The holder of a common stock equivalent can expect to participate in the appreciation in the value of the common stock and share in the earnings of the corporation.

 2. Preferred stock that is convertible to common stock would be considered a common stock equivalent only if it derives its primary value from the common stock. Preferred stock may be assumed to derive its primary value from common stock if the dividend rate on the preferred stock provides its holder with a yield significantly less than he could obtain elsewhere. In general, preferred stock would be considered a common stock equivalent if its yield at the time of issue was less than 2/3 of the prevailing prime bank lending rates.

 3. If, in computing earnings per share, it is assumed that certain securities will be converted into common stock and thereby increase the number of common shares outstanding, then it is necessary to give consideration also to the impact of such conversion on the earnings of the company (i.e., the numerator of the fraction). Interest or preferred stock dividends that the company will no longer have to pay if certain bonds or shares of preferred stock are converted into common stock should therefore be added back to net earnings.

 4. Moreover, if the firm is to receive cash in connection with warrants that will be used to purchase additional shares of common stock, it is

necessary to give consideration to the use to which such cash shall be put. It should be assumed that any cash received will be used by the firm to acquire, and immediately retire, as many shares of its own common stock as it could purchase at the prevailing market price.

E. In calculating <u>fully diluted</u> earnings per share, the denominator of the ratio should ordinarily include shares of stock that the company would have to issue if securities which are not considered to be common stock equivalent (e.g., preferred stock that does not meet the criteria of a common stock equivalent) were converted into common stock. The numerator, earnings, would be the same as that used to determine primary earnings per share but would be adjusted to take into account the savings in interest or dividends that would result from the conversion of any additional shares which were used in calculating the denominator of the ration, number of shares outstanding.

VII. **Interim Financial Reports**

A. Interim financial reports are those that cover less than a full year; commonly they cover a quarter or half year period.

B. The accounting principles to be followed in calculating income for an interim period are the same as those followed for a full year. But problems of income determination increase as the length of the period covered by the financial statements decreased. It becomes considerably more difficult to associate revenue with productive effort and to match costs with revenues.

C. Moreover, some revenues and expenses are calculated on an annual basis. The rate at which income is taxed, for example, is based on earnings for the entire year. It is sometimes difficult to compute them for periods of less than a year.

D. Interim reports should be viewed as covering a period that is an integral part of the annual period. Hence, adjustments should be made to revenues and expenses to take into account related revenues and expenses to be incurred in future interim periods. Thus, for example, income taxes for each period should be based on the most likely annual tax rate; such rate would be dependent upon an estimate of earnings for the entire year.

KEY ISSUES FOCUSED UPON IN THIS CHAPTER

1. How, and at what date, should the value of an employee stock option and the related compensation be measured?

    When an employee stock option is issued it is not yet known if and when the option might be exercised. Since the transaction will not be completed until the option is actually exercised or is allowed to lapse, it is not clear what value should be assigned in the interim to both the option and the employee services in return for which it was issued.

2. In what accounting period should losses be recognized?

    Some accountants believe that as soon as a firm is aware that a loss is possible it should establish a reverse for contingencies and report the loss on its statement of income. Others believe that losses should not be charged against earnings until they actually occur.

3. Should the income statement be indicative only of current operating performance or should it include all transactions that affect the equity of owners?

    Some accountants believe that an income statement that focuses upon current operating performance is more useful--i.e., has greater value in predicting future financial results--than one which includes unusual transactions. Others believe that the income statement should provide a complete record of all transactions, excluding dividends, that have an impact upon retained earnings.

KEY WORDS AND PHRASES

Common Stock Equivalents	Primary Earnings Per Share
Contingency	Prior Period Adjustments
Date of Record	Self-Insurance
Dividend in Kind	Stock Dividend
Earnings Per Share (EPS)	Stock Option
Extraordinary Item	Stock Split
Fully Diluted Earnings Per Share	
Interim Financial Reports	

ILLUSTRATIONS FOR REVIEW

1. The following information relates to the capital structure of the Parker Corporation for the year 1992.

    Common Stock: 300,000 shares issued and outstanding.

Class A Preferred Stock: 150,000 shares issued and outstanding. Each share is convertible into one share of common stock. Each share is entitled to a dividend of $6. The stock was initially sold to yield shareholders a return of 8 percent--a yield approximately equal to the rate that prevailed at the time of issuance for bank loans to prime borrowers.

Class B Preferred Stock: 75,000 shares issued and outstanding. Each share is convertible into one share of common stock. Each share is entitled to a dividend of $2. The stock was initially sold to yield shareholders a return of 4 percent--a yield considerably below the 7 percent bank rate that prevailed at the time.

Executive Stock Options Outstanding: Options to purchase 135,000 shares at a price of $40 per share.

The current market price of common stock is $60 per share.

The firm had net earnings in 1992 of $4,625,000. Of this amount $900,000 was paid in dividends to holders of class A preferred stock; $150,000 was paid in dividends to holders or class B preferred stock; therefore, earnings available to common stockholders were $3,575,000.

A. Determination of primary earnings per share (EPS)

1. Is the class A preferred stock considered to be a common stock equivalent?

The class A preferred stock would not be considered a common stock equivalent, since it has value in its own right--its yield at the time of initial issue was greater than 2/3 of the prevailing prime lending rate.

2. Is the class B preferred stock considered to be a common stock equivalent?

The class B preferred stock would be considered a common stock equivalent, since it would apparently derive its value directly from the common stock--its yield at the time of initial issue was less than 2/3 (4/7 in this case) of the prevailing prime lending rate.

3. If the options under the executive stock option plan were to be exercised, and the proceeds used to purchase and retire shares of the company's common

stock, how many shares could be purchased and retired? (It is unlikely that the company would in fact elect to use the proceeds from the exercise of the options to purchase and retire shares of common stock. However, current pronouncements of professional rule-making authorities require that such an assumption be made in the computation of earnings per share.)

The 135,000 stock options could be exercised at a price of $40 per share. If the options were exercised, the company would receive $5,400,000 (135,000 shares X $40). The proceeds received from the exercise of the stock options could be used to purchase and retire 90,000 shares of common stock ($5,400,000 ÷ 60).

4. How many shares of common stock would be considered to be outstanding for purpose of calculating primary EPS?

The number of shares outstanding for the primary EPS calculation would be:

```
Common stock issued and outstanding                    300,000 shares
Common stock equivalents:
  Preferred stock, Class B.                              75,000
  Options                                135,000 shares
  Less: Shares of common stock
        assumed to be purchased
        and retired                       90,000         45,000
Shares outstanding for primary EPS calculation         420,000 shares
```

5. What is the income to be used in calculating primary EPS?

The income to be used for the primary EPS calculation would be:

```
Earnings available to common stockholders              $3,575,000
Plus: Dividends on class B preferred stock
      (considered to be a common stock equivalent)        150,000
Income for primary EPS calculation                     $3,725,000
```

6. Determine primary EPS

The primary EPS may be calculated by dividing the income available to the shares of common stock and the common stock equivalents, by the sum of the common stock shares and common stock equivalents considered to be outstanding. Thus,

$$\text{Primary EPS} = \frac{\$3,725,000}{420,000 \text{ shares}} = \$8.87$$

B. Determination of the fully diluted earnings per share.

1. How many shares of common stock are considered to be outstanding for purposes of calculating the fully diluted EPS?

The number of shares may be calculated by adding the number of shares of common stock which can be converted into common stock from other securities to the number of shares of common stock used for the primary EPS calculation. Thus,

Shares considered to be outstanding for primary EPS calculations	420,000 shares
Plus: Class A preferred stock (not a common stock equivalent, but nevertheless convertible into common stock)	150,000
Shares outstanding for the fully diluted EPS calculations	570,000 shares

2. What is the income to be used in calculating fully diluted EPS?

The income may be calculated by adding the dividends and interest paid on the Securities which might be converted into common stock to the income used for the primary EPS calculation. Thus,

Income used for the primary EPS calculation $3,725,000
Plus: Dividends on Class A preferred stock
(assumed in the calculation of the number of
shares outstanding to be converted into
common stock) 900,000
Income for the fully diluted EPS calculation $4,625,000

3. Determine fully diluted EPS.

The fully diluted EPS may be calculated by dividing the total earnings available to the shares of common stock, common stock equivalents, and securities which might be converted into common stock, by the total number of shares of common stock, common stock equivalents, and securities which might be converted into common stock. Thus:

$$\text{Fully diluted EPS} = \frac{\$4,625,000}{570,000 \text{ shares}} = \$8.11$$

2. The following are transactions of the Irvine Corporation in the areas of stock options, warrants, and rights.

A. If Irvine issued stock rights which entitled the holder to purchase a share of common stock for $40 when the current market price of the stock is $65, what would be the price at which the stock right is most likely to be traded?

Twenty-five dollars, the difference between the market price of the stock and the right price ($65-40).

B. If the company granted its employees a stock option plan which entitled them to purchase 1,000 shares of the common stock at a price of $15 per share at the end of 3 years, what would be the journal entry to record the issuance of stock options? Assume that the market price of the stock was $22 per share on the date the stock options were granted.

        Employee compensation $7,000
          Capital received-
            stock options $7,000

C. If the company were to declare a 10 percent stock dividend when it had 4,000 shares of $1 par value common stock outstanding, each with a market value of $10, how much would have to be transferred from retained earnings to permanent capital accounts to record this stock dividend?

$$\$4,000 = 400 \text{ shares} \times \$10 \text{ each}$$

D. If the Irvine Corporation had earnings after taxes of $900,000, and it paid preferred stock dividends of $300,000, and it had 200,000 shares of common stock outstanding for the entire year, what would its earnings per share of common stock be?

$$\$3.00 = \frac{\$9,000,000 - \$300,000}{200,000 \text{ shares}}$$

EXERCISES

1. The capital section of the Farnell Corporation is presented below and is to be used in the various sections of this illustration. (Each section of the illustration is independent of the other section.)

Farnell Corporation
Stockholders' Equity
As of December 31, 1992

	Shares	
4 percent cumulative preferred stock, $100 par value		
Authorized	50,000	
Issued and outstanding	35,000	$3,500,000
Common stock, $4.00 par value		
Authorized	2,000,000	
Issued and outstanding	100,000	400,000
Contributed capital in excess of par value, Common stock		2,100,000
Retained earnings		6,352,000
Total Stockholders' Equity		$12,352,000

A. The Board of Directors has voted to pay $1,000,000 in dividends on common and preferred stocks combined.

    1. Assuming no preferred dividends are in arrears, what would be the amount of the dividend required to be paid to the preferred stockholders?

    2. How much of the $1,000,000 will remain for payment to the common stockholders?

    3. What would be the amount of the dividend to be paid to the holder of each share of common stock?

    4. Prepare a journal entry to record the <u>declaration</u> of the cash dividend of $1,000,000.

5. Prepare a journal entry to record the <u>payment</u> of the dividend.

B. The Board of Directors declares a 2 percent common stock dividend. The prevailing market price of the company's common stock is $35 per share.

1. How many shares of common stock will the company have to issue?

2. What is the amount to be transferred from the retained earnings account to the permanent capital accounts?

3. What is the amount to be added to both the common stock and contributed capital in excess of par accounts?

4. Prepare a journal entry to record the issuance of the stock dividend.

C. Assume instead that the Board of Directors votes to distribute as a dividend shares of stock of the Crescent Company in which it has an interest. Each share cost the company $4 to acquire and can be sold currently for $9.50. The directors decide to distribute two shares of Crescent Company stock for each share of common stock outstanding. The shares have been reported as marketable securities.

　　1. What value should be assigned to each share of Crescent Company stock to be distributed as a dividend?

　　2. How many shares of Crescent Company stock will the company be required to distribute?

　　3. What is the total book value (cost) of the 200,000 shares to be distributed as a dividend?

　　4. Prepare a journal entry to record the distribution of the dividend-in-kind, assuming the distribution of the dividend coincides with its declaration.

D. The Board of Directors is concerned about the marketability of the company's common stock. The present market value is $60 per share. The Board believes that the relatively high price per share will hamper company plans to acquire additional capital by issuing common stock. They have decided to split the stock four for one, meaning that each shareholder will receive an additional three shares for each share he presently holds.

　　1. What would you anticipate would be the market value per share of common stock immediately following the split?

2. What would be the par value per share of common stock following the split?

3. What would be the balance in the common stock account following the four for one stock split?

4. Prepare journal entries, as required, to record the issuance of the additional 300,000 shares issued in connection with the stock split.

2. The Whitewater Company, in an effort to stimulate employee productivity and reduce the rate of personnel turnover, establishes a stock option plan which will permit its employees to purchase shares of the firm's common stock ($4 par value) at a price of $25 per share--a price considerably below the market price of the shares at the time the plan is adopted. Employees may exercise their options only if they remain with the company for a period of three years after the options are granted.

The first options are granted shortly after the plan is adopted. They permit the employees to acquire up to 20,000 shares of common stock. The market price of the firm's common stock on the date the options are granted is $30 per share.

A. What is the value of the options to the employees on the date that the options are granted?

B. Prepare a journal entry to record the issuance of the stock options.

C. At the end of the three-year option period, the market value of the company's stock has increased to $50 per share. Employees exercise their options to acquire 18,000 shares of common stock.

    1.   Prepare a journal entry to record the sale of the stock by the company to its employees.

    2.   Is a journal entry required to record the lapsing of the options on the remaining 2,000 shares?

SOLUTIONS TO CHAPTER TWELVE EXERCISES

1. A. 1.   Each share of preferred stock is entitled to an annual payment of 4 percent of its par value. Thus, each share of preferred stock will receive a dividend of $4 ($100 X .04). Since there are 35,000 shares of preferred stock issued and outstanding (no dividend payment is required for those shares which have not been issued), the required dividend payment is $140,000 ($35,000 X 4).

    2.   The amount that will remain is $860,000 ($1,000,000 - $140,000).

    3.   Dividend per share of common stock =
$$\frac{\$860,000}{100,000} \text{ shares issued and outstanding} = \$8.60 \text{ per share}$$

    4.

Dividends, Preferred stock	$140,000	
Dividends, Common stock	860,000	
Dividends payable		$1,000,000

To record the declaration of dividends on both common and preferred stock.

    5.

Dividends payable	$1,000,000	
Cash		$1,000,000

To record the payment of dividends.

B. 1.   Number of shares of common stock to be issued =

100,000 shares issued and outstanding X .02 = 2,000 shares

2. The amount to be transferred (capitalized) may be determined by multiplying the number of shares to be issued (2,000) by the fair market value of each share ($35). Thus:

Amount of retained earnings to be capitalized = 2,000 X $35 = $70,000

3. The amount to be added to the common stock account may be determined by multiplying the number of shares to be issued (2,000) by the par value per share of common stock ($4). Thus:

Amount to be added to the common stock account = 2,000 X $4 = $8,000

The amount to be added to the contributed capital in excess of par account may be determined by subtracting the amount to be added to the common stock account from the total amount of retained earnings to be capitalized. Thus:

Amount to be added to the contributed capital in excess of par account = $70,000 - $8,000 = $62,000

4.
Retained earnings	$70,000	
Common stock		$ 8,000
Contributed capital in excess of par value, Common stock		62,000

To record the issue of a stock dividend.

C. 1. The value should be based on the fair market value to the company of the assets distributed, not their cost. Thus, each share should be valued at $9.50.

2. The total number of shares to be distributed is twice the number of common shares outstanding--100,000 shares X 2 = 200,000 shares.

3. Book value (cost) of dividend to company is $1,900,000 (200,000 shares X $9.50).

4.
Dividends	$1,900,000	
Gain on Marketable securities		$1,100,000
Marketable securities		800,000

To record the declaration and payment or a dividend-in-kind.

D. 1. Following the split, each shareholder will have four shares of common stock for each share he held previously. As a result, the market value per share should be reduced to one-fourth of its previous value. Thus:

$$\text{Expected market value per share} = \frac{\$60}{4} = \$15 \text{ per share}$$

2. Since there will be four shares of common stock for each share that existed before the stock split, the par value per share before the split will be divided among the four shares after the split. Thus:

$$\text{Par value per share following the split} = \frac{\$4}{4 \text{ shares}} = \$1 \text{ per share}$$

3. A stock split does not alter the amounts in the permanent or temporary capital accounts. Thus, the balance in the common stock account will remain unchanged at $400,000. This amount can be determined independently by multiplying the issued and outstanding shares following the split (400,000) by the new par value per share ($1).

$$400,000 \text{ shares} \times \$1 = \$400,000$$

4. No journal entry is required.

2.A. The value of both the options and the employee services would be represented by the number of shares that could be purchased (20,000) times the difference between the current market price of the stock ($30) and the exercise price of the option ($25). Thus:

$$\text{Value of the options} = \$20,000 \times (\$30 - \$25) = \$100,000$$

B. Employee compensation $100,000
        Capital received-stock options $100,000

To record the issuance of employee stock options.

C. 1.   Cash $450,000
        Capital received-stock options   90,000
            Common stock $ 72,000
            Contributed capital in excess of
            par value, common stock   468,000

To record exercise of options and issuance of common stock.

Note that the current market price of $50 per share is *not* taken into account in recording the transaction.

2. No special entries would be required, and the balance remaining in the capital received-stock options account ($10,000) will continue to be reported as part of owners' equity.

{Chapter 13}

INTERCORPORATE INVESTMENTS AND EARNINGS

There are a number of reasons why one corporation will invest in another corporation by purchasing its common stock. This chapter presents the accounting principles for long-term, intercorporate investments. The means by which one company accounts for its investment in another has important consequences for the valuation of assets and the determination of net income. As you might expect, this topic is sometimes as complex as it is controversial.

KEY POINTS

I. **Level of Influence, the Key Determinant**

    A. A corporation can account for an investment in another corporation in two ways: the cost method and the equity method.

        1. The cost method is generally used when the investor corporation exerts minor influence (defined as less than 20 percent ownership of voting stock) over the investee company.

        2. The equity method is generally used when the investor corporation exerts substantial influence (defined as between 20 and 50 percent ownership) over the investee company.

    B. The consolidation method is used when the investor corporation controls the investee company (defined as more than 50 percent ownership). The consolidation method differs from the other two methods in that it represents only a means of reporting an investment. A corporation must maintain its investment on its own books by either the cost or the equity method. For purposes of reporting only it can elect to consolidate its reports with that of its subsidiary.

II. **The Cost Method**

    A. Under the cost method a company records its investment in another company at cost, the amount paid to acquire its stock.

B. It recognizes revenues from its investment only as the investee company actually declares dividends. In the absence of unusual declines in market value it would maintain its investment at original cost.

C. In 1976, the FASB required that long term investments accounted for by the cost method be stated at the lower of cost or market. The cost of the long-term portfolio must be compared with its market value; if the market value is lower, the cost must be written down to market and an unrealized loss recognized. This unrealized loss should be reported on the balance sheet in a special owners' equity account.

III. The Equity Method

A. Under the equity method a company records its investment in another company at cost. Periodically, however, it adjusts the carrying value of its investment to take into account its share of the investee's earnings subsequent to the date of acquisition. It recognizes its share of increases or decreases in the net worth of the investee as soon as they are known.

B. The company would recognize revenue in the amount of its proportionate share of investee earnings as the earnings are reported. At that time it would increase the carrying value of its investment by the amount of revenue recognized.

C. Correspondingly, the company would decrease the carrying value of its investment upon the actual declaration of dividends by the investee company. It would decrease the carrying value of the investment by the amount of the dividend to which it is entitled and at the same time record an increase in an asset, dividends receivable. The decrease in the carrying value of the investment is necessary because by virtue of the declaration of the dividend the net assets of the investee company (and correspondingly the interest of the investor company in those assets) has been reduced.

IV. Consolidated Reports

A. Consolidated financial statements report the financial position and results of operations of two or more corporations, each a separate legal entity, as if they were a single economic and accounting entity.

B. In simplest form a consolidated balance sheet represents the sum of the balances in the accounts of the individual companies which compose the consolidated entity. However, certain eliminations and adjustments are required if double counting is to be avoided. For example, if one company is indebted to another, then one company on its own books would report an account receivable while the other company would report an account payable. From the standpoint of the consolidated entity, it would be inappropriate to report either the receivable or payable, since a company cannot be indebted to itself.

1. If consolidated statements are to be prepared immediately upon acquisition, the parent company owns 100 percent of the subsidiary and the amount paid for the stock of the subsidiary is exactly equal to its book value (as recorded on the books of the subsidiary) then the investment in the subsidiary (as recorded on the books of the parent) would be eliminated directly against the common stock and retained earnings of the subsidiary.

2. If the consolidated statements are to be prepared immediately upon acquisition, the parent company owns <u>less</u> than 100 percent of the subsidiary and the amount paid for the stock of the subsidiary is exactly equal to the book value of the interest purchased, then the investment in the subsidiary (as recorded on the books of the parent) would also be eliminated directly against the common stock and retained earnings of the subsidiary. In addition, however, the remaining balance in the common stock and retained earnings account of the subsidiary would have to be reclassified as <u>minority interest in subsidiary</u>.

3. If consolidated statements are to be prepared immediately upon acquisition and the parent company paid for its interest more than its recorded value on the books of the subsidiary, then such excess would be reclassified in a manner indicative of its nature. The excess would be either allocated to specific tangible assets (on the theory that the fair market value of the assets is greater than their recorded book value), assigned to specific intangible assets as patents and copyrights (on the theory that the subsidiary developed them internally and therefore never recorded them as assets), or classified as <u>goodwill</u> (on the theory that the parent company paid more for its interest in the subsidiary than its recorded book value because the assets taken as a whole were worth more than the sum of their individual values). Once such excess of cost over book value has been reclassified, then any remaining balance in the investment in subsidiary account would be eliminated against the common stock and retained earnings for the subsidiary. The remaining balance on the books of the subsidiary in the common stock and retained earnings accounts could then be reclassified as <u>minority interest in subsidiary</u>.

   a. <u>Goodwill</u> is a residual. It represents that portion of the cost of acquiring a subsidiary that cannot be assigned directly to any specific assets. Goodwill is the one asset that arises <u>only</u> out of business combinations.

   b. Although the "useful life" of goodwill is not readily determinable, the Accounting Principle Board has prescribed that firms should attempt to estimate the useful life of goodwill and amortize its value over such useful life. In no event, however, should the period of amortization exceed 40 years.

    C.   The consolidated income statement represents the sum of the balances in the various revenue and expense accounts of the individual companies. However, certain eliminations and adjustments are required to make certain that only transactions with outsiders and not those between related companies are included among revenues and expenses. For example, interest paid by one member of a consolidated entity to another would be recorded on the books of one company as an expense and on those of the other as revenue. From the standpoint of the consolidated entity, however, no interest was either paid or received. Therefore, the related revenue and expense should be eliminated.

V.   **Pooling of Interests**

    A.   A pooling of interests is a means of accounting for a business combination that has been effected by an exchange of common stock--where one company acquired substantially all of the voting stock of another in return for its own common stock.

    B.   Underlying the pooling of interests method is the rationale that two firms join together to operate as a single economic entity. Neither of them purchases the other and the owners of the two component companies are granted a proportionate interest in the combined enterprise.

    C.   The key feature of the pooling of interests method is that each of the component companies retains its former basis of accounting. The assets and liabilities of neither company are revalued at the time of combination. The assets and liabilities of both companies are carried forward to the consolidated balance sheet at their previously recorded amounts. No accounting recognition is given to goodwill; no other assets are restated to reflect their fair market values.

    D.   The pooling of interests method may result in higher reported earnings than the purchase method since it does not require the consolidated enterprise to increase to market values the carrying values of the assets of the acquired firm or to give recognition to goodwill. As a consequence, the firm does not have to charge additional depreciation or amortization on the amounts by which the fair market values of the assets of the acquired firm exceed their book values.

    E.   As a consequence of abuses in using the pooling of interests method, the Accounting Principles Board has carefully defined and limited the circumstances in which the method may be used.

KEY ISSUED FOCUSED UPON IN THIS CHAPTER

1. Under what circumstances is the pooling of interest method appropriate?

   At one time "pooling of interests" was used to describe a type of business combination rather than an accounting method. Two corporations of similar size joined together to carry out their operations and the new company was jointly managed by the previous managers of the two firms. Over time, however, business combinations that were not in spirit poolings of interests were accounted for as if they were. Although some abuses have been eliminated, the particular circumstances in which pooling of interests accounting results in the most fair presentation is still a subject of controversy among accountants.

2. How can an investment in another corporation produce "instant earnings" for the acquiring company?

   If one company acquires the common stock of another in exchange for shares of its own common stock, it is possible for the acquiring company to immediately increase its earnings per share, even in the absence of substantive improvement in the operations of either company.

   Such apparent improvement in earnings would result if the exchange were based on the relative market values of the shares of common stock of the two companies, and the market value of the common stock of the acquiring company in relation to earnings (i.e., its price/earnings ratio) were comparatively greater than that of the company being acquired. The acquiring company would have to issue relatively few additional shares of common stock to purchase the stock of the other company, and would be able to add the earnings of the other company to its own. Since it would have to issue relatively few shares, its earnings per share would increase.

KEY WORDS AND PHRASES

Consolidated Financial Statements	Majority Interest
Control	Minority Interest
Cost Method	Parent
Equity Method	Pooling of Interests Method
Goodwill	Purchase Method
Intercompany Transactions	Subsidiary

ILLUSTRATIONS FOR REVIEW

1. The Dufferin Corporation owns 25 percent of the outstanding shares of common stock of the Xavier Corporation. Assume for simplicity that the Dufferin Corporations's only source of income in 1992 is from its one subsidiary, the Xavier Corporation. Reported earnings of the Xavier Corporation in 1992 are $2,000,000.

    A. By which method should the Dufferin Corporation account for its investment in the Xavier Corporation?

    Since the Dufferin Corporation owns more than 20 percent of the outstanding shares of common stock of the Xavier Corporation, it should account for its investment in the subsidiary company by the equity method.

    B. By how much has the owners' equity of the Xavier Corporation increased as a result of its reported earnings in 1992?

    The owners' equity accounts must have increased by $2,000,000, the reported income of the corporation.

    C. By how much has the Dufferin Corporation's share of the owners' equity of the Xavier Corporation increased?

    Since the Dufferin Corporation owns 25 percent of the outstanding shares of common stock of Xavier Corporation, its share of the increase in the Xavier corporation's owners' equity accounts will have increased by $500,000 (25 percent of $2,000,000).

    D. How much better off is the Dufferin Corporation as a consequence of the earnings of the Xavier Corporation; that is, how much revenue should be recognized by the Dufferin Corporation in 1992.

The Dufferin Corporation is $500,000 "better off"; therefore, it should recognize that much in revenue.

E. Prepare a journal entry to record the Dufferin Corporation's share of the Xavier Corporation's reported earnings.

Investment in the Xavier Corporation $500,000
  Revenue from investments in the Xavier Corporation $500,000

To record proportionate share of 1992 revenue reported by the Xavier Corporation.

F. On March 1, 1992, the Xavier Corporation declares and pays a $1,000,000 cash dividend to its common stockholders.

  1. By how much will the assets of the Xavier Corporation be decreased as a result of the payment of the cash dividend?

The total assets of the Xavier Corporation will have decreased by the amount of the dividend - $1,000,000.

  2. By how much will the owners' equity (the retained earnings) of the Xavier Corporation be decreased as a result of the declaration of the dividend?

The declaration of the dividend will serve to reduce the retained earnings by the amount of the dividend--$1,000,000.

3. By how much will Dufferin Corporation's share of the owners' equity of the Xavier Corporation be decreased?

Since the Dufferin Corporation owns 25 percent of the outstanding shares of the common stock of Xavier Corporation, its share of the decrease in the owners' equity will be $250,000 (25 percent of $1,000,000).

4. Prepare a journal entry to record the receipt of the dividends by the Dufferin Corporation.

Since the Dufferin Corporation owns 25 percent of the common stock of the Xavier Corporation, it will receive 25 percent of the cash dividend - $250,000.

Cash	$250,000	
Investment in the Xavier Corporation		$250,000

To record the receipt of dividends declared and paid by the Xavier Corporation.

EXERCISES

1. The Ospray Company has recently acquired 24,000 shares of the common stock of the Nelson Corporation for $5 per share. Mr. Thomas Jones, the comptroller of Ospray, has asked for assistance in the preparation of the necessary journal entries to record his company's acquisition.

   A. Prepare a journal entry to record Ospray's acquisition of the common stock of the Nelson Corporation.

   B. Assume that the 24,000 shares purchased by the Ospray Company represents 10 percent of the Nelson Corporation's outstanding shares of common stock.

1. What method should the Ospray Company use to account for its investment?

2. The Nelson Corporation reported earnings of $1,000,000 for the year ending December 31, 1992. What journal entry (if any) is required to record Ospray's 10 percent share of the reported earnings?

3. On January 15, 1993, the Nelson Corporation declared a dividend of $2 per share, payable on January 31, 1993. Prepare a journal entry to record the declaration of the dividend on the books of the Ospray Company.

4. Prepare a journal entry to record the receipt of the $2 per share dividend on January 31, 1993.

C. Assume instead that the 24,000 shares purchased by the Ospray Company represent 30 percent of the outstanding shares of common stock of the Nelson Corporation.

1. What method should the Ospray Company use to account for its investment in the Nelson Corporation?

2. The Nelson Corporation reported earnings of $1,000,000 for the year ending December 31, 1992. What journal entry (if any) is required to record Ospray's 30 percent share of the reported earnings?

3. On January 15, 1993, the Nelson Corporation declared a dividend of $2 per share, payable on January 31, 1993. Prepare a journal entry to record the declaration of the dividend on the books of the Ospray Company.

2. The JPC Company has purchased 100 percent of the outstanding shares of common stock of the Astend Company. The balance sheets of the two companies immediately following the acquisition are shown below.

	JPC Company	Astend Company
Cash	$1,500,000	$ 45,000
Accounts Receivable (from Astend Company)	25,000	
Investment in Astend Company	240,000	
Other Assets	3,000,000	250,000
	$4,765,000	$ 295,000
Accounts Payable (to JPC Company)		$ 25,000
Other Liabilities	$ 765,000	30,000
Common Stock	2,000,000	100,000
Retained Earnings	2,000,000	140,000
	$4,765,000	$ 295,000

A. What are the combined total assets of the two companies as <u>shown</u> on the above balance sheets. What is the actual combined total of the assets?

B. Prepare a journal entry to eliminate the intercompany payables and receivables.

C. What is the amount of the parent company's investment in the subsidiary; how much of the subsidiary's equity may be assigned to the parent?

D. What is the actual amount of the equity of the outside owners in the combined corporation?

E. Prepare an entry to eliminate both the balance in the owner's equity accounts of the subsidiary and the investment in the subsidiary account of the parent.

F. Using the worksheet provided below, prepare a consolidated balance sheet for the two companies.

	Original Statements		Adjustment	Consolidated Balance Sheet
	JCP Company	Astend Co.	Debit Credit	
Cash	$1,500,000	$ 45,000		
Accounts Receivable (from Astend Company)		25,000		
Investment in Astend Company	240,000			
Other Assets	3,000,000	250,000		
	$4,765,000	$295,000		
Accounts Payable (to JPC Company)		$ 25,000		
Other Liabilities	$ 765,000	30,000		
Common Stock	2,000,000	100,000		
Retained Earnings	2,000,000	140,000		
	$4,765,000	$295,000		

3. The Austonite Company has purchased 80 percent of the outstanding shares of common stock of the Beltain Company. The balance sheets of the two companies, immediately following the acquisition, are shown below.

	Austonite	Beltain
Cash	$1,525,000	$ 45,000
Investment in Beltain Company	240,000	
Other Assets	3,000,000	310,000
	$4,765,000	$355,000
Total Liabilities	$ 765,000	$ 55,000
Common Stock	2,000,000	100,000
Retained Earnings	2,000,000	200,000
	$4,765,000	$355,000

A. What is the amount of Austonite's investment in the Beltain Company? What percentage and dollar amount of the owners' equity accounts of the Beltain Company can be assigned to the Austonite Company?

B. Prepare an entry to eliminate the investment of the Austonite Company against the corresponding owners' equity accounts of the Beltain Company.

C. What does the remaining balance (20 percent of the original amount) in the owners' equity accounts of the Beltain Company represent?

D. Prepare an entry to reclassify the equity attributable to the minority stockholders as "Minority Interest in Beltain Company".

E. What would be the amounts to be reported on the consolidated balance sheet as (1) common stock, (2) retained earnings, (3) minority interest in Beltain Company, and (4) investment in Beltain Company?

4. Presented below are the balance sheets of the Tyroll Corporation and the Zelta Corporation as well as other selected information prior to a merger of the two firms.

	Tyroll Corporation	Zelta Corporation
	Balance Sheets	
Miscellaneous Assets	$4,000,000	$8,000,000
Miscellaneous Liabilities	$1,500,000	$2,400,000
Common Stock, Par Value $1	100,000	400,000
Contributed Capital in Excess of Par	850,000	3,000,000
Retained Earnings	1,550,000	2,200,000
	$4,000,000	$8,000,000
Number of Shares Outstanding	100,000	400,000
Net Income, in year prior to merger	$ 300,000	$ 800,000
Earnings Per Share	$ 3	$ 2
Current Market Price per Share	$ 150	$ 30

The Board of Directors of the Tyroll and Zelta Corporations have decided to combine the operations of their companies.

A. The directors have decided that the Tyroll Corporation will issue shares of its own stock to the current stockholders of the Zelta Corporation in exchange for the shares that they currently hold.

1. How many shares of common stock will be issued by the Tyroll Corporation to the current stockholders of the Zelta Corporation, if the exchange is to be based on the current market prices of the shares?

2. At what amount would the Tyroll Corporation record its investment in the Zelta Corporation if the merger is to be accounted for as a pooling of interests?

3. Prepare a journal entry to record the issuance of the shares of Tyroll Corporation common stock to the shareholders of the Zelta Corporation.

4. Prepare an entry which can be used in the preparation of consolidated financial statements to eliminate the investment by the Tyroll corporation against the corresponding owners' equity accounts of the Zelta Corporation.

5. Provide the necessary amounts to complete the consolidated balance sheet presented below. Be sure to give effect to the entries made in the preceding sections of this exercise.

Miscellaneous Assets $_____

Miscellaneous Liabilities
Common Stock, Par Value $1
Contributed Capital in Excess of Par _____
Retained Earnings $_____

B. Assume alternatively that the Tyroll Corporation elected to purchase the currently outstanding shares of the Zelta Corporation's common stock for <u>cash</u>.

1. What will be the total price that the Tyroll Corporation will be required to pay for the outstanding shares of the Zelta Corporation?

2. At what amount would the Tyroll Corporation record the investment if the acquisition were to be recorded as a purchase?

3. Prepare a journal entry to record the acquisition.

4. Determine the excess of the cost of the Zelta Corporation common stock over its book value.

5. Prepare an entry which would be posted to the consolidated worksheet to eliminate the investment by the Tyroll Corporation against the corresponding owners' equity accounts of the Zelta Corporation. Consider any excess of cost over book value to represent goodwill.

6. Provide the necessary amounts to complete the consolidate balance sheet presented below. Assume that the Tyroll Corporation borrowed the amount necessary to acquire its interest in the Zelta Corporation.

Miscellaneous Assets $_____
Goodwill _____
$_____

Miscellaneous Liabilities
Common Stock, Par Value $1 $_____
Contributed Capital in Excess of Par
Retained Earnings _____
$_____

SOLUTIONS TO CHAPTER THIRTEEN EXERCISES

1. A. Investment in Nelson Corporation $120,000
    Cash $120,000

    To record the purchase of 24,000 shares of the Nelson Corporation's common stock.

   B. 1. The company should account for its investment using the cost method.

   2. Since the Ospray Company employs the cost method to account for its investment in the Nelson Corporation, no journal entry is required to record the reported earnings of the investee company.

   3. Since the Ospray Company owns 24,000 shares of the Nelson Corporation's common stock, it will receive a dividend of $48,000 (24,000 shares X $2 per share).

    Dividends receivable $48,000
         Revenue from investment in
             Nelson Corporation $48,000

    To record dividends to be received from the Nelson Corporation.

   4. Cash $48,000
         Dividends receivable $48,000

    To record the receipt of dividends from the Nelson Corporation.

   C. 1. The company should account for its investment by the equity method.

   2. Since the Ospray Company reports its investment under the equity method, it must report earnings of $300,000 (.30 X $1,000,000) in 1992.

    Investment in Nelson Corporation $300,000
         Revenue from investment in Nelson Corporation $300,000

    To record proportionate share of 1992 revenue reported by the Nelson Corporation.

   3. Since the Ospray Company owns 24,000 shares of the Nelson Corporation's common stock, it will be entitled to a dividend of $48,000 (24,000 X $2 per share).

    Dividends receivable $48,000
         Investment in Nelson Corporation $48,000

    To record dividends to be received from the Nelson Corporation.

2. A. The combined total is the sum of the total assets of the two companies. Thus, the combined total assets are $4,765,000 + $295,000 = $5,060,000.

    The actual total assets would not include the intercompany payables and receivables ($25,000) and the investment in the subsidiary ($240,000). Thus, the actual total assets are $4,795,000 ($5,060,000-$25,000-$240,000).

B. Accounts payable (Astend) $25,000
    Accounts receivable (JPC) $25,000

    To eliminate intercompany payables and receivables.

C. The JPC Company has an investment of $240,000 in the Astend Company. Inasmuch as the JPC Company owns 100 percent of the Astend Company, the entire owners' equity of the Astend Company may be assigned to the JPC Company.

D. The actual amount of the equity of outside owners in the consolidated company is the balance in the owners' equity accounts of the parent company, $4,000,000. From the perspective of the consolidated enterprise, the parent's equity in the subsidiary must not be added to the outside owners' equity in the parent. (A company cannot have an ownership interest in itself.)

E. Common stock $100,000
    Retained earnings   140,000
        Investment in Astend Company $240,000

    To eliminate investments in subsidiary and the corresponding subsidiary owners' equity accounts.

F.

	Original Statements JCP Company	Astend Co.	Adjustment Debit	Credit	Consolidated Balance Sheet
Cash	$1,500,000	$ 45,000			$1,545,000
Accounts Receivable (from Astend Company)	25,000			(B) 25,000	
Investment in Astend Company	240,000			(E) 240,000	
Other Assets	3,000,000	250,000			3,250,000
	$4,765,000	$295,000			$4,795,000
Accounts Payable (to JPC Company)		$ 25,000	(B) 25,000		
Other Liabilities	$ 765,000	30,000			$ 795,000
Common Stock	2,000,000	100,000	(E) 100,000		2,000,000
Retained Earnings	2,000,000	140,000	(E) 140,000		2,000,000
	$4,765,000	$295,000			$4,795,000

3. A. The amount of Austonite's investment in the Beltain Company is $240,000. Eighty percent ($240,000) of the $300,000 in the owners' equity accounts of the Beltain Company can be assigned to the Austonite Company.

B. Common Stock $ 80,000
Retained Earnings 160,000
    Investment in Beltain Company $240,000

To eliminate investment in subsidiary and corresponding amounts in owners' equity accounts.

C. The remaining 20 percent represents the interest of the minority stockholders in the Beltain Company.

D. Common stock $20,000
Retained earnings 40,000
    Minority interest in Beltain Company $60,000

To reclassify equity of minority stockholders in Beltain Company

E. 1. Common stock - $2,000,000.
   2. Retained earnings - $2,000,000.
   3. Minority interest in Beltain Company - $60,000
   4. Investment in Beltain Company - $0.

4. A. 1. Since the current market value of the outstanding shares of the Zelta Corporation common stock is $12,000,000 (400,000 shares at $30 per share), the Tyroll Corporation will have to issue 80,000 shares ($12,000,000 divided by $150, the current market value of the Tyroll Corporation stock).

    2. Since the merger is to be accounted for as a pooling of interests, assets are recorded at their previous book values. The investment in the Zelta Corporation would be recorded at its value on the books of the Zelta Corporation. Such value, $5,600,000, is represented by either the sum of the balances in the owners' equity account ($400,000+$3,000,000+$2,200,000) or the total assets ($8,000,000) less the total liabilities ($2,400,000).

    3. Investment in Zelta Corporation $5,600,000
        Common stock $ 80,000
        Contributed capital in excess of par value,
           common stock   5,520,000

To record the issuance of common stock in exchange for 100 percent of the outstanding shares of common stock of the Zelta Corporation.

4.
Common stock, par value $1	$ 400,000
Contributed capital in excess of par value, common stock	$5,200,000
Investment in Zelta Corporation	$5,600,000

To eliminate the investment in Zelta Corporation and corresponding balances in contributed owners' equity accounts.

5.
Miscellaneous Assets	$12,000,000
Miscellaneous Liabilities	$ 3,900,000
Common Stock, Par Value $1	180,000
Contributed Capital in Excess of Par	4,170,000
Retained Earnings	3,750,000
	$12,000,000

B. 1. Since the current market value of the outstanding shares of the Zelta Corporation common stock is $30 per share, the acquisition price will be $12,000,000 (400,000 shares at $30 per share).

2. Since the merger is to be recorded as a purchase, the Tyroll Corporation would record its investment in the Zelta Corporation at the amount it paid to acquire the shares of common stock of the Zelta Corporation--$12,000,000.

3.
Investment in Zelta Corporation	$12,000,000
Cash	$12,000,000

To record the purchase of 100 percent of the Zelta Corporation's common stock.

4. The excess of cost over book value may be determined by subtracting the book value of the Zelta Corporation common stock ($5,600,000) from the price paid for the shares. Thus:

Excess of cost over book value = $12,000,000 - $5,600,000 = $6,400,000

5.
Common stock, par value $1	$ 400,000
Contributed capital in excess of par value, common stock	3,000,000
Retained earnings	2,200,000
Goodwill	6,400,000
Investment in Zelta Corporation	$12,000,000

To eliminate investment in subsidiary and corresponding amounts in owners' equity accounts.

6. | Miscellaneous Assets | $12,000,000 |
    | Goodwill | 6,400,000 |
    | | $18,400,000 |

Miscellaneous Liabilities	$15,900,000*
Common Stock, Par Value $1	100,000
Contributed Capital in Excess of Par	850,000
Retained Earnings	1,550,000
	$18,400,000

*The sum of the liabilities of the two companies before the purchase of the Zelta Corporation common shares, plus the $12,000,000 liability established when the Tyroll Corporation borrowed the funds required to purchase the shares of Zelta Corporation common stock.

{Chapter 14}

STATEMENT OF CASH FLOWS

The balance sheet and the income statement provide vital information with respect to a firm's financial position and results of operations. But these statements fail to focus directly upon certain other types of transactions that are of significant concern to investors, creditors, and other users of financial reports. This chapter focuses on the third primary financial statement, the Statement of Cash Flows, which was required by FASB 95 as a replacement for the Statement of Changes in Financial position, required in 1971 by APB Opinion 19.

KEY POINTS

I. **The Nature of the Statement of Cash Flows**

   A. The Statement of Cash Flows is designed to provide information about a firm's cash receipts and disbursements. It reconciles cash at year end with cash at the beginning of the year. According to FASB Concepts Statement No. 5, such information is necessary to assess a firm's liquidity, financial flexibility, profitability, and risk.

   B. Many consider this report to be a complement to the income statement. Some consider accrual accounting net income to be more subjective than net cash flow information. Many activities reported on the Statement of Cash Flows are not reported on the income statement.

II. **Cash and the Classification of Cash Flows**

   A. The "cash" of a firm typically includes currency on hand and deposits in banks. Other, short term investments, can also be considered as "near cash." The FASB adopted a narrow definition of cash: cash and cash equivalents (short term investments readily marketable into cash, such as Treasury bills and money market funds). Short term investments in marketable stocks and bonds are excluded.

   B. The Statement of Cash Flows classifies cash flows into three categories along activity lines;

      1. Operating activities, which include producing and selling a firm's goods and services and administering its functions.

2. Investing activities, including buying and selling property, making and collecting loans, and purchasing and selling the securities of other firms.

3. Financing activities, including issuing and redeeming stock and borrowing and repaying loans.

C. If a firm has cash flows denominated in foreign currencies, it must translate them into U.S. dollars at the exchange rate in effect at the time of the flow. If rates change, the overall effect must be reported on the Statement of Cash Flows.

D. Some transactions are noncash but significant to the users of the financial statements. For example, a firm might acquire plant and equipment by issuing long-term debt. The FASB required that such transactions be disclosed in the Statement of Cash Flows.

III. **Two Approaches to the Statement**

A. There are two methods for reporting the operating activity section of the Statement: the direct method and indirect method. Both methods report the investing and financing activities the same.

1. The direct method reports all operating receipts and payments and shows the net cash provided by operating activities.

2. The indirect method starts with accounting net income and reconciles it to cash flow.

Although the FASB preferred that firms would use the direct method, they permit the use of the indirect method.

IV. **Preparing the Statement Using the Direct Method**

A. By definition, changes in cash are equal to changes in the noncash accounts (liabilities, owners' equity, and other assets). For example, decreases in cash are associated with decreases in liabilities and owners' equity and increases in other assets. The basic approach makes sure that all changes in noncash balance sheet accounts have been explained.

B. To prepare the Statement, obtain a comparative balance sheet and current income statement. Other information, such as firm financing and investing activities, should also be obtained. The basic strategy is to examine each change in the noncash accounts and analyze its effect on cash flows, categorized into one of the three activity groups. Reconstructing the transactions that caused the change in the account balance often explains effect on cash flows and the appropriate classification. For example, the balance in the Investment in Marketable Securities account might have increased by $55 during the period. Since this likely arose from the purchase of securities, it represents a decrease in cash and an investing activity.

C. Some transactions must be analyzed carefully to determine the cash flow implications.

1. For example, if equipment had been sold and a gain realized of $3, that may not be the full cash flow implications of that event. Further analysis may show, for example, that the actual sale realized ($5) in terms of cash inflows and should be reported for at that amount in the Statement.

2. Usually, the statements do not show the cash collected from customers or paid to creditors. That information is generated by an analysis of the accounts receivable and sales accounts or accounts payable, inventory and cost of goods sold accounts.

D. The final statement also must contain a schedule in which accounting net income is reconciled to cash provided by operating activities. This is computed by taking the accounting net income and adjusting it for the noncash revenues and expenses. A separate schedule showing noncash investing activities must also be disclosed.

V. **Working Capital**

A. Working capital represents the current assets of a firm (cash, marketable securities, accounts receivable, and inventories) less its current liabilities (wages and salaries payable, accounts payable, and short-term notes payable).

B. Changes in working capital can result only from changes in those accounts which do not directly compose working capital--that is, in non-current assets, non-current liabilities and owners' equity. Increases (sources of working capital and decreases (uses) of working capital can be summarized as follows:

Sources of Working Capital	minus	Uses of Working Capital	=	Increase in Working Capital
Increases in non-current liabilities		Decreases in non-current liabilities		Current assets
Increases in owners' equity (including those attributable to periodic income).		Decreases in owners' equity (including those attributable to periodic periodic losses).		minus
Decreases in non-current assets		Increases in non-current assets		Current liabilities

KEY ISSUES FOCUSED UPON IN THIS CHAPTER

1. Of what value is cash flow information to the investor and creditor who already have an income statement and balance sheet to analyze?

    The statement of cash flows is a supplement to the income statement. Income, although superior to cash flows, is subjective and depends upon accrual accounting. Cash flow information is more objective, and does provide financing and investing information that is not disclosed on the balance sheet.

2. How does the Statement of Cash Flows differ from the Statement of Changes in Financial Position which preceded it?

    The Statement of Changes was based on a "funds concept" and permitted considerable flexibility in its preparation. Some firms defined funds as working capital; others, as cash. The FASB confirmed the trend toward a cash definition by issuing FASB No. 95 in 1987.

KEY WORDS AND PHRASES

Cash Equivalents   Funds

Cash Flows Statement   Working Capital

Direct Method

ILLUSTRATIONS FOR REVIEW

A. Calculate the net increase (decrease) in cash during the year.

   $50 - 40 = $10 increase

B. Calculate the cash flow from operating activities:

   1. Determine the cash collected from customers.

      Collected = sales + or - change in accounts receivable
      $500,000 = $520,000 - 20,000

   2. Calculate the cash paid to suppliers.

      Purchases = cost of goods sold + or - change in inventory
      $340,000 = $300,000 + 40,000

      Payments = purchases + or - change in accounts payable
      $390,000 = $340,000 + 50,000

3. Calculate interest expense and taxes expense.

Interest = $7,500
Taxes = $34,500 - 2,000 = $32,500

4. Calculate other expenses.

Other expenses = $60,000

C. Calculate the cash flow from sales of equipment.

Information shows that the equipment was sold for $8,000.

D. Calculate other cash flow activities.

1. The firm sold 800 shares of common stock for $20,000.

2. The firm purchased equipment for $25,000.

The balance of the buildings and equipment account on December 31, 1992 was $110,000; to this is added the cost of the equipment sold during the year, $15,000; the beginning balance of the account, $100,000 is deducted to show that $25,000 was purchased.

3. Long-term debt of $2,000 was retired.

Assuming that no new bonds were issued during the year, the bonds payable account balance declined $2,000 during the year.

4. The firm purchased $1,000 of its own stock.

E. Prepare the statement of Cash Flows:

Dunell Corporation
Statement of Cash Flows
Year Ended December 31, 1992

Increases (Decreases) in Cash
In Thousands

Cash flow from Operating Activities:		
Collections from customers	$500.00	
Payments to suppliers	(390.00)	
Interest expense	(7.5)	
Taxes expenses	(32.5)	
Other expenses	(10.00)	
Net cash provided by operations		$10
Cash flow from Investing Activities:		
Proceeds from sale of Equipment	$ 8	
Purchases of equipment	(25)	
Net cash used in investing		(17)
Cash flow from Financing Activities:		
Proceeds from issuing stock	$20	
Purchases of treasury stock	(1)	
Retirement of long-term debt	(2)	
Net cash used in financing		17
Net increase in cash		$10

EXERCISES

1. For each of the following, indicate whether the transaction would increase, **decrease**, or have no effect on the firm's cash position. (Hint: consider the journal **entry that** would commonly be made to record the transaction and its effect upon **the equation:** cash = liabilities + owners' equity - other assets).

    A. Write-off of an uncollectible account receivable against the **allowance** provided.

    B. A stock dividend.

    C. Purchase of treasury stock.

    D. A cash dividend declared.

E. Sale of machinery subject to group depreciation.

2. Suppose that the income statement for the Staple Company for 1992 is as follows:

Revenue from Sales		$100,000
Less: Cost of goods sold	$50,000	
Wages and salaries	20,000	
Depreciation	10,000	
Total Expenses		80,000
Net Income		$20,000

Suppose further that:

a. Staple collected only $94,000 of the sales revenue.
b. The firm paid suppliers only $42,000.
c. Staple paid employees $24,000 ($20,000 of current year wages and $4,000 of past year wages).

Prepare the operations section of the Statement of Cash Flows using:

A. the direct method

B. the indirect method

SOLUTIONS TO CHAPTER FOURTEEN EXERCISES

1. A. No effect on cash. A decrease in accounts receivable and the allowance for uncollectible accounts.

    B. No effect on cash. A decrease in retained earnings and an increase in common stock.

    C. Decrease in cash.

    D. No effect on cash. A decrease in retained earnings and an increase in a liability, Dividends Payable.

    E. Increase in cash equal to the proceeds of the sale.

2. A. $94,000 - (42,000 + 24,000) = $28,000

    B.
Net income	$20,000
Adjustments to reconcile net income to cash flow:	
Depreciation expense	10,000
Increase in accounts receivable	(6,000)
Increase in accounts payable	8,000
Decrease in wages payable	(4,000)
Net cash provided by operating activities	$28,000

{Chapter 15}

ACCOUNTING FOR CHANGES IN PRICES

One of the assumptions underlying traditional accounting is that the basic unit of measure, the dollar, is stable. In recent years, the United States has experienced exceedingly high rates of inflation. Thus, this assumption has become considerably less tenable than it may have been previously when inflation was lower and even insignificant. Chapter 15 explores the major approach for modifying the conventional historical cost model to take into account changes in the value of the basic monetary unit.

It also examines two alternatives to the historical cost basis of accounting by which accounting recognition may be given to changes in the underlying values of assets when they occur. Lastly, it examines another controversial area--translating the financial statements of foreign operations into dollars for inclusion in the consolidated financial statements.

KEY POINTS

I. **Nature of the Price-Level Problem**

    A. Changes in specific process must be distinguished from changes in the overall level of process. Changes in specific process result from changes in the supply of or demand for specific goods of services. Changes in the overall level of process are associated with a general decline in the purchasing power of the monetary unit. Price-level adjusted financial statements are designed to take into account changes only in the overall level of prices-not in specific prices.

    B. Inflation works to the benefit of some parties and the detriment of others. As a general rule, debtors benefit from inflation inasmuch as they can repay loans with dollars that are worth less (can be used to buy goods or services of less value) than those that they initially borrowed. On the other hand, creditors are injured by inflation since they will be repaid with dollars worth less than those which they originally lent. Conventional financial statements fail to indicate the extent to which a firm benefits or suffers from inflation.

    C. It is possible to express dollars of one period in terms of dollars of another. If, for example, $1.50 was required in 1991 to acquire goods and services that in 1976 could have been purchased for $1.00 then the historical cost of an asset that was purchased in 1976 for $100,000 could be expressed as either $1000,000 (1976) or $150,000 (1991). Many accountants believe that information should be expressed on financial statements in terms of dollars prevailing as of the end of the period covered by the statements. Stated values of goods or services which were acquired with differing monetary units (e.g., 1976 dollars) should be translated into current monetary units (e.g., 1991 dollars).

D. Proposals to express values in terms of current dollars do not represent an abandonment of the historical cost approach to accountants. Assets will <u>not</u> be expressed in terms of their current market values. Rather they will be stated at <u>historical costs expressed in terms of current dollars.</u>

II. **Restating Financial Statements in Current Dollars**

A. The key to restating financial statements so that they are expressed in common (current) dollar terms is the translation of dollars of the past into dollars of the present. Each value on the unadjusted statements (with the exception noted in "B" below) expressed in terms of original dollars, is multiplied by the ratio of an index (such as the GNP deflator) of prices as of the balance sheet date to those of a prior date--that of the transaction on which the value is based. Suppose for example, that a parcel of the land was acquired in 1981 for $100,000 when the index of prices was at 60. If, in 1991, when the price index was at 120, the land were still in the possession of the firm, its book value could be translated to current dollars as follows:

$$\$100,000 \times 120/60 = \$200,000$$

B. Not all balance sheet values, however, need to be translated from original to current dollars. Assets and liabilities that are considered to be <u>monetary items</u> should be reported at their unadjusted amounts. Monetary items are assets and liabilities that are fixed, or that are convertible into a fixed number of dollars, regardless of changes in prices. Accounts receivable, for example, are considered to be monetary items. Regardless of changes in the general price level, accounts receivable can be converted into no more than the original agreed upon number of dollars. Marketable securities, by contrast, are non-monetary items. The price at which a marketable security can be sold reflects the general level of prices prevailing at the time of sale.

1. Other examples of monetary items are cash, notes receivable, accounts and notes payable, and bonds receivable and payable.

2. Other examples of non-monetary items are prepaid interest, inventory, land, plant and equipment, common stock and retained earnings.

C. One of the important measures to be derived and reported on a price-level adjusted statement of income is the net gain or loss from holding monetary items. Insofar as a company holds monetary assets during a period in which the level of prices is increasing, it suffers a monetary (purchasing power) loss. The dollars or promises of dollars are worth less--they could be used to acquire fewer goods of services--at the end of the period than they were at the beginning. Correspondingly, insofar as a firm has debts, (monetary liabilities) during inflationary periods, it realizes a monetary gain.

1. The gain or loss associated with a monetary item within a particular period may be computed by subtracting the purchasing power of the item (expressed in current dollars) at the start of the period from that at the end of the period. The purchasing power at the start of the period may be determined by multiplying the monetary item by the ratio of the price index at the end of the period to that at the beginning.

2. The gain or loss on a monetary item acquired during the year must be measured from the date acquired to the end of the year. That on a monetary item disposed of during the period must be determined from the start of the year to the date of disposal.

3. To determine the overall gain or loss on purchasing power during a period the following procedure is recommended:

    a. Determine the net monetary assets at the beginning of the period. Express them in current dollar terms.

    b. Determine all inflows of net monetary assets during the period (e.g., those resulting from sale of merchandise or fixed assets or collection of rent, interest, or other revenues). Express them in terms of current dollars, taking into account the level of the price index when the inflow took place.

    c. Determine all outflows of net monetary assets during the period (e.g., those resulting from purchases of merchandise or fixed assets, or from other costs incurred). Express them in current dollar terms, taking into account the level of the price index when the outflow took place.

    d. Add the adjusted net monetary assets at the start of the period to the adjusted cash inflows and subtract the adjusted cash outflows. The resultant amount will be the adjusted net monetary assets as of the end of the period.

    e. Determine the unadjusted net monetary assets at the end of the period. This amount represents the actual monetary assets less the actual monetary liabilities of the firm.

    f. Subtract the unadjusted net monetary assets at period-end from the adjusted net monetary assets. The resultant amount represents the net gain of low in purchasing power during the period.

4. The conventional statement of income can be translated into end-of-the period dollars by adjusting each of the individual revenues and expenses and by adding or subtracting the purchasing power gains or losses attributable to holding monetary items. In making the adjustments each revenue and expense must be related to the transaction from which it arose and the conversion factor must be based on the level of prices that existed at the time the transaction took place.

   a. Depreciation expense arises from the acquisition of fixed assets; it must be adjusted by the ratio of current value of the price index to the value of the index at the time the fixed assets were acquired.

   b. Cost of goods sold arises from the purchase of merchandise. In adjusting this expense the different times at which the merchandise sold during the period was acquired must be taken into account.

III. **Rationale for Price-Level Adjustments**

   A. Price-level adjustments increase the internal consistency of financial statements. They assure that all amounts that appear on the financial statements are expressed in dollars of the same value rather than in a mixture of dollars of different values.

   B. Price-level adjusted statements enable managers and stockholders to determine whether the "real" capital of the business, taking into account the effects of inflation, has increased or decreased.

IV. **Factors Which Determine the Magnitude of Differences Between Price-Level Adjusted Earnings and Conventional Earnings**

   A. Rate of inflation. The greater the rate of inflation, the greater the impact on earnings.

   B. Rate of turnover of non-monetary assets and liabilities. The slower the turnover, the greater will be the differences between adjusted and unadjusted statements.

   C. Composition of balance sheet. The greater the proportion of net monetary assets or liabilities, the greater will be the purchasing power of gains or losses; the greater the proportion of fixed assets, the greater will be the difference in depreciation charges.

V. The Replacement Cost Alternative

A. Price level accounting is really just the financial statements of traditional accounting (the historical cost model) expressed in terms of common dollars.

B. Another model which takes into account changed prices is the replacement cost model which is based on current values. Under this approach, increases in the replacement cost of assets would be recognized when the increases were identified.

C. The resulting financial statements would report monetary assets and liabilities at their stated values and non-monetary assets would be presented at their current replacement cost (the best approximation of what the firm would have to spend to replace them). Since under this approach non-monetary assets such as inventory and fixed assets would have to be written up to their replacement value, the resulting increases would have to be reported in the income statement of the period as unrealized gains and realized gains, depending upon whether or not the asset in question was sold or used up in that period.

D. The replacement cost model offers the following advantages: it provides more relevant information on the current value of the resources of the firm and the source of increases in those resources; it allow a more meaningful evaluation of the past performance of the firm and its management, and it facilitates intercorporate comparisons. However, the valuation process may be subjective; the replacement cost may not be relevant if the firm does not plant to replace the assets, and the approach may be incomplete because it does not include future revenue as part of the model.

VI. Accounting for Foreign Currency Transactions

A. A related measurement problem area of importance today to many firms with international operations concerns the accounting for transactions in foreign currencies. Accounting requires that all transactions of a firm be reported in one common currency.

B. In 1975, the FASB issued Statement No. 8 which contains the rules for translating foreign currency transactions into dollars. Basically, this statement requires for the translation of foreign currency financial statements into dollars that the monetary assets and liabilities in the foreign currency be translated into dollars using the exchange rate in effect as of the time of the translation, usually year end. The non-monetary items in the foreign financial statement are to be translated with the exchange rate in effect when the underlying transaction took place. Any dollar imbalance resulting from the translation process must be included in net income of the period on the income statement.

C. FASB 8 was superseded in 1981 by FASB 52. This new accounting standard required the use of the current rate of exchange for translating foreign functional currency financial statements into U.S. dollars. Translation gains and losses are shown in a separate component of stockholders' equity on the balance sheet. An important new concept in FASB 52 is the functional currency, defined as the currency of the primary economic environment in which the foreign unit operates. Both the translation methodology and gain/loss treatment are greatly influenced by the functional currency determination under FASB 52.

KEY ISSUES FOCUSED UPON IN THIS CHAPTER

1. How should changes in the general level of prices be taken into account?

In the view of may accountants, the assumption underlying conventional financial statements that the basic unit of measure is stable has become untenable. Price-level adjusted statements represent an effort to give accounting recognition to the impact of changes in the overall level of prices. Certain assets, liabilities, and income statement items are restated in units of common dollars using measures of the change in the general price level.

2. How should changes in underlying values of a firm's resources be taken into account?

Conventional financial statements are cost-based; they fail to take into account changes in the market prices of specific assets or in their value to specific users. This chapter considered briefly two accounting "models" that are not based primarily on historical costs--one that values the resources of a firm in terms of their potential earning power; the other that is founded upon current market prices.

KEY WORDS AND PHRASES

Gross National Product Implicit Price Deflator (GNP Deflator)

Monetary Items

Non-monetary Items

Purchasing Power Gains (Losses)

ILLUSTRATIONS FOR REVIEW

The Harrington Corporation was organized on January 2, 1992. Common stock was issued to stockholders in exchange for $100,000 cash. On January 3, 1992 the company acquired fixed assets, which have a useful life of five years, at a cost of $100,000.

The income statement and balance sheet prepared on December 31, 1992 revealed the following:

Harrington Corporation
Income Statement
For the Year Ended December 31, 1992

Sales revenue		$100,000
Less: Expenses		
Cost of goods sold	$60,000	
Depreciation	20,000	
Other expenses	10,000	90,000
Net Income		$ 10,000

Harrington Corporation
Balance Sheet
As of December 31, 1992

Assets

Cash		$ 20,000
Accounting receivable		10,000
Inventory		20,000
Fixed Assets	$100,000	
Less: Accumulated depreciation	20,000	80,000
Total Assets		$130,000

Liabilities and Owners' Equity

Accounts payable	$ 20,000
Common stock	100,000
Retained earnings	10,000
Total Liabilities and Owners' Equity	$130,000

Additional Information:

1. As of January 1, 1992 the GNP deflator index was at 100. During 1992 the deflator averaged 120 and at year-end it was at 140.

2. All sales, purchases of merchandise (including that on hand at year-end) and all other expenses may be assumed to have taken place evenly throughout the year.

A. Gain or Loss in Purchasing Power

1. Determine the December 31, 1992 net monetary assets in both adjusted and unadjusted dollars.

Since there were no assets at the start of the year (the company was not formed until January 2nd), the determination of the gain of loss in purchasing power may be calculated by translating each of the monetary inflows and outflows into year-end 1992 dollars (GNP deflator = 140), by multiplying the amount of the flow by the ratio of the deflator at year-end to that existing at the time of the flow. Since the flows occurred evenly throughout the year, the average value (120) of the GNP deflator may be used in the conversion. Thus,

	Unadjusted Amounts	Conversion Factor	Adjusted Amounts (12/31/92 dollars)
Net monetary assets January 1, 1992	0	0	0
Add: Sales	$100,000	140/120	$116,667
	$100,000		$116,667
Less: Purchases	$ 80,000*	140/120	$ 93,333
Other expenses	10,000	140/120	11,667
	$ 90,000		$105,000
Net monetary assets December 31, 1992	$ 10,000		$ 11,667

* Beginning Inventory + Purchases - Ending Inventory = Cost of Goods Sold
Purchases = Cost of Goods Sold + Ending Inventory - Beginning Inventory
Purchases = $60,000 + $20,000 - 0 = $80,000

2. Determine the gain or loss in purchasing power in 1992.

The loss or gain in purchasing power may be calculated by subtracting unadjusted net monetary assets from adjusted net monetary assets. If the balance is greater than zero, there will be a loss, otherwise there will be a gain. Thus,

Purchasing power gain or loss in 1992 =

$11,667 - $10,000 = $1,667 (loss)

B. Adjusting the Income Statement

1. Express sales revenue in terms of December 31, 1992 dollars.

Since sales took place evenly throughout the year, sales may be restated by multiplying the unadjusted sales by the ratio of the year-end value of the GNP deflator (140) to the average value (120). Thus,

$100,000 X 140/120 = $116,667.

2. Restate cost of goods sold in terms of December 31, 1992 dollars.

Since purchases may be assumed to have taken place evenly throughout the entire year, the cost of goods sold may be restated by multiplying both purchases and year-end inventories by the ratio of the value of the GNP deflator at year-end (140) to that during the year (120). Thus,

	Unadjusted Amounts	Conversion Factor	Adjusted Amounts (12/31/92 dollars)
Beginning inventory	0	0	0
Purchases, 1992*	$80,000	140/120	$93,333
Goods available for sale	$80,000		$93,333
Inventory, 12/31/92	20,000	140/120	23,333
Cost of goods sold, 1992	$60,000		$70,000

* Beginning Inventory + Purchases - Ending Inventory = Cost of Goods Sold
  Purchases = Cost of Goods Sold + Ending Inventory = Beginning Inventory
  Purchases = $60,000 + $20,000 - 0 = $80,000

3. Restate the depreciation expense in terms of December 31, 1992 dollars.

Depreciation expense may be associated with the acquisition of fixed assets. The firm's fixed assets were acquired on January 3, 1992, when the GNP deflator was at 100. Thus, depreciation expense may be adjusted as follows:

$20,000 X 140/100 = $28,000

4. Restate other expenses in terms of December 31, 1992 dollars.

Since the other expenses ($10,000) were incurred evenly throughout the year, they may be restated by multiplying the unadjusted amount by the ratio of the value of the GNP deflator at the end of the year (140) to the average (120) during the year. Thus,

$10,000 X 140/120 = $11,667

5. Determine 1992 net income expressed in terms of year-end dollars. Be certain to take into account the loss in purchasing power calculated earlier.

Harrington Corporation
Income Statement
For the Year Ending December 31, 1992

Sales revenue		$116,667
Less: Expenses		
Cost of goods sold	$70,000	
Depreciation	28,000	
Other expenses	11,667	
Loss of purchasing power	1,667	111,334
Net Income		$ 5,333

C. <u>Adjusting the Balance Sheet.</u>

The balance sheet account adjustments can be made by raising the following question and adhering to the following procedures.

1. Which balance sheet accounts do not require adjustment inasmuch as they are already expressed in terms of current (December 31, 1992) dollars?

Monetary assets and liabilities need not be adjusted. The amounts to be paid or received are contractually fixed. Monetary assets and liabilities include cash, accounts receivable and accounts payable.

2. Restate the balance in year-end inventories in terms of December 31, 1992 dollars.

Since the purchases of inventory took place evenly throughout the year, and the ending inventory is considered to be composed of items purchased evenly throughout 1992, inventories may be restated by multiplying them by the ratio of the GNP deflator at year-end (140) to the average during the year (120). Thus,

$$\$20,000 \times 140/120 = \$23,333$$

3. Restate the value of fixed assets in terms of December 31, 1992 dollars.

Since the fixed assets were acquired on January 3, 1992, the GNP deflator value (100) for that date may be used to restate the value of the fixed assets in term of December 31, 1992 dollars. Thus,

$$\$100,000 \times 140/100 = \$140,000$$

4. Restate the balance of the accumulated depreciation associated with the fixed assets in terms of December 31, 1992 dollars.

Since accumulated depreciation is associated with the fixed assets acquired on January 3, 1992, the GNP deflator value (100) for that date may be used to restate the accumulated depreciation in terms of December 31, 1992 dollars. Thus,

$$\$20,000 \times 140/100 = \$28,000$$

5. Restate the value of common stock in terms of December 31, 1992 dollars.

Since the common stock was sold on January 2, 1992, the GNP deflator value (100) for that date may be used to restate the value of the common stock in terms of December 31, 1992 dollars. Thus,

$$\$100,000 \times 140/100 = \$140,000$$

6. Prepare a balance sheet as of December 31, 1992 expressed entirely in terms of current 1992 dollars.

Harrington Corporation
Balance Sheet
As of December 31, 1992

<u>Assets</u>

Cash		$ 20,000
Accounts receivable		10,000
Inventory		23,333
Fixed assets	$140,000	
Less: Accumulated depreciation	<u> 28,000</u>	<u>112,000</u>
Total Assets		<u>$165,333</u>

<u>Liabilities and Owners' Equity</u>

Accounts payable	$ 20,000
Common stock	140,000
Retained earnings *	<u> 5,333</u>
Total Liabilities and Owner's Equity	<u>$165,000</u>

* Represents the net income figure (as adjusted) expressed in current, 12/31/92 dollars. Alternatively, it may have been determined by adding to the unadjusted value of net income ($10,000) the difference between unadjusted and adjusted amounts of total assets, and subtracting the difference between unadjusted and adjusted amounts of liabilities and common stock.

EXERCISES

1. Presented below are comparative balance sheets of the Reed Land Company as of December 31, 1992 and 1993. Also shown are a statement of income and a statement of changes in financial position for the year ending December 31, 1993.

Reed Land Company
Balance Sheet
As of December 31,

	1993	1992
Assets		
Current Assets:		
Cash	$ 60,000	$ 40,000
Accounts receivable	100,000	80,000
Inventories	140,000	150,000
Total current assets	$300,000	$270,000
Other Assets:		
Plant and equipment	$320,000	$320,000
Less: Accumulated depreciation	160,000	120,000
Total other assets	$160,000	$200,000
Total Assets	$460,000	$470,000
Equities		
Current Liabilities:		
Accounts payable	$ 50,000	$ 60,000
Other Liabilities:		
Bonds payable	$ 90,000	$100,000
Total Liabilities	$140,000	$160,000
Owners' Equity:		
Common stock	$200,000	$200,000
Retained earnings	120,000	110,000
Total Owners' Equity	$320,000	$310,000
Total Equities	$460,000	$470,000

Reed Land Company
Statement of Income
For the Year Ending December 31, 1993

Sales		$900,000
Less: Expenses		
Cost of goods sold	$780,000	
Depreciation	40,000	
Other expenses	70,000	890,000
Net Income		$ 10,000

Reed Land Company
Statement of Changes in Financial Position
For the Year Ending December 31, 1993

Changes in Working Capital

	December 31, 1993	December 31, 1992	Increase (Decrease)
Current Assets:			
Cash	$ 60,000	$ 40,000	$ 20,000
Accounts receivable	100,000	80,000	20,000
Inventory	140,000	150,000	(10,000)
Total Current Assets	$300,000	$270,000	$ 30,000
Current Liabilities:			
Accounts payable	$ 50,000	$ 60,000	$(10,000)
Working Capital	$250,000	$210,000	$ 40,000*

* Changes in working capital - $40,000 = Changes in current assets ($30,000) minus Changes in current liabilities (10,000).

Sources of Working Capital

From operations		
Net income	$ 10,000	
Add: Depreciation (a non-working capital expense)	40,000	$ 50,000

Uses of Working Capital

Repayment of bonds		10,000
Net increases in Working Capital		$ 40,000

The firm began operations in 1988. In that year it issued $200,000 in common stock and acquired the plant and equipment that it presently uses. The price index on January 2, 1988, when the stock was sold and the plant and equipment was acquired, was at a level of 110.

Inventory on hand as of December 31, 1992 was acquired at the end of 1992, when the price index was at 130. The inventory on hand as of December 31, 1993 was acquired at the end of the year, when the price index was at 140.

A leading price index reflected the following values:

Date	Price Index
1/2/88	110
12/31/92	130
Average for 1993	135
12/31/93	140

A. Determine the loss in purchasing power incurred during 1993 by completing parts 1 and 2.

1. Determine net monetary assets (liabilities) as of December 31, 1992 and 1993.

	December 31, 1993	December 31, 1992
Monetary Assets		
Monetary Liabilities		
Net Monetary Assets (Liabilities)		

2. Complete the following table, which converts the inflows and outflows of monetary items to current (December 31, 1993) dollars. The unadjusted inflows and outflows are multiplied by the ratio of the price index as of December 31, 1993 to that at the time of the inflow or outflow.

	Unadjusted Amounts	Conversion Factor	Adjusted Amounts
Net monetary assets (liabilities), 12/31/92	$(40,000)		
Add: Sales	900,000		
	$860,000		
Less: Purchases	$770,000		
Other expenses	70,000		
	$840,000		
Net monetary assets (liabilities), 12/31/93	$ 20,000		
Less: Net monetary assets unadjusted 12/31/93			$ 20,000
Loss: (Gain) in purchasing power			$

241

B. Express cost of goods sold in terms of current (December 31, 1993) dollars by completing the following table:

	Unadjusted Amounts	Conversion Factor	Adjusted Amounts
Inventory, 12/31/93	$150,000		$
Add: Purchases, 1993	770,000		_____
	$920,000		$
Subtract: Inventory, 12/31/93	140,000		_____
Cost of goods sold, 1993	$780,000		$

C. Prepare a statement of income, for the year ending December 31, 1993, expressed in terms of current (December 31, 1993) dollars, by completing the following schedule:

	Unadjusted Amounts	Conversion Factor	Adjusted Amounts
Sales	$900,000		$
Gain in purchasing power	-	(see previous computation)	_____
Total revenues	$900,000		$
Less: Cost of goods sold	$780,000	(see previous computation)	
Depreciation	40,000		
Other expenses	70,000		$_____
Other expenses	$890,000		_____
Net Income (Loss)	$ 10,000		$_____

D. Prepare a balance sheet, as of December 31, 1993, expressed in terms of current (December 31, 1993) dollars by completing the schedule that follows. The adjusted retained earnings is provided for you.

	Unadjusted Amounts	Conversion Factor	Adjusted Amounts
Assets			
Current Assets:			
Cash	$ 60,000	-	$
Accounts receivable	100,000	-	
Inventories	140,000		_____
Total Current Assets	$300,000		$_____
Other Assets:			
Plant and equipment	$320,000		
Less: Accumulated depreciation	160,000		
Total Other Assets	$160,000		$_____
Total Assets	$460,000		$_____

Equities

Current Liabilities:			
Accounts payable	$ 50,000	-	$
Other Liabilities:			
Bonds payable	$ 90,000	-	$
Owners' Equity:			
Common stock	$200,000		$
Retained earnings	120,000	-	$109,092
Total Owners' Equity	$320,000	-	$
Total Equities	$460,000		$

2. The Catalina Company began operations on January 2, 1992. The balance sheet immediately after the formation of the company was as follows:

Balance Sheet
January 2, 1992

Assets:
Cash $ 2,500
Inventory   12,500
Plant and equipment   25,000
                           $40,000

Equities:
Owners' Equity $40,000

Below are the financial statements for the year 1992, based on the traditional accounting model (historical cost):

Income Statement For Year Ended 12/31/92		Balance Sheet 12/31/92	
Cash sales	$50,000	Assets	
Cost of goods sold	30,000	Cash	$27,500
Depreciation expense	2,500	Inventory	7,500
Total expenses	32,500	Plant & Equipment (net)	22,500
Net Income	$17,500	Total Assets	$57,500
		Equities:	
		Owners' Equity	$57,500

Additional information:

1. During the year, Catalina purchased merchandise for $25,000 cash. The current cost to replace the goods sold during 1992 was $33,000. The current cost to replace the ending inventory was $10,000.

2. The useful life of the plant and equipment was 10 years, with no salvage value. During the year, the replacement cost of those assets increased from $25,000 to $30,000.

Prepare a balance sheet and income statement for 1992 for the Catalina Company based on the replacement cost model. Be sure the identify on the income statement the realized and unrealized holding gains.

SOLUTIONS TO CHAPTER FIFTEEN EXERCISES

A. 1.

	December 31, 1993	December 31, 1992
Monetary Assets:		
Cash	$ 60,000	$ 40,000
Accounts receivable	100,000	80,000
Total monetary assets	$160,000	$120,000
Monetary Liabilities		
Accounts payable	$ 50,000	$ 60,000
Bonds payable	90,000	100,000
Total monetary liabilities	$140,000	$160,000
Net Monetary Assets (Liabilities)	$ 20,000	$(40,000)

2.

	Unadjusted Amounts	Conversion Factor	Adjusted Amounts
Net monetary assets (liabilities), 12/31/92	$(40,000)	140/130	$(43,077)
Add: Sales	900,000	140/135	$933,333
	$860,000		$890,256
Less: Purchases	$770,000	140/135	$798,519
Other expenses	70,000	140/135	72,593
	$840,000		$871,112
Net monetary assets (liabilities), 12/31/93	$ 20,000		$19,144
Less: Net monetary assets, unadjusted, 12/31/93			$20,000
Loss (Gain) in Purchasing Power			$ (856)

B.

	Unadjusted Amounts	Conversion Factor	Adjusted Amounts
Inventory	$150,000	140/130	$161,538
Add: Purchases, 1993	770,000	140/135	798,519
	$920,000		$960,057
Subtract: Inventory, 12/31/93	140,000	140/140	140,000
Cost of goods sold, 1993	$780,000		$820,057

C.

	Unadjusted Amounts	Conversion Factor	Adjusted Amounts
Sales	$900,000	140/130	$933,333
Gain in purchasing power	-	(see previous computation)	856
Total revenues	$900,000		$934,189
Less: Cost of goods sold	$780,000	(see previous computation)	$820,057
Depreciation	40,000	140/110	50,909
Other expenses	70,000	140/135	72,593
Total expenses	$890,000		$943,559
Net Income (Loss)	$ 10,000		$ (9,370)

	Unadjusted Amounts	Conversion Factor	Adjusted Amounts

Assets

Current Assets			
Cash	$ 60,000	-	$60,000
Accounts receivable	100,000	-	100,000
Inventories	140,000	140/140	140,000
Total Current Assets	$300,000		$300,000
Other Assets:			
Plant and equipment	$320,000	140/110	$407,273
Less: Accumulated depreciation	160,000	140/110	203,636
Total Other Assets	$160,000		$203,637
Other Assets	$460,000		$503,637

Equities

Current Liabilities:			
Accounts payable	$ 50,000	-	$ 50,000
Other Liabilities:			
Bonds payable	$ 90,000	-	$ 90,000
Owners' Equity:			
Common stock	$200,000	140/110	$254,545
Retained earnings	120,000	-	109,092
Total Owners' Equity	$320,000		$363,637
Total Equities	$460,000		$503,637

Catalina Company
Income Statement
For Year Ended 12/31/92

Cash Sales	$50,000
Cost of Goods Sold	33,000
Depreciation Expense	3,000
Total Expenses	36,000
Operating Income	$14,000
Holding Gains	
Realized	
On goods sold	3,000
On plant and equipment used	500
Total Realized	$ 3,500
Unrealized	
On ending inventory	2,500
On plant and equipment	4,500
Total Unrealized	$ 7,000
Total Holding Gains	10,500
Net Income	$24,500

Balance Sheet
12/31/92

Assets:	
Cash	$27,500
Inventory	10,000
Plant and equipment (net)	27,000
	$64,500
Equities:	
Owners' Equity	$64,500

{Chapter 16}

FINANCIAL REPORTING AND ANALYSIS IN PERSPECTIVE

If financial statements are to be useful, they must be relevant--they must bear upon or be associated with the decisions they are designed to facilitate. Chapter 16 focuses upon the decisions made by investors, one of the groups that financial statements are designed to serve. To a large extent, Chapter 16 represents a summary of the preceding chapters.

The chapter conveys two important but somewhat contradictory messages. The first is that financial statements do provide an abundance of information about the company whose financial affairs they describe. A measure of expertise is usually necessary to properly interpret them. The second is that the importance of financial statements can easily be overemphasized. Before any decision is made as to whether to invest in a firm, other, non-financial information must be taken into account.

This chapter introduces some basic techniques that assist in the analysis of financial statements and discusses the important concepts of corporate personality and quality of earnings.

KEY POINTS

I. **Accrual Accounting**

   A. According to the FASB, financial reports should be useful to investors and creditors in making investment, credit, and other similar decisions. Financial reports should provide data that will help such users to predict the cash that a firm will generate. Generally, firms report on the basis of accrual accounting, which measures changes in a firm's financial resources when they have their economic impact. Accrual accounting provides more useful information than cash accounting, and is necessarily more complex.

   B. Additionally, financial reports should assist the users to assess an enterprise during a time period. Accrual accounting concentrates on income, rather than cash flows, to meet this informational need of users.

II. **Quality of Earnings**

    A. High quality earnings are those in which the recognition of revenue is postponed until the actual receipt of cash and expenses are charged no later than the period in which the cash is disbursed. Conversely, lower quality earnings are those in which revenue is recognized before collection of cash can reasonably be assured and recognition of expenses is delayed beyond the period in which the cash disbursements are made. High quality earnings are associated with both conservatism and low reported income.

    B. It is essential that an analyst be aware of those areas in which a firm has flexibility in the application of, or choice among, accounting policies of practices. Selection of one policy or practice over another may have significant impact upon reported earnings.

        1. <u>Timing or Revenue</u>. There are several points in time at which firms can recognize revenue: in the course of production; when title passes from seller to buyer; upon collection of cash; etc.

        2. <u>Gains from Appreciation</u>. Increases in market value are recognized only at time of sale. By judicious timing of sales of assets which have appreciated in value a firm may be able, at its discretion, to increase of decrease reported income.

        3. <u>Losses on Receivables</u>. There are no set rules as to when accounts receivable should be written-off or how much should be added to the allowance for uncollectible accounts each year. Reported bad debt expense is to a large extent based on the good-faith judgements of corporate management and their accountants.

        4. <u>Cost of Goods Sold</u>. Corporations have the option of employing three basic methods of accounting for inventories-first-in, first-out; weighted average and last-in, first-out-along with several variations of each. Choice of method has a direct bearing upon reported cost of goods sold.

        5. <u>Depreciation</u>. Corporations can choose among several methods of depreciation, including straight-line, sum-of-the-years' digits, and double-declining balance. Moreover, reported depreciation expense is influenced by estimates of the asset's useful life.

        6. <u>Other Determinants of Income</u>. Other revenues and expenses for which management has broad discretion in the manner by which they are accounted include income taxes (and more specifically the investment tax credit), pensions, and gains or losses on the retirement of long-term debt.

III. **Disclosure**

    A. Footnotes supply information which supplements that contained in the body of the three financial statements.

    B. Among the typical matters disclosed in footnotes are:

        1. Accounting policies (for example, inventory and depreciation methods used).

        2. Supporting details of amounts contained in the body of the financial statements.

        3. Outstanding commitments with respect to contracts entered into by the firm.

        4. Contingent liabilities, such as those which may result from pending legal actions.

IV. **Ratio and Percentage Analysis**

    A. Ratios and percentages should be computed in a manner that best serves to facilitate the specific decisions at hand. There are no absolutely correct forms for any of the ratios and percentages illustrated.

    B. Ratios must never be evaluated in a vacuum. An analyst should focus upon trends over time and comparisons with firms in the same or related industries.

    C. There are three major types of ratios: Profitability and activity ratios; liquidity ratios; financing ratios.

    D. <u>Profitability and activity</u> ratios measure the profitability and efficiency of the activities carried out by an enterprise.

        1. <u>Return on investment</u> is the single most significant measure of corporate profitability and efficiency.

$$\text{Return on Investment (all capital)} = \frac{\text{Net Income} + \text{Interest After Taxes}}{\text{Average Assets}}$$

or

$$\text{Return on Investment (stockholders' equity)} = \frac{\text{Net Income}}{\text{Average Stockholders' Equity}}$$

The first ratio (all capital) measures profitability of the enterprise without regard to the manner in which it has been financed. The alternative form (stockholders' equity) measures profitability with respect to the owners--the stockholders--of the enterprise. Return on investment alone is not an adequate measure of performance since it is based on accrual accounting with its inherent limitations. Return on investment may also not reflect the interests of existing owners. Some actions can be taken by the management of the firm to boost return on investment and yet be counter to the interests of current owners. This is dysfunctional behavior. One way to avoid this dysfunctional behavior in divisionalized firms is to use residual income (measured by net income before interest minus an imputed cost of capital).

2. The Price-Earnings Ratio compares the market price at which the common stock of a company is being traded with the earnings of the company expressed on a per share basis.

$$\text{Price-Earnings Ratio} = \frac{\text{Market Price Per Share}}{\text{Earnings Per Share}}$$

3. Activity ratios measure the effectiveness of management in utilizing specific resources under its command. They are often referred to as turnover ratios. They relate specific asset accounts to the revenue or expense accounts with which they are logically associated. Some examples of activity ratios are:

a. $$\text{Inventory Turnover} = \frac{\text{Cost of Goods Sold}}{\text{Average Inventory}}$$

b. $$\text{Number of days' sales in accounts receivable} = \frac{\text{Accounts Receivable}}{\text{Average Sales per Day}}$$

c. $$\text{Plant and Equipment Turnover} = \frac{\text{Sales}}{\text{Average Plant and Equipment}}$$

E. Liquidity ratios indicate the ability of the firm to meet its obligations as they mature.

1. The current ratio compares current assets with current liabilities.

$$\text{Current Ratio} = \frac{\text{Current Assets}}{\text{Current Liabilities}}$$

2. A test of liquidity more severe than the current ratio is the quick ratio. The quick ratio compares cash, as well as those current assets that can be most readily converted into cash, with current liabilities.

$$\text{Quick Ratio} = \frac{\text{Cash + Marketable Securities + Accounts Receivable}}{\text{Current Liabilities}}$$

F. <u>Financial Ratios</u> compare the claims of the firm's creditors with the equity of its owners.

1. The <u>debt to equity ratio</u> compares capital provided by creditors with that supplied by owners.

$$\text{Debt to Equity Ratio} = \frac{\text{Total Debt}}{\text{Total Equity}}$$

2. <u>Times interest earned</u> is a measure of a firm's ability to satisfy its fixed obligations to creditors. It compares earnings (before taxes and the interest charges themselves) with interest charges.

$$\text{Times Interest Earned} = \frac{\text{Net Income + Interest + Income Taxes}}{\text{Interest}}$$

KEY ISSUES FOCUSED UPON IN THIS CHAPTER

What is meant by the phrase, "quality of earnings?" Why is it important in financial analysis.

Quality of earnings refers to whether or not the reported earnings of a firm are closely related to the underlying cash flows. Today's corporate management has flexibility in the selection of accounting methods, many of which will have a significant impact on the reported earnings of the firm. When analyzing the financial statements of a given firm, one must keep in mind the accounting methods that produced those statements, and assess the quality of the earnings reported in light of the underlying accounting methods.

KEY WORDS AND PHRASES

Accrual Concept	Liquidity Ratios
Contingent Liabilities	Profitability and Activity Ratios
Financial Ratios	Profit Margin
Gross Margin	Turnover Ratios

ILLUSTRATION FOR REVIEW

The president of the Troy Corporation wants your assistance in evaluating the financial strengths and weaknesses of his company. The analysis is to be based on the financial statements presented below and is to be made for the year ended December 31, 1993.

Troy Corporation
Statement of Income
For the year-ended December 31

	1994	1993	1992
Sales	$4,274,000	$2,524,500	$3,547,000
Less: Expenses			
Cost of Goods Sold	$1,514,500	$ 910,000	$1,285,000
Depreciation	31,000	26,000	28,000
Amortization	3,000	3,000	3,000
Interest	92,000	92,000	90,000
Contributions to employees' retirement fund	94,000	82,000	89,000
Selling	1,191,700	573,500	741,000
General and administrative	898,000	811,000	878,000
Total expenses	$3,824,200	$2,497,500	$3,114,000
Net income before taxes	449,800	27,000	433,000
Taxes on income	234,200	6,400	213,500
New income	$ 215,600	$ 20,600	$ 219,500
Earnings per share of common stock	$3.59	$.34	$3.65
Average number of common shares outstanding	60,000	60,000	60,000
Total dividends declared during year	$ 150,000	$ 124,000	$ 100,000
Market price per share of common stock at year-end	$63	$31	$58

Troy Corporation
Balance Sheet
As of December 31

	1994	1993	1992
Assets			
Current Assets:			
Cash on hand	$ 4,000	$ 3,700	$ 3,800
Cash in bank	157,500	98,000	96,500
Marketable securities	119,500	89,800	81,300
Accounts receivable	$ 207,600	$ 241,300	$ 238,600
Less: Allowance for doubtful accounts	26,000	31,000	30,000
	$ 181,600	$ 210,300	$ 208,600
Inventories	$ 478,000	$ 396,000	$ 409,300
Prepaid insurance	18,000	36,000	54,000
Prepaid rent	0	50,000	100,000
Total Current Assets	$ 958,600	$ 883,800	$ 953,500
Other Assets:			
Notes receivable	$ 15,000	$ 15,000	$ 15,000
Delivery vehicles	$ 110,000	$ 110,000	$ 110,000
Less: Accumulated depreciation	42,000	31,000	20,000
	$ 68,000	$ 79,000	$ 80,000
Machinery and equipment	$ 85,000	$ 70,000	$ 70,000
Less: Accumulated depreciation	25,000	15,000	10,000
	$ 60,000	$ 55,000	$ 60,000
Buildings	$ 250,000	$ 250,000	$ 250,000
Less: Accumulated depreciation	45,000	35,000	25,000
	$ 205,000	$ 215,000	$ 225,000
Land	$ 100,000	$ 100,000	$ 100,000
Patents	57,500	59,500	61,500
Goodwill	38,000	39,000	40,000
Total Other Assets	$ 543,500	$ 562,500	$ 581,500
Total Assets	$1,502,100	$1,446,300	$1,535,000
Liabilities and Owners' Equity			
Current Liabilities:			
Accounts payable	$ 104,500	$ 95,100	$ 94,700
Accrued wages payable	15,400	12,100	14,300
Accrued interest payable	29,000	29,000	22,500
Total Current Liabilities	$ 148,900	$ 136,200	$ 131,500
Other Liabilities			
Long-term debt	$ 160,000	$ 185,000	$ 180,000
Deferred federal income taxes	31,500	29,000	24,000
Bonds payable	500,000	500,000	500,000
Total Other Liabilities	$ 691,500	$ 714,000	$ 704,000

Owners' Equity
   Common stock ($10 par) $ 500,000 $ 500,000 $ 500,000
   Contributed capital in excess of
      par value   50,000   50,000   50,000
   Retained earnings   111,700   46,100   149,500
                                              $ 661,700 $ 596,100 $ 699,500
Total Liabilities and Owners' Equity $1,502,100 $1,446,300 $1,535,000

A. **Profitability and activity ratios.**

   1. How effectively is the company employing the total resources under its command during 1993; what is the percent return earned by the company on its total capital (all funds invested in the company)?

       To calculate the return earned on all investments, interest expense must be added back to net income. The total is then divided by the average total assets held by the company during 1993. Thus,

       $$\text{Average total assets} = \frac{\text{Total assets, 12/31/92} + \text{Total assets, 12/31/93}}{2}$$

       $$\text{Average total assets} = \frac{\$1,535,000 + \$1,446,300}{2} = \$1,490,650$$

       $$\text{Return on investment} = \frac{\text{Net income} + \text{interest}}{\text{Average total assets}} = \frac{\$20,600 + \$92,000}{\$1,490,650}$$

       Return on investment (all capital) - 7.6 percent

   2. How effectively is the company using the capital provided by its owners; what is the return provided the owners of the company on their invested capital?

       The return earned on the investment of the owners may be determined by dividing net income by the average investment of the owners during the year. Thus,

       $$\text{Average stockholders' equity} = \frac{\text{Stockholders' equity 12/31/92} + \text{Stockholders' equity 12/31/93}}{2}$$

       $$\text{Average stockholders' equity} = \frac{\$699,500 + \$596,100}{2} = \$647,800$$

$$\text{Return on investment (stockholders' equity)} = \frac{\text{Net Income}}{\text{Average stockholders' equity}}$$

$$\text{Return on investment (stockholders' equity)} = \frac{\$20,600}{\$647,800} = 3.2 \text{ percent}$$

3. What is the company's price-earnings ratio as of the end of 1993?

The price-earnings ratio may be calculated by dividing the market price of a single share at year-end by the earnings per share for the year. This ratio enables the owners of common stock to compare the return that they are presently receiving with that which they could receive were they to sell their shares and reinvest the proceeds elsewhere. Thus,

$$\text{Price-earnings ratio} = \frac{\text{Market price per share}}{\text{Earnings per share}} = \frac{\$31}{.34} = 91.2 \text{ to } 1$$

4. What is the company's profit margin on sales; that is, of what percent sales revenue is net income?

The profit margin is calculated by dividing net income by total sales revenue. Thus:

$$\text{Profit margin} = \frac{\text{Net income}}{\text{Sales revenue}} = \frac{\$20,600}{\$2,524,500} = .8 \text{ percent}$$

5. What is the rate of inventory turnover; that is, what is the number of times the average inventory has been sold during the year?

The inventory turnover ratio may be computed by dividing cost of goods sold by average inventory. The ratio indicates how efficiently the company is employing its inventories. The more often the inventory "turns over," the more efficiently it is being used. Thus:

Average inventory = $\dfrac{\text{Beginning inventory + Ending inventory}}{2}$

Average inventory = $\dfrac{\$409,300 + \$396,000}{2}$ = $402,650

Inventory turnover = $\dfrac{\text{Cost of goods sold}}{\text{Average inventory}}$ = $\dfrac{\$910,000}{\$402,650}$ = 2.26 times per year

6. What is the accounts receivable turnover rate; that is, what is the number of times that the average balance in accounts receivable has been turned over?

The accounts receivable turnover rate may be computed by dividing the sales by the average balance in accounts receivable. The greater the accounts receivable turnover rate, the smaller is the amount of funds "tied up" in accounts receivable. Thus:

Average accounts receivable = $\dfrac{\text{Accounts receivable, 12/31/92 + Accounts Receivable 12/31/93}}{2}$

Average accounts receivable = $\dfrac{\$208,600 + \$210,300}{2}$ = $209,450

Accounts receivable turnover = $\dfrac{\text{Sales}}{\text{Average accounts receivable}}$

Accounts receivable turnover = $\dfrac{\$2,524,500}{\$209,450}$ = 12.05 times per year

7. How many days' sales are represented by the December 31, 1993 balance of accounts receivable; that is, what is the average number of days during which sales are tied up in accounts receivable before collection?

The number of days sales in accounts receivable may be determined by dividing the balance in accounts receivable as of December 31, 1993 by the average sales per day. Thus,

Average sales per day = $\dfrac{\text{Total sales}}{360} = \dfrac{\$2{,}524{,}500}{360} = \$7{,}012.50$ per day

Number of days sales in accounts receivable = $\dfrac{\text{Accounts receivable}}{\text{Average sales per day}}$
(as of 12/31/92)

Number of days sales in accounts receivable = $\dfrac{\$210{,}300}{\$7{,}012.50} = 29.99$ days
(as of 12/31/92)

8. What is the plant and equipment turnover ratio; that is, what is the relationship between the average balance of plant and equipment and total sales for the year?

The plant and equipment turnover ratio may be calculated by dividing the annual sales by the average balance of the plant and equipment accounts. This ratio provides a measure as to how efficiently the plant and equipment are being employed. The higher the ratio, the greater the efficiency. Thus,

Average plant and equipment =

$$\dfrac{\text{Plant \& Equipment 12/31/92*} + \text{Plant \& Equipment 12/31/93*}}{2}$$

* Balance of plant and equipment may be calculated by adding the net balances in delivery vehicles account, machinery and equipment account and the building accounts.

$$\text{Average plant and equipment} = \frac{\$365,000 + \$349,000}{2} = \$357,000$$

$$\text{Plant and equipment turnover} = \frac{\text{Sales}}{\text{Average plant and equipment}}$$

$$\text{Plant and equipment turnover} = \frac{\$2,524,500}{\$357,000} = 7.07 \text{ times per year}$$

B. <u>Liquidity ratios</u>

    1.   What is the company's current ratio; that is, how many times greater is the balance of current assets than that of current liabilities?

           The current ratio may be calculated by dividing the balance of current assets by the balance of current liabilities. The ratio compares the liabilities that require payment within one year with the resources available to satisfy such liabilities.

$$\text{Current ratio} = \frac{\text{Current assets}}{\text{Current liabilities}} = \frac{\$883,800}{\$136,200} = 6.49 \text{ to } 1$$

    2.   What is the quick ratio; that is, how many times greater is the balance of current assets less inventories and prepaid expenses greater than the balance of current liabilities?

           The quick ratio may be calculated by dividing the sum of cash, marketable securities and accounts receivable by the balance of current liabilities. It is a more severe measure of liquidity than the current ratio.

$$\text{Quick ratio} = \frac{\text{(Cash + Marketable securities + Accounts receivable)*}}{\text{Current liabilities}}$$

$$\text{Quick ratio} = \frac{\$101{,}700 + \$89{,}800 + \$210{,}300}{\$136{,}200} = 2.95 \text{ to } 1$$

* This is the same as total current assets less the balances in the inventory and prepaid expense accounts.

C. <u>Financing ratios</u>

1. What is the debt to equity ratio; that is, what is the portion of total equity provided by creditors?

The debt to equity ratio may be calculated by dividing total liabilities by the owners' equity. The debt to equity ratio indicates the portion of total equities provided by creditors.

$$\text{Debt to equity ratio} = \frac{\text{Total debt}}{\text{Total equity}} = \frac{\$850{,}200}{\$596{,}100} = 1.43 \text{ to } 1$$

2. What is the times interest is earned; that is, what is the number of times the company's earnings will satisfy the required payment of interest?

Times interest earned is calculated by dividing income before deducting both interest and income taxes by the required interest payments. Thus,

$$\text{Times interest earned} = \frac{\text{Net income + Interest expense + Income taxes}}{\text{Interest expense}}$$

$$\text{Times interest earned} = \frac{\$20{,}600 + \$92{,}000 + \$6{,}400}{\$92{,}000} = 1.29 \text{ times}$$

EXERCISES

1. A. Presented below is the 1994 income statement.

Troy Corporation
Income Statement
For the year-ended December 31, 1994

			Percentage of sales
Sales		$4,274,000	
Less: Expenses			
Cost of goods sold	$1,514,500		
Depreciation	31,000		
Amortization	3,000		
Interest	92,000		
Contributions to employees' retirement fund	94,000		
Selling expenses	1,191,700		
General and administrative	898,000		
Total expenses		3,824,000	
Net income before taxes		$ 449,800	
Taxes on income		234,200	
Net income		$ 215,600	

B. Determine the profit margin.

C. Determine the gross margin.

2. The following question are based on the financial statements of the Troy Corporation presented in the ILLUSTRATIONS FOR REVIEW.

A. What is the return earned by the Troy Corporation, in 1994, on its total assets?

B. Is the return earned by Troy's stockholders on their equity greater than, less than or equal to that earned by Troy on its total assets?

C. 1. Did the Troy Corporation successfully apply financial leverage to increase the return to its stockholders in 1993?

   2. Was financial leverage used successful in 1994?

D. Did Troy's profit margin improve in 1994 over that in 1993? 1992?

SOLUTIONS TO CHAPTER SIXTEEN EXERCISES

1. A. The profit margin may be calculated by dividing net income by net sales revenue. Thus,

   $$\text{Profit margin} = \frac{\text{Net income}}{\text{Net sales revenue}} = \frac{\$215,600}{\$4,274,000} = 5.04 \text{ percent}$$

   B. The gross margin may be calculated by subtracting the cost of goods sold percentage to the net sales revenue percentage. Thus,

   Gross margin = Net sales revenue percentage - Cost of goods sold percentage

   Gross margin = 100.0 percent - 35.4 percent = 64.6 percent

2. A. Return on total assets (return on investments, all capital) is calculated in the following manner:

   $$\text{Average total assets} = \frac{\text{Total assets, 12/31/93 + Total assets, 12/31/94}}{2}$$

$$\text{Average total assets} = \frac{\$1,446,300 + \$1,502,100}{2} = \$1,474,200$$

Return on investments = Net income + Interest
(all capital)   Average total assets

$$\text{Return on investments} = \frac{\$215,600 + \$92,000}{\$1,474,200} = 20.87 \text{ percent}$$

B. The return on total owners' equity (stockholders' equity) is calculated in the following manner:

$$\text{Average stockholders' equity} = \frac{\text{Stockholders' equity 12/31/93} + \text{Stockholders' equity 12/31/94}}{2}$$

$$\text{Average stockholders' equity} = \frac{\$596,100 + \$661,700}{2} = \$628,900$$

Return on investment   =   Net income
(stockholders' equity)   Average Stockholders' equity

$$\text{Return on investment (stockholders' equity)} = \frac{\$215,600}{\$628,900} = 34.28 \text{ percent}$$

The return on stockholders' equity (34.28 percent) is greater than the return on the total assets (20.87 percent).

C. 1. A comparison of the return on investment (all capital) 7.6 percent (per illustrations) - with that on investment (stockholders' equity) 3.2 percent-indicated that the return available to stockholders was reduced as a consequence of the amounts borrowed from outsiders.

2. A comparison of the return on investment (all capital) 20.87 percent--and return on investment (stockholders' equity) 34.28 percent--shows that the return to stockholders was increased. The dollar return on assets acquired by borrowed funds exceeded the required interest payments to creditors.

D. The profit margins for each of these years may be calculated as follows:

$$\text{Profit margin} = \frac{\text{Net income}}{\text{Net sales revenue}}$$

$$\text{Profit margin, 1992} = \frac{\$219,500}{\$3,547,000} = 6.19 \text{ percent}$$

Profit margin, 1993 = $\dfrac{\$20,600}{\$2,524,500}$ = .82 percent

Profit margin, 1994 = $\dfrac{\$215,600}{\$4,274,000}$ = 5.04 percent

The 1994 profit margin is substantially higher (4.22 percent) than that of 1993, and slightly lower than that of 1992.

GLOSSARY

A

Accelerated Methods. Methods of calculating depreciation which results in declining depreciation charges over the useful life of an asset. Depreciation charges are thereby greater in the early years of the assets' life than in the later years. Accelerated methods include double-declining balance and sum-of-the-years' digit methods.

Accounting Cycle. The procedures that lead from the initial recognition of a financial event to the preparation of financial statements.

Accounts Receivable. Amounts owed to the firm by customers or others which can be expected to be collected within one year (or one operating cycle of business if greater than one year). Claims resulting from the sale of goods or services which are not supported by written notes or secured by specific collateral (assets to which a creditor has rights in the event the debtor defaults on his obligation). Accounts receivable usually does no require the payment of interest.

Accrual Concept. The concept that the effect of transactions on the assets and liabilities of an enterprise should be accorded accounting recognition at the time that they have heir primary economic impact, not necessarily when cash is received or disbursed. Revenues should be assigned to the period in which they are earned; costs should be charged as expenses in the period in which they provide their expected services.

Accrued. A term used to reflect the fact that an expense or revenue has been earned or incurred but the related asset or liability is not yet legally receivable or due; examples include accrued rent receivable and accrued utility costs payable.

Accrued Pension Expense (Liability). The accumulated excess of the required payment into the pension fund as determined by the actuarial cost method over the amount actually pain into the fund.

Actuarial Cost Method. The specific method a firm uses to determine the amount of its required payments to a pension fund, taking into account life expectancy of employees, employee turnover, rate of return on pension fund investments, and benefits to which employees will be entitled.

Actuary. A statistician who computes insurance risks and premiums.

Aging Schedule. A worksheet which indicates the age of each account receivable; that is, whether it is current, 0 to 30 days pay due, 31 to 60 days past due, etc.

All-Inclusive Concept. The concept that the income statement should include all transactions, excluding dividends, that affect the retained earnings of a business.
Amortization. The process of allocating the cost of developing or acquiring intangible assets over the periods in which they provide their benefits.

Annuity. A series of equal payments at fixed intervals.

Annuity Due. An annuity in which payments are made or received at the beginning of each period. (compare with ordinary annuity)

Annuity in Arrears. See Ordinary Annuity.

Appropriation of Retained Earnings. The process of segregating and reporting separately a portion of retained earnings which has been reserved for a specific purpose. Appropriations are commonly made to provide for debt retirement, plant expansion, or various contingencies.

Arm's Length Transaction. A transaction between two independent (unrelated) parties.

Assets. Economic resources of an enterprise that are recognized and measured in conformity with generally accepted accounting principles; future benefits or service potentials.

Audit. An examination of the financial books and records of an enterprise leading to an opinion as to whether the financial statements derived from them present fairly the organization's financial position and results of operation.

Authorized Shares. The maximum number or shares of stock a company is permitted to issue under its corporate charter.

B

Balance Sheet. A financial statement which indicates a firm's assets, liabilities and interests of owners as of a particular point in time.

Bank Reconciliation. The means by which a firm accounts for differences between its cash balances per its own record and that of the bank per a statement from the bank.

Betterments. Costs incurred to enhance an asset's service potential from what as first anticipated by extending its useful life or increasing its productivity.

Bond Discount. The difference between the face amount of a bond and the amount actually paid when the purchaser acquires a bond for more than its face value.

Bond Premium. The differences between the face amount of a bond and the amount actually paid when the purchaser acquires a bond for more than its face value.

Bonds. Certificates which provide evidence of long-term (usually five years of more) indebtedness. Bonds generally require that the borrower make periodic interest payments and repay the principal or face amount of the bond upon its maturity.

Book Value. The original cost of an asset less accumulated depreciation to date. Also known as depreciated cost.

C

Call. The right of a company to redeem an issue of bonds or preferred stock after it has been outstanding for a certain period of time.

Call Premium. An amount greater than the par value of the bond which the borrower (issuer of the bond) must pay to the lender in the event he exercises his option to retire the debt prior to its maturity. The excess amount to be paid above par is a penalty for depriving the lender of his right to receive interest payments for the original term of the loan.

Capital in Excess of Par. Amounts received by a firm from buyers at the issuance of its own capital stock in excess of the par (face) value of the stock. Also referred to as additional paid in capital.

Capitalize. To record as assets those costs which are intended to provide future services until such time as the services are actually provided.

Cash. Money. Includes currency and balances on deposit in banks.

Closely-Held Corporation. A corporation in which all outstanding shares of common stock are held by a small number of stockholders.

Closing Entries. Entries which terminate an account (bring to zero its balance) at the end of an accounting period. Closing entries are made to revenue and expense accounts--not to asset and liability accounts. Their balances are transformed to the retained earnings account. New accounts are established for the next accounting period.

Common Stock. The class of capital stock (as distinguished form preferred stock) that represents the residual interest of owners of the company in the assets of the firm after all liabilities and claims by preferred stockholders have been satisfied. Generally grants its holder the right to vote for members of the corporations board of directors as well as on other corporate matters and the right to share in the corporate profits.

Common Stock Equivalents. Securities that are not, in form, common stock, but which are convertible into common stock. They derive their value primarily from common stock inasmuch as they can eventually be exchanged for common shares.

Compensating Balance. A minimum cash balance which a back requires a firm to keep on deposit in return for a loan or promise to make credit available in the future. It is usually in the form of a checking account deposit, and thus earns no interest. The effect of such an arrangement is to reduce the amount borrowed by the firm and to increase its effective rate of interest.

Completed Contract Method. A method of revenue recognition whereby revenue is recognized at the completion of the production process. The completed contract method is especially applicable to those mining and agricultural firms which face stable prices and have a guaranteed market for their commodities.

Conservatism. The concept that it is usually preferable that any possible errors in measurement be in the direction of understatement rather than overstatement of net income and net assets. In case of doubt, the recognition of events having favorable consequences should be postponed, while those having unfavorable consequences should be immediately recognized.

Consolidated Financial Statements. Statements which report the financial position and earnings of two of more corporations as if they were a single economic and accounting entity.

Contingency. An uncertain event, one that if it occurs will usually result in a financial loss.

Contingent Liabilities. Potential liabilities which will be transformed into actual liabilities only if certain unfavorable events occur. They often arise from pending legal proceedings.

Contra Account. An offsetting account which is reported on the financial statements directly beneath the account with which it is associated. Examples of contra accounts are accumulated depreciation and allowance for doubtful accounts.

Control. Ownership of more than 50 percent of a company's outstanding voting stock.

Control Accounts. Accounts in the general ledger which summarize the individual, detailed accounts of the subsidiary ledgers.

Corporation. A legal entity which operates under a grant of authority by a state or other political body. Typical characteristics include limited liability, continued existence and ownership interests which are readily transferable.

Correcting Entries. Adjustments to the financial records which are required because firms, in order to obtain a measure of bookkeeping convenience, permit out-of-date or incorrect data to remain in the accounts.

Cost Accounting. A branch of accounting which focuses on the determination of the cost of goods manufactured.

Cost Method. A method used by a company to record its investment in the stock of another company. The investment is maintained on the books of the investor at original cost, unless there are unusual circumstances indicating that the initial value of the investment has been impaired. Revenue from the investment is recognized only to the extent the investee company actually declares dividends.

Cost of Goods Sold. The sum of the expenditures directly or indirectly attributable to an item in order to bring it to its salable condition and location. Thus, all costs reasonably identifiable with the manufacture or acquisition, storage and preparation or sale of goods should be included as part of the cost of the goods sold. Such costs will be charged as cost of goods sold only in the period in which the merchandise is actually sold.

Coupon Bonds. Bonds containing a series of coupons which can be redeemed (generally semi-annually) for the interest due.

Coupon Rate. The interest rate set by the borrower that determines the dollar amount to be paid to the lender each interest period; that which is stated in the bond agreement.

Credit. An entry to the right side of an account. Credits represent decreases in assets or increases in liabilities or owners' equities.

Current Assets. Cash and other such assets which will either be sold or consumed within one year (or one operating cycle of the business if greater than one year).

Current Liabilities. Obligations of the company that are expected to be satisfied within a relatively short period of time, generally one year (or one operating cycle of the business if greater than one year).

Current Operating Performance Concept. The view that only the transactions which are representative of the normal, recurring operations of the firms should be considered in calculating net income. Any transactions of an unusual, non-recurring nature should be segregated and reported separately from the main body of the income statement.

Current Replacement Cost. The cost of replacing as asset with one of similar quality and condition.

D

Date of Record. The date on which stock records are closed and ownership of outstanding shares is determined for the purpose of identifying the stockholders who are to receive payments.

Debentures. Bonds which are unsecured (not backed by collateral). The lender (purchaser of the bond) must rely primarily upon the good faith and financial integrity of the borrower for repayment.

Debit. An entry to the left side of an account. Debits signify increases in assets or decreases in liabilities or owners' equities. Debits are sometimes referred to as charges.

Deferred Charges. Expenditures made in one period but not recognized as an expense of that period. Rather, they are carried forward as assets to be charged as expenses in future periods. Examples include prepaid expenses (such as prepaid rent or prepaid interest) and organizational costs.

Deferred Credits. Obligations of a firm, often arising out of customer advances, to provide goods or services in the future; revenue received before it is earned. Examples include unearned rent, subscription charges representing magazines not yet delivered, and advance ticket sales.

Depletion. The process of allocating the cost of natural recourses over the periods in which their benefits are received. Depletion charges are generally calculated on a unit or output basis.

Depletion Cost. Acquisition cost of an asset less accumulated depreciation. Accumulated depreciation consists of the portion of acquisition cost representing the services of the asset already utilized.

Depreciation. The process of allocating the cost of a tangible asset, such as plant and equipment, over its useful life, so as to match the cost of the asset with the revenue it will serve to generate.

Direct Costs. Manufacturing costs, such as factory labor and raw materials, which can be directly associated with specific units of production.

Discount. (verb) To lend or borrow money with interest taken out in advance; often used to refer to the sale of notes receivable to a factor or other lending institution.

Discount Rate. The rate of interest at which a future payment is converted to a present value.

Discounted Note. A note in which the amount actually loaned is less than the face amount of the note. That is, the face amount includes both principal and interest.

Dividend in Kind. A dividend in property or assets other than cash.

Dividends. Distribution of the assets of an enterprise to its owners. The asset distributed is most often cash, but it could be other properties as well.

Dollar-Value LIFO. A variation of the last-in, first-out method of inventory valuation by which products are grouped into one or more inventory pools and are valued on the basis of the ratio of current average prices to those of prior periods.

Double-Entry Bookkeeping. The method by which transactions are conventionally recorded. It is based on the basic accounting equation, assets = liabilities + owners' equity. When a transaction (financial event) causes a net increase or decrease on the left side of the equation, it must cause a corresponding increase or decrease of an identical amount on the right side.

E

Earnings Per Share (EPS). A measure of corporate performance, calculated by dividing net earnings (after deducting preferred stock dividends) by the number of shares of common stock outstanding.

Equities. The rights to or claims against the assets of an enterprise. There are two categories of equities: liabilities and owners' equity (capital stock and retained earnings).

Equity Method. A method used by a firm to record its investment in the stock of another company. The investment is recorded initially at cost but the carrying value is periodically adjusted to take into account the investor's share of the investee's earnings subsequent to the date of acquisition. Revenue or expenses are recognized as soon as the investee's net worth increases or decreases. Carrying value of the investment is decreased each time the investee company declares a dividend, because dividends result in a decrease of investee's net worth.

Exchange Prices. The fair market values of the goods, services, or monetary consideration received or surrendered by the parties to a transaction.

Executory Contracts. Those contract contingent upon the mutual performance of both parties to the contract. As a general rule, assets and liabilities arising out of such contracts are recorded only to the extent that at least one of the parties has fulfilled its contractual obligations.

Expenses. Outflows of cash or other assets attributable to the profit directed activities of an enterprise. Expenses are measures of the efforts exerted on the part of the enterprise in its attempt to realize revenues.

Extraordinary Item. A gain or loss arising from an event or transaction which is both unusual in nature and infrequent in occurrence. Examples of such events include major casualties such as earthquakes, and expropriations of property by foreign governments.

F

Factor. A type of lending institution which specializes in buying notes or accounts receivable.

Factory Overhead Costs. Costs which cannot readily be associated with specific units of production, such as those for utilities, maintenance, and rent.

Financial Accounting. The branch of accounting primarily concerned with reporting to parties outside of the firm.

Financing Ratios. Ratios used to compare the claims of the creditors with the equity of owners.

First-in, First-out (FIFO) Method. A method of inventory valuation which assumes that goods acquired first are sold first.

Fiscal Year. An Accounting period of twelve successive calendar months, not necessarily starting from January.

Fixed Assets. The long-lived assets (resources) of an enterprise, including plant and equipment, motor vehicles and land.

Fixed Costs. Those costs that do not vary with number of units produced. For example, within broad ranges of output, a firm's costs of rent, power, and executive salaries are fixed; they remain constant regardless of the number of units produced.

Fully Diluted Earnings Per Share. A calculation of EPS in which the denominator includes all shares of common stock currently outstanding plus all shares which the firm might have to issue in the future.

Funds. Working capital. Sometimes is used to refer to cash alone or to the excess of current assets, excluding inventories, over current liabilities.

Future Value. The amount to which a payment or series of payments would accumulate if invested so as to earn interest at a specified rate.

G

General Ledger. A book of accounts which contains all of the various accounts maintained by an enterprise.

Going Concern Concept. The assumption that an enterprise will continue operating indefinitely and thereby realize the anticipated benefits of its recorded assets.

Goodwill. The portion of the cost of acquiring a subsidiary that cannot be assigned directly to any specific assets. It arises only when one firm purchases another and the excess of cost of the assets acquired over their book value cannot be specifically attributed to other assets.

Gross Margin. One minus cost of goods sold, expressed as a percentage of sales.

Gross National Product Implicit Price Deflator (GNP Deflator). An index which expressed prices of all goods and services included in gross national product as a percentage of prices of a selected base year.

Group Depreciation Method. A method of calculating depreciation under which groups of similar assets are recorded as a unit and depreciation is taken on the group as a whole rather than on individual assets. Characteristic of the group depreciation method is the practice that no gain or loss is recognized on the sale or retirement of individual assets.

H

Historical Cost. The amount paid to acquire an asset.

Holding Gain (Loss). Gain (Loss) attributable to the increase (decrease) in replacement cost between the date on which an item is purchased and that on which it is sold.

I

Imprest Basis. A means of accounting for petty cash, by which the recorded general ledger balance is fixed. At any given time the actual balance in the petty cash fund would consist of either cash or cash plus expenditure receipts in an amount equal to the reported general ledger balance. Periodically the fund is replenished with cash and debit specific expense accounts for the amounts indicated on the expenditure receipts.

Income. A measure of financial performance determined by subtracting expenses from revenues. Often referred to as profit or earnings.

Income Statement. A financial statement which indicates a firm's revenues and expenses as well as the difference between the two (income or loss) for a particular period of time.

Input Price. The price which would have to be paid to obtain the same assets or its equivalent; replacement cost.

Installment Method. A method of revenue recognition whereby revenue is recognized when cash is collected. The installment method is often used to account for certain types of real estate or other property transactions in which the collectibility of the receivables is in doubt.

Installment Sale. A sale of property in which a series of payments is made over a specified period of time. A down payment at the time of sale is generally required.

Intangible Asset. An asset characterized by the rights, privileges, and benefits of possession rather than by physical existence. Examples include patents, copyrights, organizational costs, and goodwill.

Intangible Drilling Costs. Costs incurred by oil companies in searching for active oil wells. Intangible drilling costs may include those of drilling productive wells as well as those of drilling dry ones.

Intercompany Transactions. Transactions between a parent company and its subsidiary. Examples are purchases, sales, and loans. In preparing consolidated financial statements, the effect of such transactions must be eliminated.

Interim Financial Reports. Financial reports that cover less than a full year.

Inter-period Tax Allocation. The procedure by which the reported tax expense is based upon reported income rather than the actual legal tax obligation. It has the effect of matching the reported income tax expense with the reported income which it is based on.

Inventory. Goods that are in various stages of production or are awaiting sale. It includes supplies, raw materials, work in process and finished goods.

Investment Tax Credit. A direct reduction of income tax liability, the amount of which is tied to the acquisition of certain eligible fixed assets.

Issued Shares. The shares of stock that have been put into circulation.

J

Journal. A book which maintains a comprehensive history of all transactions that affect the various accounts of a company. It is the book of original entry of the transactions. Original entries are referred to as journal entries.

L

Last-in, First-out (LIFO) Method. A method of inventory valuation which assumes that the goods acquired last are sold first.

Lease. The right to use property for a stated period of time in return for rent or some other form of compensation.

Leverage. The ability of a firm to increase or decrease the return on investment of its common stockholders. Leverage results when a firm acquires capital by issuing securities, such as bonds or preferred stock, that acquire fixed payments of interest or dividends. All income, after the fixed payments are made, accrues entirely to the common stockholders. Small fluctuations in operating income may produce large fluctuations in earnings available to common stockholders.

Liabilities. Claims by outsiders against the assets of an enterprise. They may be payable in money, goods, or services.

Liquidation Value. The amount which would be realized if a firm were to be dissolved (terminated) and its assets sold. Assets should be reported at liquidation values if there is evidence that a firm will not be able to survive.

Liquidity Ratios. Ratios used to indicate the ability of the firm to meet its obligations as they mature.

Long-Lived Assets. Assets that will not be consumed within a single operating cycle of the business, but which will serve to benefit several accounting periods. Examples of long-lived assets are land, buildings, equipment, natural resources, and most intangible assets. Tangible long-lived assets are often referred to as fixed assets.

Loss. An unrecoverable and involuntary expense which provides no present or future benefits.

Lower of Cost or Market Rule. The rule by which the carrying value of an asset is compared to its market price. If the market price is less than the historical cost less accumulated depreciation, then the asset is written down to and reported at its current market value; otherwise it is reported ass its carrying value. The rule is applied primarily to assets intended for resale in the normal course of business, such as inventories and marketable securities.

M

Maintenance (Repair) Costs. Costs incurred to keep assets in good operating condition which do not add to the productivity of the assets or extend their originally estimated useful lives.

Majority Interest. The interest of the stockholders of the parent company in a subsidiary. Consolidated financial statements are prepared from the standpoint of the majority stockholders.

Managerial Accounting. The branch of accounting primarily concerned with reports that are used within an organization to facilitate improved planning, management, and control.

Market Value. The price that would have to be paid to replace an asset with one of comparable age and quality; the price at which an asset can be bought or sold in a fair exchange with an unrelated party.

Marketable Securities. Stocks, bonds, or other securities which a company holds as a temporary investment and can readily sell in the open market as it has a need for cash; are usually classified as current assets.

Matching Principle. The principle that all costs should be associated with the particular revenues that they generate and recorded as expenses in the same periods in which the revenues are given accounting recognition.

Minority Interest. The equity of the minority stockholders of a subsidiary in a consolidated corporation. Such interest represents a liability from the standpoint of the majority stockholders.

Monetary Items. Assets and Liabilities which are fixed, or which are convertible into a fixed number of dollars regardless of changes in prices. Examples include accounts and notes receivable, cash, and most forms of debt.

N

Negotiable Note. A note which may be freely bought and sold and whose owner at the date of maturity can present the note to its maker for collection.

Net Assets. Assets less liabilities; equal to owners' equity.

Non-Current Assets. Assets that are not expected to be sold, consumed, or converted into cash within one year (or one operating cycle of the business if the cycle is greater than one year).

Non-Current Liabilities. Obligations that are not expected to be satisfied within one year (or one operating cycle of the business if the cycle is greater than one year).

Non-Monetary Items. Assets and liabilities which are not contractually fixed in terms of a specific dollar amount. These include all items which are not classified as monetary items. Examples are inventories, marketable securities, plant and equipment, and common stock.

Notes Receivable. Claims resulting from sales of goods, performance of services which are evidenced by written notes. Notes receivable generally require the payment of interest.

O

Operating Cycle. The period of time between the purchase of raw materials or other inventory and their eventual conversion into cash.

Opportunity Cost. The amount that could be earned if an asset were sold and the proceeds used in the best possible alternative.

Ordinary Annuity. An annuity in which payments are made or received at the end of each period; also called annuity in arrears.

Organizational Costs. Costs incurred in forming a firm, such as legal and accounting fees. These costs are considered intangible assets, incurred to benefit future accounting periods.

Output Price. The net realizable value of an asset; the amount for which an asset could be sold reduced by any costs that must be incurred to bring it to a salable condition.

Outstanding Shares. The shares currently in circulation; the number of shares issued less those that are currently held by the company as treasury stock.

Owners' Equity. The residual interest of the owners of an enterprise in its assets after all claims by outside parties have been satisfied. Owners' equity is equal to the assets of the firm less its liabilities. It is composed of the contributions of the owners to the enterprise (common stock and capital in excess of par, for example) as well as the earnings accumulated since the formation of the enterprise (retained earnings).

P

Parent. A company that has control over another company.

Partnership. A firm owned by two or more parties.

Participating Preferred Stock. An issue of preferred stock which entitles the preferred stockholders to share with common stockholders in income in excess of a stipulated dividend.

Par Value. The principal or face value of a bond which represents the amount payable on the maturity of the bond.

Payee. The person or organization to whom the payment required by a note is to be made.

Payor. The party that agrees to make the payment required by a note.

Pensions. Periodic payments to retired or disabled employees owing to their years of employment. Pension plans usually require that a company make fixed monthly payments to an employee from the time of his retirement to the date of either his death or that of his surviving spouse.

Percentage Depletion. A method of calculating depletion whereby the annual charge is determined by applying a pre-established percentage to revenues attributed to the property. Depletion may be charged on a particular mineral deposit even after the full cost of the deposit has been depleted. The percentage depletion method may be used for tax purposes only--not for general reporting purposes.

Percentage of Completion Method. A method of revenue recognition whereby revenue is recognized in the course of production. The amount of revenue to be recognized in each accounting period is indicated by the percentage of the total project completed in that period times the total contract price. This method is most applicable to firms which provide goods or services under long-term contracts.

Period Costs. Costs which are charged as expenses in the period in which they are incurred, regardless of when the products produced by the enterprise are sold. Examples of period costs are salaries of officers and other "home-office" costs.

Perpetual Inventory Method. The method of accounting for inventory whereby the accounting records are updated each time inventory is acquired, used, or sold, and are, thereby, always on a current basis.

Petty Cash. Small amounts of cash maintained to meet disbursements of amounts too small to justify the time and inconvenience of writing checks.

Pooling of Interests Method. A means of accounting for a business combination that has been effected by an exchange of common stock, whereby the assets and liabilities of each of the component companies are carried forward to the new enterprise at their previously recorded amounts. No recognition is given to any excess of the fair market values of the securities over the book values of the assets exchanged.

Posting. The process of transferring information from a journal to a ledger. For example, journal entries are posted to the general ledger account which they affect.

Preferred Stock. The class of capital stock (as distinguished from common stock) which has a claim prior to that of common stock upon the earnings of the company and upon assets distributed in liquidation. Often guarantees the holder a specified annual dividend.

Prepaid Expenses. Assets which represent services or rights to services which have been paid for but not yet consumed; a type of deferred charge. Examples include prepaid insurance and prepaid utility costs.

Present Value. The amount which, if invested today so as to earn interest at a specified rate, would accumulate in value to a specified payment or series of payments to be received in the future.

Primary Earnings Per Share. A calculation of EPS in which the denominator (shares outstanding) is based on common stock presently outstanding and other types of securities which are considered to be common stock equivalents.

Prime Rate. The interest rate that a bank offers to its most credit worthy customers.

Principal. The amount of a note on which interest is charged or earned.

Prior Period Adjustment. The correction of earnings of a previous period by a credit or charge <u>directly</u> to retained earnings. Such correction would be <u>excluded from reported income</u> of the year in which the correction is made. Prior period adjustments should be made only for those items which: (1) are directly related to the business activities of a specific prior period; (2) are not attributable to economic events occurring after the prior period; (3) depend mainly no determinations by persons other than managements; (4) and were not susceptible of reasonable estimation prior to such determination. Examples of events for which prior period adjustments are appropriate include resolution of disputes over income taxes and settlement of litigation relating to a previous period.

Product Costs. Costs that can be associated with and assigned to particular products and are included as part of their total cost. Such costs are charged to expense (cost of goods sold) only upon the sale of the products. Examples of product costs are raw materials, direct labor, and factory overhead.

Profitability and Activity Ratios. Ratios used to measure the profitability and efficiency of the activities carried out by the enterprise.

Profit Margin. Net income expressed as a percentage of sales revenue.

Promissory Note. A legal instrument providing formal written documentation of a borrower's obligation to make timely payment and to pay interest for the use of the funds.

Promoters. Individuals who form a corporation. They contribute cash or other assets or services in exchange for all or part of the stock to be issued. The promoters have a fiduciary obligation to the corporation and must not benefit at the expense of others who may later buy shares of the firm's stock.

Purchase Method. A means of accounting for a corporate acquisition whereby the total value assigned to the net assets of the acquired company is based on the fair market value of the consideration surrendered by the acquiring company.

Purchasing Power Gains (Losses). Gains or losses in ability to acquire real goods or services. Purchasing power gains or losses are attributable to holding monetary assets and liabilities over a period in which there is a change in the value of the existing monetary unit (e.g., the dollar).

R

Recognize. To give expression in the accounts to a transaction or financial event' as in "to recognize revenue," "to recognize expenses."

Redemption. The retirement of bonds by the issuer, usually by repurchase.

Research and Development Costs. Expenditures made with the expectation that they will result in new or improved products or processes.

Retain Inventory Method. A method of inventory valuation by which inventory records of goods on hand are maintained at retail prices rather than at acquisition costs. In order to convert the value of goods on hand from a value based on selling prices to one based on acquisition costs, the recorded balance in the inventory account is multiplied by a ratio of average cost to average selling price.

Retained Earnings. The sum of the earnings of each accounting period since a company has been in existence less the amounts distributed to stockholders in the form of dividends. Retained earnings represent stockholders' claims against the assets of the firm, but they cannot be identified with either cash or other specific assets.

Revenues. Inflows of cash or other assets attributable to the goods or services provided by the enterprise.

S

Salvage Value. The amount that can be recovered when an asset is either sold, traded in for a new asset, or scrapped.

Self-Correcting Errors. Errors which will automatically be eliminated either upon liquidation of the asset or liability involved or when other routine adjustments to the accounts are made. The errors may, however, cause the financial reports of intervening accounting period to be incorrect.

Self-Insurance. The means by which a firm provides for potential losses by appropriating retained earnings and/or by establishing a reserve of cash or other assets.

Sinking Fund. A fund composed of cash or other assets which is segregated in the accounts in order to repay an outstanding obligation when it matures or to make some specified payments in the future.

Sole Proprietorship. A firm owned by a single individual.

Sources of Funds. Under the working capital concept of the statement of changes in financial position, they represent increases in funds due to increases in non-current liabilities, increases in owners' equity, and decreases in non-current assets.

Specific Identification Method. An inventory valuation method that requires an enterprise to account for the cost of each individual item bought and sold. This method is largely used by enterprises that sell small quantities of high cost items.

Statement of Changes in Financial Position. A financial statement which indicates changes in funds (generally defined as working capital but sometimes defined as cash alone) as well as in the specific accounts which funds are composed of, and which reveals the sources and uses of funds during the period covered by the statement.

Stock Dividend. A form of stock split; the distribution to each shareholder, on a pro rata basis, of additional shares of stock. A stock dividend is often issued in lieu of a dividend in cash or other property. Its purpose is to provide shareholders with tangible evidence of an increase in their ownership interest attributable to corporate earnings. Commonly the number of new shares to be issued is less than 20 percent of previously outstanding shares.

Stock Option. A certificate which allows the holder to purchase a specific number of shares of a firm's stock at an established price. Stock options are often used as a means of compensating employees. Should the market price of the firm's common stock increase above the established exercise price, the employee has the opportunity to acquire the stock at less than its market price.

Stock Right. A certificate which permits the holder to purchase directly from the issuing corporation a set number of shares at an established price. Stock rights are ordinarily issued by a company to its existing shareholders, but they are freely negotiable. They enable the company to raise additional capital and at the same time permit the stockholders to maintain their proportionate ownership interests in their company.

Stock Split. The issue of additional shares of stock for each share currently outstanding. For example, should a company split its stock three-for-one, then, for each one share presently held, a shareholder would receive two additional shares. The purpose of a stock split is to reduce the market price per share, obtain a wider distribution of ownership, and improve the marketability or outstanding shares.

Straight-Line Method. A method of calculating depreciation which results in equal depreciation charges during each year of an asset's useful life.

Subsidiary. A company that is controlled by another company, its parent.

Subsidiary Ledgers. The ledgers in which the individual, more detailed accounts are maintained. Among subsidiary ledgers commonly maintained are those for accounts receivable and fixed assets.

T

T-Account. A representation of a ledger account in the form of the letter "T."

Time Value of Money. The concept that a dollar received today is worth considerably more than a dollar to be received in the future, since it can be invested so as to earn a periodic return.

Trial Balance. A complete listing of the balances in each of the accounts. The total debt balances must equal the total credit balances. Otherwise an error has been made. A pre-closing trial balance is one taken before the closing entries are made. One taken after the closing entries are made is called a post-closing trial balance. The post-closing trial balance consists only of asset, liability, and owners' equity accounts, since by the time it is taken, revenue and expense accounts would have zero balances.

Turnover. Replacing an asset by a like asset; as in inventory turnover or fixed asset turnover.

Turnover Ratios. Activity ratios which measure the effectiveness of management in utilizing specific resources under its command.

U

Updating (Adjusting) Entries. Journal entries which recognize ongoing revenues and expenses in order to bring the accounts up to date.

Uses of Funds. Under the working capital concept of the statement of changes in financial position, they represent decreases in funds due to decreases in non-current liabilities, decreases in owners' equity, and increases in non-current assets.

W

Warrant. An option to purchase an established number of shares at a stated price. Warrants are usually issued in connection with the sale of bonds in order to make the bonds more attractive to investors. Warrants are a form of stock rights but normally can be exercised only after a specified period of time has elapsed.

Wasting Assets. Natural resources.

Weighted Average Method. An inventory valuation method which assumes that all costs can be aggregated and the cost to be assigned to a particular unit should be the weighted average of the costs of all units held for sale during the accounting period.

Working Capital. Cash and other liquid assets that could be transformed into cash within a relatively short period of time, less accounts payable and other liabilities that are expected to consume cash within the same short period of time; that is, current assets minus current liabilities.

Y

Yield Rate. The actual or effective interest rate which is established by adjusting the selling price of the bond instead of changing its coupon rate; the anticipated period cash (interest payments divided by the selling price of the bond).

APPENDIX

table 1

Future Value of $1

No. of periods	2%	3%	4%	5%	6%	7%	8%	9%	10%	11%	12%	13%	14%	15%
1	1.0200	1.0300	1.0400	1.0500	1.0600	1.0700	1.0800	1.0900	1.1000	1.1100	1.1200	1.1300	1.1400	1.1500
2	1.0404	1.0609	1.0816	1.1025	1.1236	1.1449	1.1664	1.1881	1.2100	1.2321	1.2544	1.2769	1.2996	1.3225
3	1.0612	1.0927	1.1249	1.1576	1.1910	1.2250	1.2597	1.2950	1.3310	1.3676	1.4049	1.4429	1.4815	1.5209
4	1.0824	1.1255	1.1699	1.2155	1.2625	1.3108	1.3605	1.4116	1.4641	1.5181	1.5735	1.6305	1.6890	1.7490
5	1.1041	1.1593	1.2167	1.2763	1.3382	1.4026	1.4693	1.5386	1.6105	1.6851	1.7623	1.8424	1.9254	2.0114
6	1.1262	1.1941	1.2653	1.3401	1.4185	1.5007	1.5869	1.6771	1.7716	1.8704	1.9738	2.0820	2.1950	2.3131
7	1.1487	1.2299	1.3159	1.4071	1.5036	1.6058	1.7138	1.8280	1.9487	2.0762	2.2107	2.3526	2.5023	2.6600
8	1.1717	1.2668	1.3686	1.4775	1.5938	1.7182	1.8509	1.9926	2.1436	2.3045	2.4760	2.6584	2.8526	3.0590
9	1.1951	1.3048	1.4233	1.5513	1.6895	1.8385	1.9990	2.1719	2.3579	2.5580	2.7731	3.0040	3.2519	3.5179
10	1.2190	1.3439	1.4802	1.6289	1.7908	1.9672	2.1589	2.3674	2.5937	2.8394	3.1058	3.3946	3.7072	4.0456
11	1.2434	1.3842	1.5395	1.7103	1.8983	2.1049	2.3316	2.5804	2.8531	3.1518	3.4785	3.8359	4.2262	4.6524
12	1.2682	1.4258	1.6010	1.7959	2.0122	2.2522	2.5182	2.8127	3.1384	3.4985	3.8960	4.3345	4.8179	5.3503
13	1.2936	1.4685	1.6651	1.8856	2.1329	2.4098	2.7196	3.0658	3.4523	3.8833	4.3635	4.8980	5.4924	6.1528
14	1.3195	1.5126	1.7317	1.9799	2.2609	2.5785	2.9372	3.3417	3.7975	4.3104	4.8871	5.5348	6.2613	7.0757
15	1.3459	1.5580	1.8009	2.0789	2.3966	2.7590	3.1722	3.6425	4.1772	4.7846	5.4736	6.2543	7.1379	8.1371
16	1.3728	1.6047	1.8730	2.1829	2.5404	2.9522	3.4259	3.9703	4.5950	5.3109	6.1304	7.0673	8.1372	9.3576
17	1.4002	1.6528	1.9479	2.2920	2.6928	3.1588	3.7000	4.3276	5.0545	5.8951	6.8660	7.9861	9.2765	10.7613
18	1.4282	1.7024	2.0258	2.4066	2.8543	3.3799	3.9960	4.7171	5.5599	6.5436	7.6900	9.0243	10.5752	12.3755
19	1.4568	1.7535	2.1068	2.5270	3.0256	3.6165	4.3157	5.1417	6.1159	7.2633	8.6128	10.1974	12.0557	14.2318
20	1.4859	1.8061	2.1911	2.6533	3.2071	3.8697	4.6610	5.6044	6.7275	8.0623	9.6463	11.5231	13.7435	16.3665
21	1.5157	1.8603	2.2788	2.7860	3.3996	4.1406	5.0338	6.1088	7.4002	8.9492	10.8038	13.0211	15.6676	18.8215
22	1.5460	1.9161	2.3699	2.9253	3.6035	4.4304	5.4365	6.6586	8.1403	9.9336	12.1003	14.7138	17.8610	21.6447
23	1.5769	1.9736	2.4647	3.0715	3.8197	4.7405	5.8715	7.2579	8.9543	11.0263	13.5523	16.6266	20.3616	24.8915
24	1.6084	2.0328	2.5633	3.2251	4.0489	5.0724	6.3412	7.9111	9.8497	12.2392	15.1786	18.7881	23.2122	28.6252
25	1.6406	2.0938	2.6658	3.3864	4.2919	5.4274	6.8485	8.6231	10.8347	13.5855	17.0001	21.2305	26.4619	32.9190
26	1.6734	2.1566	2.7725	3.5557	4.5494	5.8074	7.3964	9.3992	11.9182	15.0799	19.0401	23.9905	30.1666	37.8568
27	1.7069	2.2213	2.8834	3.7335	4.8223	6.2139	7.9881	10.2451	13.1100	16.7386	21.3249	27.1093	34.3899	43.5353
28	1.7410	2.2879	2.9987	3.9201	5.1117	6.6488	8.6271	11.1671	14.4210	18.5799	23.8839	30.6335	39.2045	50.0656
29	1.7758	2.3566	3.1187	4.1161	5.4184	7.1143	9.3173	12.1722	15.8631	20.6237	26.7499	34.6158	44.6931	57.5755
30	1.8114	2.4273	3.2434	4.3219	5.7435	7.6123	10.0627	13.2677	17.4494	22.8923	29.9599	39.1159	50.9502	66.2118
31	1.8476	2.5001	3.3731	4.5380	6.0881	8.1451	10.8677	14.4618	19.1943	25.4104	33.5551	44.2010	58.0832	76.1435
32	1.8845	2.5751	3.5081	4.7649	6.4534	8.7153	11.7371	15.7633	21.1138	28.2056	37.5817	49.9471	66.2148	87.5651
33	1.9222	2.6523	3.6484	5.0032	6.8406	9.3253	12.6760	17.1820	23.2252	31.3082	42.0915	56.4402	75.4849	100.6998
34	1.9607	2.7319	3.7943	5.2533	7.2510	9.9781	13.6901	18.7284	25.5477	34.7521	47.1425	63.7774	86.0528	115.8048
35	1.9999	2.8139	3.9461	5.5160	7.6861	10.6766	14.7853	20.4140	28.1024	38.5749	52.7996	72.0685	98.1002	133.1755
36	2.0399	2.8983	4.1039	5.7918	8.1473	11.4239	15.9682	22.2512	30.9127	42.8181	59.1356	81.4374	111.8342	153.1519
37	2.0807	2.9852	4.2681	6.0814	8.6361	12.2236	17.2456	24.2538	34.0039	47.5281	66.2318	92.0243	127.4910	176.1246
38	2.1223	3.0748	4.4388	6.3855	9.1543	13.0793	18.6253	26.4367	37.4043	52.7562	74.1797	103.9874	145.3397	202.5433
39	2.1647	3.1670	4.6164	6.7048	9.7035	13.9948	20.1153	28.8160	41.1448	58.5593	83.0812	117.5058	165.6873	232.9248
40	2.2080	3.2620	4.8010	7.0400	10.2857	14.9745	21.7245	31.4094	45.2593	65.0009	93.0510	132.7816	188.8835	267.8635
41	2.2522	3.3599	4.9931	7.3920	10.9029	16.0227	23.4625	34.2363	49.7852	72.1510	104.2171	150.0432	215.3272	308.0431
42	2.2972	3.4607	5.1928	7.7616	11.5570	17.1443	25.3395	37.3175	54.7637	80.0876	116.7231	169.5488	245.4730	354.2495
43	2.3432	3.5645	5.4005	8.1497	12.2505	18.3444	27.3666	40.6761	60.2401	88.8972	130.7299	191.5901	279.8392	407.3870
44	2.3901	3.6715	5.6165	8.5572	12.9855	19.6285	29.5560	44.3370	66.2641	98.6759	146.4175	216.4968	319.0167	468.4950
45	2.4379	3.7816	5.8412	8.9850	13.7646	21.0025	31.9204	48.3273	72.8905	109.5302	163.9876	244.6414	363.6791	538.7693
46	2.4866	3.8950	6.0748	9.4343	14.5905	22.4726	34.4741	52.6767	80.1795	121.5786	183.6661	276.4448	414.5941	619.5847
47	2.5363	4.0119	6.3178	9.9060	15.4659	24.0457	37.2320	57.4176	88.1975	134.9522	205.7061	312.3826	472.6373	712.5224
48	2.5871	4.1323	6.5705	10.4013	16.3939	25.7289	40.2106	62.5852	97.0172	149.7970	230.3908	352.9923	538.8065	819.4007
49	2.6388	4.2562	6.8333	10.9213	17.3775	27.5299	43.4274	68.2179	106.7190	166.2746	258.0377	398.8813	614.2395	942.3108
50	2.6916	4.3839	7.1067	11.4674	18.4202	29.4570	46.9016	74.3575	117.3909	184.5648	289.0022	450.7359	700.2330	1083.6574

Present Value of $1

table 2

No. of periods	2%	3%	4%	5%	6%	7%	8%	9%	10%	11%	12%	13%	14%	15%
1	.9804	.9709	.9615	.9524	.9434	.9346	.9259	.9174	.9091	.9009	.8929	.8850	.8772	.8696
2	.9612	.9426	.9246	.9070	.8900	.8734	.8573	.8417	.8264	.8116	.7972	.7831	.7695	.7561
3	.9423	.9151	.8890	.8638	.8396	.8163	.7938	.7722	.7513	.7312	.7118	.6931	.6750	.6575
4	.9238	.8885	.8548	.8227	.7921	.7629	.7350	.7084	.6830	.6587	.6355	.6133	.5921	.5718
5	.9057	.8626	.8219	.7835	.7473	.7130	.6806	.6499	.6209	.5935	.5674	.5428	.5194	.4972
6	.8880	.8375	.7903	.7462	.7050	.6663	.6302	.5963	.5645	.5346	.5066	.4803	.4556	.4323
7	.8706	.8131	.7599	.7107	.6651	.6227	.5835	.5470	.5132	.4817	.4523	.4251	.3996	.3759
8	.8535	.7894	.7307	.6768	.6274	.5820	.5403	.5019	.4665	.4339	.4039	.3762	.3506	.3269
9	.8368	.7664	.7026	.6446	.5919	.5439	.5002	.4604	.4241	.3909	.3606	.3329	.3075	.2843
10	.8203	.7441	.6756	.6139	.5584	.5083	.4632	.4224	.3855	.3522	.3220	.2946	.2697	.2472
11	.8043	.7224	.6496	.5847	.5268	.4751	.4289	.3875	.3505	.3173	.2875	.2607	.2366	.2149
12	.7885	.7014	.6246	.5568	.4970	.4440	.3971	.3555	.3186	.2858	.2567	.2307	.2076	.1869
13	.7730	.6810	.6006	.5303	.4688	.4150	.3677	.3262	.2897	.2575	.2292	.2042	.1821	.1625
14	.7579	.6611	.5775	.5051	.4423	.3878	.3405	.2992	.2633	.2320	.2046	.1807	.1597	.1413
15	.7430	.6419	.5553	.4810	.4173	.3624	.3152	.2745	.2394	.2090	.1827	.1599	.1401	.1229
16	.7284	.6232	.5339	.4581	.3936	.3387	.2919	.2519	.2176	.1883	.1631	.1415	.1229	.1069
17	.7142	.6050	.5134	.4363	.3714	.3166	.2703	.2311	.1978	.1696	.1456	.1252	.1078	.0929
18	.7002	.5874	.4936	.4155	.3503	.2959	.2502	.2120	.1799	.1528	.1300	.1108	.0946	.0808
19	.6864	.5703	.4746	.3957	.3305	.2765	.2317	.1945	.1635	.1377	.1161	.0981	.0829	.0703
20	.6730	.5537	.4564	.3769	.3118	.2584	.2145	.1784	.1486	.1240	.1037	.0868	.0728	.0611
21	.6598	.5375	.4388	.3589	.2942	.2415	.1987	.1637	.1351	.1117	.0926	.0768	.0638	.0531
22	.6468	.5219	.4220	.3418	.2775	.2257	.1839	.1502	.1228	.1007	.0826	.0680	.0560	.0462
23	.6342	.5067	.4057	.3256	.2618	.2109	.1703	.1378	.1117	.0907	.0738	.0601	.0491	.0402
24	.6217	.4919	.3901	.3101	.2470	.1971	.1577	.1264	.1015	.0817	.0659	.0532	.0431	.0349
25	.6095	.4776	.3751	.2953	.2330	.1842	.1460	.1160	.0923	.0736	.0588	.0471	.0378	.0304
26	.5976	.4637	.3607	.2812	.2198	.1722	.1352	.1064	.0839	.0663	.0525	.0417	.0331	.0264
27	.5859	.4502	.3468	.2678	.2074	.1609	.1252	.0976	.0763	.0597	.0469	.0369	.0291	.0230
28	.5744	.4371	.3335	.2551	.1956	.1504	.1159	.0895	.0693	.0538	.0419	.0326	.0255	.0200
29	.5631	.4243	.3207	.2429	.1846	.1406	.1073	.0822	.0630	.0485	.0374	.0289	.0224	.0174
30	.5521	.4120	.3083	.2314	.1741	.1314	.0994	.0754	.0573	.0437	.0334	.0256	.0196	.0151
31	.5412	.4000	.2965	.2204	.1643	.1228	.0920	.0691	.0521	.0394	.0298	.0226	.0172	.0131
32	.5306	.3883	.2851	.2099	.1550	.1147	.0852	.0634	.0474	.0355	.0266	.0200	.0151	.0114
33	.5202	.3770	.2741	.1999	.1462	.1072	.0789	.0582	.0431	.0319	.0238	.0177	.0132	.0099
34	.5100	.3660	.2636	.1904	.1379	.1002	.0730	.0534	.0391	.0288	.0212	.0157	.0116	.0086
35	.5000	.3554	.2534	.1813	.1301	.0937	.0676	.0490	.0356	.0259	.0189	.0139	.0102	.0075
36	.4902	.3450	.2437	.1727	.1227	.0875	.0626	.0449	.0323	.0234	.0169	.0123	.0089	.0065
37	.4806	.3350	.2343	.1644	.1158	.0818	.0580	.0412	.0294	.0210	.0151	.0109	.0078	.0057
38	.4712	.3252	.2253	.1566	.1092	.0765	.0537	.0378	.0267	.0190	.0135	.0096	.0069	.0049
39	.4619	.3158	.2166	.1491	.1031	.0715	.0497	.0347	.0243	.0171	.0120	.0085	.0060	.0043
40	.4529	.3066	.2083	.1420	.0972	.0668	.0460	.0318	.0221	.0154	.0107	.0075	.0053	.0037
41	.4440	.2976	.2003	.1353	.0917	.0624	.0426	.0292	.0201	.0139	.0096	.0067	.0046	.0032
42	.4353	.2890	.1926	.1288	.0865	.0583	.0395	.0268	.0183	.0125	.0086	.0059	.0041	.0028
43	.4268	.2805	.1852	.1227	.0816	.0545	.0365	.0246	.0166	.0112	.0076	.0052	.0036	.0025
44	.4184	.2724	.1780	.1169	.0770	.0509	.0338	.0226	.0151	.0101	.0068	.0046	.0031	.0021
45	.4102	.2644	.1712	.1113	.0727	.0476	.0313	.0207	.0137	.0091	.0061	.0041	.0027	.0019
46	.4022	.2567	.1646	.1060	.0685	.0445	.0290	.0190	.0125	.0082	.0054	.0036	.0024	.0016
47	.3943	.2493	.1583	.1009	.0647	.0416	.0269	.0174	.0113	.0074	.0049	.0032	.0021	.0014
48	.3865	.2420	.1522	.0961	.0610	.0389	.0249	.0160	.0103	.0067	.0043	.0028	.0019	.0012
49	.3790	.2350	.1463	.0916	.0575	.0363	.0230	.0147	.0094	.0060	.0039	.0025	.0016	.0011
50	.3715	.2281	.1407	.0872	.0543	.0339	.0213	.0134	.0085	.0054	.0035	.0022	.0014	.0009

table 3

Future Value of an Annuity of $1 in Arrears

No. of periods	2%	3%	4%	5%	6%	7%	8%	9%	10%	11%	12%	13%	14%	15%
1	1.0000	1.0000	1.0000	1.0000	1.0000	1.0000	1.0000	1.0000	1.0000	1.0000	1.0000	1.0000	1.0000	1.0000
2	2.0200	2.0300	2.0400	2.0500	2.0600	2.0700	2.0800	2.0900	2.1000	2.1100	2.1200	2.1300	2.1400	2.1500
3	3.0604	3.0909	3.1216	3.1525	3.1836	3.2149	3.2464	3.2781	3.3100	3.3421	3.3744	3.4069	3.4396	3.4725
4	4.1216	4.1836	4.2465	4.3101	4.3746	4.4399	4.5061	4.5731	4.6410	4.7097	4.7793	4.8498	4.9211	4.9934
5	5.2040	5.3091	5.4163	5.5256	5.6371	5.7507	5.8666	5.9847	6.1051	6.2278	6.3528	6.4803	6.6101	6.7424
6	6.3081	6.4684	6.6330	6.8019	6.9753	7.1533	7.3359	7.5233	7.7156	7.9129	8.1152	8.3227	8.5355	8.7537
7	7.4343	7.6625	7.8983	8.1420	8.3938	8.6540	8.9228	9.2004	9.4872	9.7833	10.0890	10.4047	10.7305	11.0668
8	8.5830	8.8923	9.2142	9.5491	9.8975	10.2598	10.6366	11.0285	11.4359	11.8594	12.2997	12.7573	13.2328	13.7268
9	9.7546	10.1591	10.5828	11.0266	11.4913	11.9780	12.4876	13.0210	13.5795	14.1640	14.7757	15.4157	16.0853	16.7858
10	10.9497	11.4639	12.0061	12.5779	13.1808	13.8164	14.4866	15.1929	15.9374	16.7220	17.5487	18.4197	19.3373	20.3037
11	12.1687	12.8078	13.4864	14.2068	14.9716	15.7836	16.6455	17.5603	18.5312	19.5614	20.6546	21.8143	23.0445	24.3493
12	13.4121	14.1920	15.0258	15.9171	16.8699	17.8885	18.9771	20.1407	21.3843	22.7132	24.1331	25.6502	27.2707	29.0017
13	14.6803	15.6178	16.6268	17.7130	18.8821	20.1406	21.4953	22.9534	24.5227	26.2116	28.0291	29.9847	32.0887	34.3519
14	15.9739	17.0863	18.2919	19.5986	21.0151	22.5505	24.2149	26.0192	27.9750	30.0949	32.3926	34.8827	37.5811	40.5047
15	17.2934	18.5989	20.0236	21.5786	23.2760	25.1290	27.1521	29.3609	31.7725	34.4054	37.2797	40.4175	43.8424	47.5804
16	18.6393	20.1569	21.8245	23.6575	25.6725	27.8881	30.3243	33.0034	35.9497	39.1899	42.7533	46.6717	50.9804	55.7175
17	20.0121	21.7616	23.6975	25.8404	28.2129	30.8402	33.7502	36.9737	40.5447	44.5008	48.8837	53.7391	59.1176	65.0751
18	21.4123	23.4144	25.6454	28.1324	30.9057	33.9990	37.4502	41.3013	45.5992	50.3959	55.7497	61.7251	68.3941	75.8364
19	22.8406	25.1169	27.6712	30.5390	33.7600	37.3790	41.4463	46.0185	51.1591	56.9395	63.4397	70.7494	78.9692	88.2118
20	24.2974	26.8704	29.7781	33.0660	36.7856	40.9955	45.7620	51.1601	57.2750	64.2028	72.0524	80.9468	91.0249	102.4436
21	25.7833	28.6765	31.9692	35.7193	39.9927	44.8652	50.4229	56.7645	64.0025	72.2651	81.6987	92.4699	104.7684	118.8101
22	27.2990	30.5368	34.2480	38.5052	43.3923	49.0057	55.4568	62.8733	71.4027	81.2143	92.5026	105.4910	120.4360	137.6316
23	28.8450	32.4529	36.6179	41.4305	46.9958	53.4361	60.8933	69.5319	79.5430	91.1479	104.6029	120.2048	138.2970	159.2764
24	30.4219	34.4265	39.0826	44.5020	50.8156	58.1767	66.7648	76.7898	88.4973	102.1742	118.1552	136.8315	158.6586	184.1678
25	32.0303	36.4593	41.6459	47.7271	54.8645	63.2490	73.1059	84.7009	98.3471	114.4133	133.3339	155.6196	181.8708	212.7930
26	33.6709	38.5530	44.3117	51.1135	59.1564	68.6765	79.9544	93.3240	109.1818	127.9988	150.3339	176.8501	208.3327	245.7120
27	35.3443	40.7096	47.0842	54.6691	63.7058	74.4838	87.3508	102.7231	121.0999	143.0786	169.3740	200.8406	238.4993	283.5688
28	37.0512	42.9309	49.9676	58.4026	68.5281	80.6977	95.3388	112.9682	134.2099	159.8173	190.6989	227.9499	272.8892	327.1041
29	38.7922	45.2189	52.9663	62.3227	73.6398	87.3465	103.9659	124.1354	148.6309	178.3972	214.5828	258.5834	312.0937	377.1697
30	40.5681	47.5754	56.0849	66.4388	79.0582	94.4608	113.2832	136.3075	164.4940	199.0209	241.3327	293.1992	356.7868	434.7451
31	42.3794	50.0027	59.3283	70.7608	84.8017	102.0730	123.3459	149.5752	181.9434	221.9132	271.2926	332.3151	407.7370	500.9569
32	44.2270	52.5028	62.7015	75.2988	90.8898	110.2182	134.2135	164.0370	201.1378	247.3236	304.8477	376.5161	465.8202	577.1005
33	46.1116	55.0778	66.2095	80.0638	97.3432	118.9334	145.9506	179.8003	222.2515	275.5292	342.4294	426.4632	532.0350	664.6655
34	48.0338	57.7302	69.8579	85.0670	104.1838	128.2588	158.6267	196.9823	245.4767	306.8374	384.5210	482.9034	607.5199	765.3654
35	49.9945	60.4621	73.6522	90.3203	111.4348	138.2369	172.3168	215.7108	271.0244	341.5896	431.6635	546.6808	693.5727	881.1702
36	51.9944	63.2759	77.5983	95.8363	119.1209	148.9135	187.1021	236.1247	299.1268	380.1644	484.4631	618.7493	791.6729	1014.3457
37	54.0343	66.1742	81.7022	101.6281	127.2681	160.0374	203.0703	258.3759	330.0395	422.9825	543.5987	700.1867	903.5071	1167.4975
38	56.1149	69.1594	85.9703	107.7095	135.9042	172.5610	220.3159	282.6298	364.0434	470.5106	609.8305	792.2110	1030.9981	1343.6222
39	58.2372	72.2342	90.4091	114.0950	145.0585	185.6403	238.9412	309.0665	401.4478	523.2667	684.0102	896.1984	1176.3378	1546.1655
40	60.4020	75.4013	95.0255	120.7998	154.7620	199.6351	259.0565	337.8824	442.5926	581.8261	767.0914	1013.7042	1342.0251	1779.0903
41	62.6100	78.6633	99.8265	127.8398	165.0477	214.6096	280.7810	369.2919	487.8518	646.8269	860.1424	1146.4858	1530.9086	2046.9539
42	64.8622	82.0232	104.8196	135.2318	175.9505	230.6322	304.2435	403.5281	537.6370	718.9779	964.3595	1296.5289	1746.2358	2354.9969
43	67.1595	85.4839	110.0124	142.9933	187.5076	247.7765	329.5830	440.8457	592.4007	799.0655	1081.0826	1466.0777	1991.7088	2709.2465
44	69.5027	89.0484	115.4129	151.1430	199.7580	266.1209	356.9496	481.5218	652.6408	887.9627	1211.8125	1657.6678	2271.5481	3116.6334
45	71.8927	92.7199	121.0294	159.7002	212.7435	285.7493	386.5056	525.8587	718.9048	986.6386	1358.2300	1874.1646	2590.5648	3585.1285
46	74.3306	96.5015	126.8706	168.6852	226.5081	306.7518	418.4261	574.1860	791.7953	1096.1688	1522.2176	2118.8060	2954.2439	4123.8977
47	76.8172	100.3965	132.9454	178.1194	241.0986	329.2244	452.9002	626.8628	871.9749	1217.7474	1705.8838	2395.2508	3368.8380	4743.4824
48	79.3535	104.4084	139.2632	188.0254	256.5645	353.2701	490.1322	684.2804	960.1723	1352.6996	1911.5898	2707.6334	3841.4753	5456.0047
49	81.9406	108.5406	145.8337	198.4267	272.9584	378.9990	530.3427	746.8656	1057.1896	1502.4965	2141.9806	3060.6258	4380.2819	6275.4055
50	84.5794	112.7969	152.6671	209.3480	290.3359	406.5289	573.7702	815.0836	1163.9085	1668.7712	2400.0182	3459.5071	4994.5213	7217.7163

table 4

Present Value of an Annuity of $1 in Arrears

No. of periods	2%	3%	4%	5%	6%	7%	8%	9%	10%	11%	12%	13%	14%	15%
1	.9804	.9709	.9615	.9524	.9434	.9346	.9259	.9174	.9091	.9009	.8929	.8850	.8772	.8696
2	1.9416	1.9135	1.8861	1.8594	1.8334	1.8080	1.7833	1.7591	1.7355	1.7125	1.6901	1.6681	1.6467	1.6257
3	2.8839	2.8286	2.7751	2.7232	2.6730	2.6243	2.5771	2.5313	2.4869	2.4437	2.4018	2.3612	2.3216	2.2832
4	3.8077	3.7171	3.6299	3.5460	3.4651	3.3872	3.3121	3.2397	3.1699	3.1024	3.0373	2.9745	2.9137	2.8550
5	4.7135	4.5797	4.4518	4.3295	4.2124	4.1002	3.9927	3.8897	3.7908	3.6959	3.6048	3.5172	3.4331	3.3522
6	5.6014	5.4172	5.2421	5.0757	4.9173	4.7665	4.6229	4.4859	4.3553	4.2305	4.1114	3.9975	3.8887	3.7845
7	6.4720	6.2303	6.0021	5.7864	5.5824	5.3893	5.2064	5.0330	4.8684	4.7122	4.5638	4.4226	4.2883	4.1604
8	7.3255	7.0197	6.7327	6.4632	6.2098	5.9713	5.7466	5.5348	5.3349	5.1461	4.9676	4.7988	4.6389	4.4873
9	8.1622	7.7861	7.4353	7.1078	6.8017	6.5152	6.2469	5.9952	5.7590	5.5370	5.3282	5.1317	4.9464	4.7716
10	8.9826	8.5302	8.1109	7.7217	7.3601	7.0236	6.7101	6.4177	6.1446	5.8892	5.6502	5.4262	5.2161	5.0188
11	9.7868	9.2526	8.7605	8.3064	7.8869	7.4987	7.1390	6.8052	6.4951	6.2065	5.9377	5.6869	5.4527	5.2337
12	10.5753	9.9540	9.3851	8.8633	8.3838	7.9427	7.5361	7.1607	6.8137	6.4924	6.1944	5.9176	5.6603	5.4206
13	11.3484	10.6350	9.9856	9.3936	8.8527	8.3577	7.9038	7.4869	7.1034	6.7499	6.4235	6.1218	5.8424	5.5831
14	12.1062	11.2961	10.5631	9.8986	9.2950	8.7455	8.2442	7.7862	7.3667	6.9819	6.6282	6.3025	6.0021	5.7245
15	12.8493	11.9379	11.1184	10.3797	9.7122	9.1079	8.5595	8.0607	7.6061	7.1909	6.8109	6.4624	6.1422	5.8474
16	13.5777	12.5611	11.6523	10.8378	10.1059	9.4466	8.8514	8.3126	7.8237	7.3792	6.9740	6.6039	6.2651	5.9542
17	14.2919	13.1661	12.1657	11.2741	10.4773	9.7632	9.1216	8.5436	8.0216	7.5488	7.1196	6.7291	6.3729	6.0472
18	14.9920	13.7535	12.6593	11.6896	10.8276	10.0591	9.3719	8.7556	8.2014	7.7016	7.2497	6.8399	6.4674	6.1280
19	15.6785	14.3238	13.1339	12.0853	11.1581	10.3356	9.6036	8.9501	8.3649	7.8393	7.3658	6.9380	6.5504	6.1982
20	16.3514	14.8775	13.5903	12.4622	11.4699	10.5940	9.8181	9.1285	8.5136	7.9633	7.4694	7.0248	6.6231	6.2593
21	17.0112	15.4150	14.0292	12.8212	11.7641	10.8355	10.0168	9.2922	8.6487	8.0751	7.5620	7.1016	6.6870	6.3125
22	17.6580	15.9369	14.4511	13.1630	12.0416	11.0612	10.2007	9.4424	8.7715	8.1757	7.6446	7.1695	6.7429	6.3587
23	18.2922	16.4436	14.8568	13.4886	12.3034	11.2722	10.3711	9.5802	8.8832	8.2664	7.7184	7.2297	6.7921	6.3988
24	18.9139	16.9355	15.2470	13.7986	12.5504	11.4693	10.5288	9.7066	8.9847	8.3481	7.7843	7.2829	6.8351	6.4338
25	19.5235	17.4131	15.6221	14.0939	12.7834	11.6536	10.6748	9.8226	9.0770	8.4217	7.8431	7.3300	6.8729	6.4641
26	20.1210	17.8768	15.9828	14.3752	13.0032	11.8258	10.8100	9.9290	9.1609	8.4881	7.8957	7.3717	6.9061	6.4906
27	20.7069	18.3270	16.3296	14.6430	13.2105	11.9867	10.9352	10.0266	9.2372	8.5478	7.9426	7.4086	6.9352	6.5135
28	21.2813	18.7641	16.6631	14.8981	13.4062	12.1371	11.0511	10.1161	9.3066	8.6016	7.9844	7.4412	6.9607	6.5335
29	21.8444	19.1885	16.9837	15.1411	13.5907	12.2777	11.1584	10.1983	9.3696	8.6501	8.0218	7.4701	6.9830	6.5509
30	22.3965	19.6004	17.2920	15.3725	13.7648	12.4090	11.2578	10.2737	9.4269	8.6938	8.0552	7.4957	7.0027	6.5660
31	22.9377	20.0004	17.5885	15.5928	13.9291	12.5318	11.3498	10.3428	9.4790	8.7331	8.0850	7.5183	7.0199	6.5791
32	23.4683	20.3888	17.8736	15.8027	14.0840	12.6466	11.4350	10.4062	9.5264	8.7686	8.1116	7.5383	7.0350	6.5905
33	23.9886	20.7658	18.1476	16.0025	14.2302	12.7538	11.5139	10.4644	9.5694	8.8005	8.1354	7.5560	7.0482	6.6005
34	24.4986	21.1318	18.4112	16.1929	14.3681	12.8540	11.5869	10.5178	9.6086	8.8293	8.1566	7.5717	7.0599	6.6091
35	24.9986	21.4872	18.6646	16.3742	14.4982	12.9477	11.6546	10.5668	9.6442	8.8552	8.1755	7.5856	7.0700	6.6166
36	25.4888	21.8323	18.9083	16.5469	14.6210	13.0352	11.7172	10.6118	9.6765	8.8786	8.1924	7.5979	7.0790	6.6231
37	25.9695	22.1672	19.1426	16.7113	14.7368	13.1170	11.7752	10.6530	9.7059	8.8996	8.2075	7.6087	7.0868	6.6288
38	26.4406	22.4925	19.3679	16.8679	14.8460	13.1935	11.8289	10.6908	9.7327	8.9186	8.2210	7.6183	7.0937	6.6338
39	26.9026	22.8082	19.5845	17.0170	14.9491	13.2649	11.8786	10.7255	9.7570	8.9357	8.2330	7.6268	7.0997	6.6380
40	27.3555	23.1148	19.7928	17.1591	15.0463	13.3317	11.9246	10.7574	9.7791	8.9511	8.2438	7.6344	7.1050	6.6418
41	27.7995	23.4124	19.9931	17.2944	15.1380	13.3941	11.9672	10.7866	9.7991	8.9649	8.2534	7.6410	7.1097	6.6450
42	28.2348	23.7014	20.1856	17.4232	15.2245	13.4524	12.0067	10.8134	9.8174	8.9774	8.2619	7.6469	7.1138	6.6478
43	28.6616	23.9819	20.3708	17.5459	15.3062	13.5070	12.0432	10.8380	9.8340	8.9886	8.2696	7.6522	7.1173	6.6503
44	29.0800	24.2543	20.5488	17.6628	15.3832	13.5579	12.0771	10.8605	9.8491	8.9988	8.2764	7.6568	7.1205	6.6524
45	29.4902	24.5187	20.7200	17.7741	15.4558	13.6055	12.1084	10.8812	9.8628	9.0079	8.2825	7.6609	7.1232	6.6543
46	29.8923	24.7754	20.8847	17.8801	15.5244	13.6500	12.1374	10.9002	9.8753	9.0161	8.2880	7.6645	7.1256	6.6559
47	30.2866	25.0247	21.0429	17.9810	15.5890	13.6916	12.1643	10.9176	9.8866	9.0235	8.2928	7.6677	7.1277	6.6573
48	30.6731	25.2667	21.1951	18.0772	15.6500	13.7305	12.1891	10.9336	9.8969	9.0302	8.2972	7.6705	7.1296	6.6585
49	31.0521	25.5017	21.3415	18.1687	15.7076	13.7668	12.2122	10.9482	9.9063	9.0362	8.3010	7.6730	7.1312	6.6596
50	31.4236	25.7298	21.4822	18.2559	15.7619	13.8007	12.2335	10.9617	9.9148	9.0417	8.3045	7.6752	7.1327	6.6605